INTERPRETING
INFORMATION SYSTEMS
IN ORGANIZATIONS

John Wiley
SERIES IN INFORMATION SYSTEMS

Editors

Richard Boland
Case Western Reserve University

Rudy Hirschheim
University of Houston

INTERPRETING
INFORMATION SYSTEMS
IN ORGANIZATIONS

Geoff Walsham

University of Cambridge, UK

 John Wiley
SERIES IN INFORMATION SYSTEMS

JOHN WILEY & SONS
Chichester · New York · Brisbane · Toronto · Singapore

Other Wiley Editorial Offices

John Wiley & Sons, Inc., 605 Third Avenue,
New York, NY 10158–0012, USA

Jacaranda Wiley Ltd, G.P.O. Box 859, Brisbane,
Queensland 4001, Australia

John Wiley & Sons (Canada) Ltd, 22 Worcester Road,
Rexdale, Ontario M9W 1L1, Canada

John Wiley & Sons (SEA) Pte Ltd, 37 Jalan Pemimpin #05–04,
Block B, Union Industrial Building, Singapore 2057

Library of Congress Cataloging-in-Publication Data

Walsham, Geoffrey.
  Interpreting information systems in organizations / Geoff Walsham.
    p. cm. — (John Wiley series in information systems)
  Includes bibliographical references and indexes.
  ISBN 0-471-93814-9
  1. Management information systems. 2. Business—Data processing.
I. Title. II. Series.
T58.6.W328 1993
650'.0285—dc20   92–29754
                                                               CIP

British Library Cataloguing in Publication Data

A catalogue record for this book is available from the British Library

ISBN 0-471-93814-9

Typeset in 10/12pt Baskerville from author's disks by Photo·graphics, Honiton, Devon
Printed and bound in Great Britain by Biddles Ltd, Guildford and King's Lynn

To
Alison

CONTENTS

SERIES FOREWORD

In order for all types of organization to succeed, they need to be able to process data and use information effectively. This has become especially true in today's rapidly changing environment. In conducting their day-to-day operations, organizations use information for functions such as planning, controlling, organizing, and decision-making. Information, therefore, is unquestionably a critical resource in the operation of all organizations. Any means, mechanical or otherwise, which can help organizations process and manage information presents an opportunity they can ill afford to ignore.

The arrival of the computer and its use in data processing has been one of the most important organizational innovations in the past thirty years. The advent of computer-based data processing and information systems has led to organizations being able to cope with the vast quantities of information which they need to process and manage to survive. The field which has emerged to study this development is *information systems* (IS). It is a combination of two primary fields: computer science and management, with a host of supporting disciplines, e.g. psychology, sociology, statistics, political science, economics, philosophy, and mathematics. IS is concerned not only with the development of new information technologies but also with questions such as: how they can best be applied, how they should be managed, and what their wider implications are.

Partly because of the dynamic world in which we live (and the concomitant need to process more information), and partly because of the dramatic recent developments in information technology, e.g. personal computers, fourth-generation languages, relational databases, knowledge-based systems, and office automation, the relevance and importance of the field of information systems has become apparent. End users, who previously had little potential of becoming seriously involved and knowledgeable in information technology and systems, are now much more aware of and interested in the new technology. Individuals working in today's and tomorrow's organizations will be expected to have some understanding of and the ability to use the rapidly developing information technologies and systems. The dramatic increase in the availability and use of information technology, however, raises fundamental questions on the guiding of technological innovation, measuring organizational and managerial productivity, augmenting human intelligence, ensuring data integrity, and establishing strategic advantage. The expanded use of information systems also raises major challenges to the traditional forms of administration and authority, the right to privacy, the nature and form of work, and the limits of calculative rationality in modern organizations and society.

The Wiley Series on Information Systems has emerged to address these questions and challenges. It hopes to stimulate thought and discussion on the key role information systems play in the functioning of organizations and society, and how their role is likely to change in the future. This historical or evolutionary theme of the Series is important because considerable insight can be gained by attempting to understand the past. The Series will attempt to integrate both description—what has been done—with prescription—how best to develop and implement information systems.

The descriptive and historical aspect is considered vital because information systems of the past have not necessarily met with the success that was envisaged. Numerous writers postulate that a high proportion of systems are failures in one sense or another. Given their high cost of development and their importance to the day-to-day running of organizations, this situation must surely be unacceptable. Research into IS failure has concluded that the primary cause of failure is the lack of consideration given to the social and behavioural dimensions of IS. Far too much emphasis has been placed on their technical side. The result has been something of a shift in emphasis from a strictly technical conception of IS to one where it is recognized that information systems have behavioural consequences. But even this misses the mark. A growing number of researchers suggest that information systems are more appropriately conceived as social systems which rely, to a greater and greater extent, on new technology for their operation. It is this social orientation which is lacking in much of what is written about IS. The present volume, *Interpreting Information Systems in Organizations*, is an excellent book which combines both the organizational and social side of IS into a cohesive whole. The insightful treatment of the subject adds much to our understanding of IS, and should be read by all individuals in the field.

The Series seeks to provide a forum for the serious discussion of IS. Although the primary perspective is a more social and behavioural one, alternative perspectives will also be included. This is based on the belief that no one perspective can be totally complete; added insight is possible through the adoption of multiple views. Relevant areas to be addressed in the Series include (but are not limited to): the theoretical development of information systems, their practical application, the foundations and evolution of information systems, and IS innovation. Subjects such as systems design, systems analysis methodologies, information systems planning and management, office automation, project management, decision support systems, end-user computing, and information systems and society are key concerns of the Series.

Rudy Hirschheim
Richard Boland

PREFACE

I have asked many people over the last few years about the computer systems
they use in their workplace, whether they are satisfied with the systems, how
they have changed the nature of their work, and what they would like to see
happen in this area in the future. A veritable flood of views, interpretations,
complaints and anxieties has normally resulted. Various messages come
through with clarity, namely that practically everybody is using computer-
based information systems (IS) of some sort, that there are different views
concerning the purpose and value of such systems, and that major problems
are often perceived to exist, in terms both of the usefulness of the systems
and of their impact on work and work lives. Computer-based IS are viewed
as important in contemporary society, but problematic in terms of interpreting
their meaning and value.

The research which underpins this book was directed towards increasing
our understanding of these concerns and issues surrounding computer systems.
A small group of research students and myself carried out in-depth case
studies in eight organizations over a period of six years. The focus of the
studies was on collecting and describing people's interpretations concerning
the development, use, and value of the computer-based IS in their organizations.
Three of the case studies are described in detail in the book, but the ideas
and concepts in the following pages were informed by the whole of the research
programme. Empirical research without theory produces a series of anecdotes,
and the research aimed to avoid this by using theory both to guide the field
work carried out and to provide ways of synthesizing the results. One main
body of theoretical literature which was drawn on, and is described in the
book, was concerned with ways of viewing organizations and the processes of
organizing. A second body of theory concerned interpretation and meaning,
both at the individual level and in interaction. The third main source for
theory was the existing literature on computer-based information systems.

The primary purpose of the book is to aid readers in their own processes
of interpretation of computer systems. Interpretive approaches adopt the
stance that knowledge is a social construction, and that our theories concerning
reality provide ways of making sense of the world rather than discoveries
about the world which represent absolute truth. Some IS literature currently
exists which adopts an interpretive stance, but it is normally found in articles
scattered across a wide range of journals. This book aims to provide a coherent
and integrated source for an interpretive approach to understanding IS in
organizations. It presupposes a reasonable level of prior knowledge on

organizations and information systems, and is thus aimed primarily at postgraduate students, the IS research community, and practitioners concerned with information systems and their management.

After an introductory chapter, the book describes theory in Part I, empirical research in Part II, and then examines a number of IS issues in Part III. The issues chosen are fairly conventional, namely strategy, evaluation, design and development, and implementation. The book aims to provide new ways of looking at these 'old' issues, and thus to stimulate readers with ideas and insights of value to their future work. The focus of these chapters is in areas such as the facilitation of improved communication and mutual understanding. The examination of such issues is not intended to downgrade the importance of more traditional technical or economic issues, but is aimed to provide a complement to such approaches, centred on human interpretation and social meaning. A final chapter brings together some of the key themes of the book, and then widens out to discuss some broad conclusions concerning the possible future with respect to information systems in organizations and society.

The various parts of the book could be used by readers for particular purposes. For example, the introductory chapter and Part I on theory provide a research source for literature on IS in organizations from an interpretive stance. The case studies in Part II could be used with student groups for analysis and discussion. The material on major IS issues in Part III could be employed directly by an IS practitioner as a source of ideas and a framework for debate. However, the various parts of the book are interconnected, and I hope that readers will take an interest in all elements in order to obtain a fuller picture relating theory, empirical research and practice.

The development of the ideas in the book has been a collaborative activity in many ways, and I would like to acknowledge firstly the contributions made by three of my ex-research students, namely Veronica Symons, Tim Waema, and Chun Kwong Han. Their work not only provided the basis for the case studies described in Chapters 4 to 6, but the close contact I had with them over an extended time period was critical in the development of the ideas and concepts in the book.

I have drawn on the work of many authors as theoretical sources, and they are too numerous to be mentioned here; they are, however, fully referenced in the text. My Management Studies colleagues in Cambridge provided a supportive intellectual environment for the research programme; I would particularly like to thank Matthew Jones for his willingness to share his knowledge on all aspects of computer-based IS, Elizabeth Garnsey and John Roberts for their stimulating conversations on issues of organizations and interpretation, and Stephen Watson for his unfailing support throughout the research programme. Dick Boland provided valuable ideas and encouragement on the writing of the book, and I would like to thank him, together with Matthew Jones and Dan Robey, for their detailed and helpful comments on earlier drafts. I wish to thank Jo Grantham who provided help with the preparation of the figures and tables, and Diane Taylor at Wiley for her valuable editorial assistance and support. Finally, I would like to thank my wife and family, who have taught me more than I can say about life and its interpretation.

Cambridge   Geoff Walsham
July 1992

INTRODUCTION

Chapter 1

AN INTERPRETIVE APPROACH TO INFORMATION SYSTEMS

This book is about computer-based information systems in the contemporary world of the late twentieth century. The concept of an information system embraces a broad category of human artefacts, such as texts and books, with a history as old as human civilization, but computers and telecommunications hardware and related software now provide a composite technology with capabilities which are quite remarkable viewed from any earlier epoch. Our forebears would no doubt be astonished by taken-for-granted modern phenomena such as robots, video transmission systems linking distant parts of the world, or whole libraries with almost instantaneous retrieval systems.

The rapid rate of development of these technological miracles, as they would have been viewed from an earlier age, has created a momentum of its own, and it is not surprising that concomitant concerns have also developed about the impact and influence of computer-based technology on human society. These concerns include the possible dehumanization and routinization of work, the invasion of human privacy and personal space, and the creation of the information rich and the information poor, both in terms of individuals and whole societies. The shrinking of time and space enabled by technology has benefits in terms of task efficiency and wider capability for communication, but it is less obvious that human life is improved at a deeper level.

The above discussion should not be taken to imply that technology determines the direction of human society. The development and use of technology is within human control and there is no inevitable future path. However, it can be argued that the quantity and quality of debate about the human and societal impact of computers and related technology has not matched the rate of development of the technologies themselves. For example, the debate concerning computers in Western business, commercial and government organizations largely centres around questions of strategic importance and value-for-money rather than deeper issues of human job satisfaction and quality of life.

The questions of the broad societal impact of computer-based technologies and of the impact on individual human lives are of major importance, but the focal level in this book is the organization rather than the individual or society in general. Most computer-based information systems at the present time are developed and used within the context of a specific organization, and the main aim of this book is to provide ways of generating a better understanding of the design, development and use of computer-based information systems in an organizational context. However, any understanding which is gained at the organizational level has implications for the individual and for human society, and these complementary levels are inevitably involved, explicitly or implicitly, in what follows.

The importance of organizational issues with respect to computer-based information systems (IS) is well recognized by practitioners. The top five key issues identified by Brancheau and Wetherbe (1987), from the results of a survey of IS executives in the USA, were strategic planning, competitive advantage, organizational learning, IS's role and contribution, and the alignment of the information systems function in the organization. It is notable that all of these have a strong organizational emphasis rather than a technical emphasis. Some relate mainly to internal organizational structures and approaches, whereas others are more concerned with the external context and environment of the organization, and the part which information systems play in addressing the world external to the organization.

Organizational issues have also become a major focus for IS researchers in recent years and the rapidly expanding number of IS journals contain many papers dealing with such issues. It is not a primary objective of this book to criticize these publications or the style of research that they represent. It is worth noting, however, that much of this literature reflects a rational-economic interpretation of organizational processes, and a positivist methodology which is based on the view that the world exhibits objective cause-effect relationships which can be discovered, at least partially, by structured observation. Many researchers have noted the limitations of such approaches. For example, Kraemer and King (1990) state that:

> Supply-push views of technical development, coupled with a rational economic interpretation of managerial behaviour have dominated MIS (management information systems) research. These explanatory perspectives have considerable power, and have yielded useful results. However, they do not explain the variance observed in the patterns and processes of adoption and routinization of information technology in various tasks, or the differences in successful use of the technology across organizations. (pp. 582–583)

It is relatively easy to criticize the approaches of others, but harder to construct a worthwhile alternative; so what style of research on information systems is being proposed in this book as a way of increasing our understanding of the critical organizational issues related to computer-based information systems? The answer is *broadly interpretive methods* of research, aimed at producing an understanding of the *context* of the information system, and the *process* whereby the information system influences and is influenced by its context. The ideas and approaches inherent in these few words are the primary focus of the book and will be expanded in detail in the subsequent chapters. For the purposes of this first chapter, a brief description of these key ideas is now given as an introduction to the later material.

Interpretive methods of research start from the position that our knowledge of reality, including the domain of human action, is a social construction by human actors and that this applies equally to researchers. Thus there is no objective reality which can be discovered by researchers and replicated by others, in contrast to the assumptions of positivist science. Our theories concerning reality are ways of making sense of the world and shared meanings are a form of intersubjectivity rather than objectivity. Interpretivism is thus an epistemological position, concerned with approaches to the understanding of reality and asserting that all such knowledge is necessarily a social construction and thus subjective.

Within the broad style of interpretive research, many specific methodologies can be used to guide the information systems researcher, but in this book emphasis will be placed on approaches which deal carefully with context and process. Context is concerned with the multi-level identification of the various systems and structures within which the information system is embedded. This can include such obvious elements as the organizational department within which the system is being used, the organization as a whole, and the various sectoral, national and international contexts within which the organization is located. A more subtle set of contexts for an information system are the various social structures which are present in the minds of the human participants involved with the system, including designers, users and any of those affected by the system. Their interpretation of reality, their shared and contested sense of the world, create complex interacting contexts within which the information system, as a human artefact, is drawn on and used to create or reinforce meaning.

The concept of context has a static flavour whereas human affairs are in a constant state of flux and change. The second strand of analysis of information systems in this book addresses this area of dynamics by taking seriously the processes of transformation and change which take place over time. Human actors draw on elements of context, such as resources or perceived authority, to carry out actions, and this activity can reinforce existing systems of resource distribution or power, or can create new systems of authority or meaning. Thus human action draws on context or structure and, in so doing, reinforces existing structures or contexts, or creates new contexts. An investigation of this dynamic process of action/context interweaving is fundamental to an understanding of the process of organizational change within which the information system is one element. The information system itself is not static, neither in the obvious physical sense of changing hardware, software, systems and data, nor in the changing human perceptions of the output of the various systems and the system itself.

The above ideas emphasize the investigation of context and process within a broad style of interpretive research. But how are such concepts operationalized in this book? The first part of the book, following this introductory chapter, deals with *theory*, in which the conceptual and methodological ideas outlined briefly above are expanded and explored in considerable detail. The second part of the book then uses three substantial *case studies* to illustrate the theoretical and methodological concepts. The third part of the book concentrates on the analysis of a number of *major issues* in information systems; these interpretive analyses draw on the theoretical and empirical work of the earlier parts and are designed to be of direct practical value.

The research which underpins this book was not conducted in isolation of the work of others in the information systems and related fields. In the next two sections of this introductory chapter, some of the existing literature will be discussed under the two headings of theory and case studies. The purpose of this is to describe some interesting work which was a forerunner and inspiration for the research presented in the main parts of the book, and, at the same time, to illustrate and discuss the role of theory and case studies within the interpretive tradition of information systems research. The final section of the chapter will then summarize the broad research perspective which forms the basis for the rest of the book.

THEORY

In the interpretive tradition, there are no correct and incorrect theories but there are interesting and less interesting ways to view the world. A reader might well ask 'interesting to whom'? An author can only respond in the first instance that the theories which he or she presents are interesting to themselves and may be interesting to others. However, although the use by an individual author of a particular theoretical approach derives no doubt from his or her personal experience and insight, the testing of the value of these insights to others can be carried out by exposing the approach through verbal and written discourse to enable broader judgements of value to be made. Theory can be compared, evaluated and improved by this form of public testing; the result is not the generation of 'best' theory, but the creation of intersubjectively tested theoretical approaches, considered of value to a broader group than a single individual. The theory used in this book falls within this intersubjective tradition.

Theory is both a way of seeing and a way of not-seeing. A particular theoretical perspective blinds us to other perspectives at its moment of application. A second, and more subtle, criticism of theory is that in any real human activity, particularly that involving others, we take action without the conscious use of theory, and certainly the action is conditioned by more than any singular theory. This latter point can be put forward as a way of understanding why many management practitioners, for example, display a healthy scepticism with respect to the theories of management and management practice.

Nevertheless, we are conditioned by theories whether we like it or not, since we are exposed to a multiplicity of theories from our earliest childhood and we are undoubtedly influenced by them. So the argument in favour of theory does not rest on it being essential to good practice; rather that an appropriate blend of theory and practice may be more valuable to an individual practitioner than practice alone, and that explicit theories may aid the synthesis of implicit practical knowledge and, equally important, may provide a means to communicate this knowledge to others.

So where does this lead us with respect to theory on information systems with an organizational focus? Some specific theories will be described in detail in Part I and some previous information systems researchers, in the interpretive tradition, who have taken theory seriously, are discussed below. A final general point, however, is that theory about the human aspects of computer-based information systems should not be considered as isolated from theory about the human condition in general, since human beings display some broad similarities in their actions and interactions over long stretches of time, at least judging by the contemporary relevance of works of fiction and non-fiction from thousands of years of history. This implies that the whole of previous theory about human life, and in particular philosophical thought, is 'relevant' to modern-day information systems. It is too much to expect any one individual to have comprehensive access to this historical legacy, but we should not be misled into divorcing IS research from earlier work and ideas. It is no coincidence that most of the work described below makes explicit acknowledgement to various earlier thinkers and philosophers. Information systems in their organizational context have holographic properties, in that their development and use can be taken to involve all aspects of human life, and thus their study can be considered to be a relevant domain for all earlier thought.

Computers and Cognition

A book of significance in the search for understanding of computers and their relationship to human beings is that by Winograd and Flores (1986). The aims of the book are very much within the spirit of the previous discussion of the role of theory in information systems and its linkage to knowledge about human action in general, as shown in the following extract:

> Our larger goal is to clarify the background of understanding in which the discourse about computers and technology takes place, and to grasp its broader implications. Ultimately we are seeking a better understanding of what it means to be human. (p. 13)

A major body of theory from which they draw is the work of the philosopher Heidegger and his quest for an understanding of what it means to exist in the world. Heidegger (1962) argued that distinguishing subject (I) from object (the thing perceived) is at odds with actual experience, where understanding operates without reflection; the separation of subject and object denies the unity of being-in-the-world. This insight is interesting in the light of the earlier discussion of practical managers and their emphasis on action rather than theory. Heidegger also discussed prejudice (or pre-understanding) as a necessary condition of being able to interpret anything in the world, and argued that the interpreter and interpreted do not exist independently: existence is interpretation and interpretation is existence. A detailed discussion of Heidegger's work is beyond the scope of this chapter. It has been introduced briefly here since it is a deep investigation of human existence and meaning which provides a philosophical underpinning for the interpretive tradition. In addition, Winograd and Flores use this work, amongst others, to draw interesting implications for computers in modern society, some of which are now briefly discussed.

They argue that a new orientation is needed with action as the primary focus for information systems design. They also maintain that commitment is the basis for language, and that in creating new computer-based information systems, we are designing new conversations, connections, and commitments. They draw on a further element of Heidegger's work which is concerned with 'breakdown'. Heidegger argued that objects only become present-at-hand (i.e. become visible as separate objects to the observer) when a breakdown occurs. An example used by Winograd and Flores (drawn from Heidegger) is that a hammer is only perceived by the hammerer as separate from the action of hammering when some breakdown occurs, such as the hammer head coming off. Winograd and Flores use the idea of breakdown to argue that, in designing computer systems, we must anticipate the range of occurrences that go outside normal functioning (breakdowns) and provide means both to understand them and to act.

The book by Winograd and Flores is excellent in stimulating thought about computers and their relationship to human action and cognition, and this author would recommend it to readers on those grounds alone. In addition, they provide some useful ideas on information systems design issues. The focus of the book is largely at the individual level, however, and it is not obvious to see how to operationalize the ideas for information systems in an organizational context. One aim of the current book is to provide elements for such an operationalization, and thus the reader should view the earlier work of Winograd and Flores as a complementary precursor to this book and within the same spirit of broadly interpretive investigation.

Phenomenology and Hermeneutics

A second body of work which is centrally based on the interpretive approach to research on information systems, and which draws heavily from earlier theoretical writings, is that carried out by Boland (1979, 1985). Boland uses phenomenology and hermeneutics as the philosophical bases for his research. Phenomenology arose from the work of Husserl (1931), who was concerned to understand the phenomena which he believed to be the totality of what we can know. Hermeneutics began as the study of the translation and interpretation of sacred texts, and is taken now to be concerned with the interpretation of any textual material. Thus hermeneutics can be thought of as a key strand of phenomenology since the interpretation of texts is an important part of the search for meaning and the essence of experience. Boland draws on the work of Gadamer (1975) in this area, who argued that language is fundamental to our being-in-the-world, and that every reading or hearing of a text constitutes a hermeneutic act of giving meaning to it through interpretation. Boland (1985) describes this as follows:

> Gadamer focuses our attention on phenomenology as an historic act of interpretation, grounded in tradition. He emphasizes the impossibility of stripping away all assumptions as a guarantee of objective knowledge. For Gadamer, prejudice is a positive not a negative thing. Prejudice is the basis of our ability to experience the world ... Understanding ... is a moving dialectic process: a dialogue in which we continuously engage all that is alien to us in a reciprocal, intersubjective relation ... Gadamer argues that the hermeneutic process of interpretation is not some esoteric problem relevant only to translators of ancient texts, but a basic problem that confronts us all as part and parcel of our existence in the social world. (p. 195)

With respect to the specific application of the theoretical ideas outlined above to the study of information systems, Boland considers that our everyday experience of the social world is a hermeneutic and that in the world we encounter a 'text' of meanings already made and being made; thus he argues that (1985, pp. 195–196):

> ... the use, design and study of information systems is best understood as a hermeneutic process ... In *using* an information system, the available output is a text that must be read and interpreted by people other than its author. This is a hermeneutic task. In *designing* an information system, the designer reads the organization and its intended users as a text in order to make an interpretation that will provide the basis for a systems design. This is also a hermeneutic task. In *studying* information systems, social scientists read the interaction during systems design and use in order to interpret the significance and potential

meanings they hold. Hence, doing research on information systems is yet another hermeneutic task.

Boland has tried to operationalize these ideas by carrying out specific empirical work in a variety of settings and we will discuss one of the most interesting of these attempts (Boland and Day 1989) later in this chapter.

It may have occurred to the reader that there are striking similarities between the ideas being presented here and those drawn on by Winograd and Flores. This is not surprising since Heidegger was a pupil of Husserl, and Gadamer was a pupil of Heidegger. It is worth noting that, despite the close similarity of the philosophical traditions from which they draw and the basic objectives of their work concerned with understanding computers in human society, Boland and Winograd/Flores do not cross-reference each other's ideas. Yet there are many interesting points of contact and opportunities for building on the interpretive foundations laid by their work. Boland's research, as with that of Winograd and Flores, has a strong focus at the level of the individual and individual acts of interpretation, but his work also addresses groups within an organization and thus moves some way towards a parallel focus at the organizational level. It is practically-oriented work that this author has used as a valuable source of ideas to inform the research described later in the main parts of the book.

Soft Systems Methodology

A third stream of work from an interpretive perspective which is of relevance to computer-based IS is based on the soft systems methodology (SSM) of Checkland (1981). SSM embodies a philosophy of organizational intervention that sees different individuals and groups as constructing interpretations of the world, the interpretations having no absolute or universal status. The purpose of the intervention is to reconcile these views sufficiently to achieve organized action:

> What is in short supply in organizations is an organized sharing of perceptions sufficiently intense that concerted action gets taken corporately. Enacting the process of SSM can help. (Checkland and Scholes 1990, p. 79)

A special feature of SSM is the use of a number of different 'human activity systems' or 'holons', which are conceptual models of the area of interest based on a 'root definition' representing a particular view of the core purpose of the activity system. These holons are compared to the real world as epistemological devices in an interpretive debate between the organizational participants.

SSM is a well-defined and subtle approach to organizational intervention, with wide application potential across a range of areas within the broad label of management science. It has already been used extensively by a variety of management practitioners in the UK (Mingers and Taylor 1992), including a considerable number of applications in the area of computer-based IS. Its specific relevance to IS design and development will be discussed later in Chapter 9. The main reason for outlining the methodology here is that it provides an interpretive philosophy and approach for organized intervention and purposeful action, which recognizes and builds on the multiple realities perceived by different stakeholders. Checkland (1981, p. 19) notes that SSM implies a model of social reality in the phenomenological tradition deriving sociologically from Weber and philosophically from Husserl. SSM thus links to the work of both Winograd/Flores and Boland, and provides a further basis for IS research in an interpretive tradition.

Soft systems methodology has certainly been influential, but it also has its critics. An early paper by Jackson (1982) argued that the use of SSM largely ignored the constraining effects of existing power relations, and thus tended to be conservative and likely to be geared to the vested interests of the powerful. Checkland himself has always disputed this analysis (see, for example, Checkland 1982), and argued that radical change can be achieved in some cases through SSM, dependent on factors such as the value systems of the participants to the debate including the intervention agents. In addition, later versions of SSM include some analysis of power and conflict (Checkland and Scholes 1990, p. 50), although the treatment of these issues is rather rudimentary. This debate on the possibly 'conservative' nature of interpretive approaches such as SSM leads on to discussion of a fourth strand of theoretical ideas, based on the work of the social philosopher Jürgen Habermas (see, for example, Habermas 1972).

Critical Theory

Habermas' writing is a development from the critical social theory of the so-called Frankfurt School in the 1930s. This school was opposed to the dominance of positivism which, it was argued, eclipses the philosopher, namely the subject who reflexively investigates the grounds of his or her own claims to knowledge. Part of Habermas' work is a theory of the link between knowledge and human interests, arguing that positivism is linked to the desire for technical control, hermeneutics and related interpretive approaches to a desire for understanding, but critical theory to a desire for emancipation. The pursuit of the goal of emancipation leads to an attempt to create circumstances in which communicative action takes place aimed at achieving mutual understanding. This is mediated through language and Habermas discusses the creation of 'ideal speech situations' in which undistorted communication can take place. This involves 'not only the rational attainment of consensus but also complete mutual understanding by participants and recognition of the authentic right of each to participate in the dialogue as an autonomous and equal partner' (Giddens 1977).

There is some debate in the literature regarding the status of Habermas' critical theory *vis-à-vis* interpretivism. Critical theory is certainly anti-positivist, but some argue that it should also be strongly distinguished from interpretive approaches. For example, Jönsson (1991) discusses action research on information systems and argues for an approach based on the philosophical underpinnings of critical theory, since 'interpretive researchers do not recognise the inherent conflict and contradiction in social relations'. Not all researchers who class their work as interpretive would agree with the substance of this statement, but nevertheless it is clear that critical theory places a strong emphasis on values and the emancipation of the individual, rather than on description and understanding as is the case with mainstream interpretive approaches.

In the information systems field, an early contribution by Lyytinen and Klein (1985) maintained that critical theory can be used 'as a basis for a theory of information systems'. For example, they argued that information systems development should be related to the concern of people for emancipation, and that this requires the removal of organizational barriers that prevent a discussion by all participants of values and norms. This seems a worthwhile goal, but it is less clear how it is to be achieved. The authors express a wish for methodologies which are more socially open, but when they argue that methodologies should 'enforce authentic communication', they are implicitly recognizing the existing structures of power and domination which necessarily constrain the openness of the debate.

A later article by Hirschheim and Klein (1989) is concerned with alternative views on the systems development process and different ways of thinking about the role of the systems analyst. The four 'paradigms' of information systems development are generated from Burrell and Morgan's (1979) widely-quoted, though contentious, typology for alternative approaches to organizational analysis, involving a subjectivist-objectivist axis and an order-conflict axis. Positivism is in the objectivist/order quadrant, interpretivism is in the subjectivist/order quadrant, whereas critical theory falls within the subjectivist/conflict area. Hirschheim and Klein generate four views of the systems analyst, corresponding to these quadrants, consisting of the analyst as a systems expert, as a facilitator, as a labour partisan, and as an emancipator or social therapist. The last of these corresponds to the critical theory discussed above, and the authors discuss some of the barriers which need to be overcome in order for the analyst to fulfil this role. These include authority and illegitimate power, peer opinion pressure, time and resource limitations, and the bias and limitation of language use.

The barriers mentioned above can be used to end this brief discussion of critical theory as a theoretical basis for information systems research and practice. A naïve reading of critical theory would imply that the goal is the removal of such barriers in order to create perfect communication. However, Habermas conceived of the 'ideal speech situation' as an analytical construct or ultimate goal. The practical message from critical theory is not that the barriers to perfect communication can be removed, but that explicit and critical reflection on the barriers is a step in the right direction of human emancipation. It is an attempt to recognize the importance of the emancipatory knowledge interest, rather than concentrating solely on technical control or on hermeneutic understanding.

In terms of the relation of critical theory to this book, the earlier statement that the book was concerned with 'interpretive methods' should be taken in its broadest sense to include the concerns and issues, such as power and control and human emancipation, raised by critical theory. A major contribution of the work of Habermas is that such issues are the explicit focus, which provides a valuable counterbalance and complement not only to positivism and concerns of technical control, but also to hermeneutics and phenomenology and the desire for increased understanding through description.

Post-modernism

No description of current social theory of potential relevance to information systems, albeit the very brief outline attempted in this section, would be complete without a mention of post-modernism (see, for example, Lyotard 1984). This is a very difficult and complex area of work since it is hard to decide which writers and thinkers to include as 'post-modernist', and the work of each of such writers tends to be rather diverse in itself and different from other post-modernists. Nevertheless, a common position of those writers who tend to be classed under the label of post-modernist is to question the 'modernist' idea of the history of human progress as an upwards curve. Post-modernists, in contrast, tend to focus on the immediacy of events and their contingent nature, and challenge the privileging of any one perspective or future vision.

The writers discussed in the preceding subsections, including Heidegger, Gadamer and Habermas, would all be seen as falling in the modernist tradition. No attempt will be made here to survey the broad counter-movement of post-modernism, nor to enter the debate concerning its possible 'nihilism'. The literature contains little of substance concerning post-modernism and information systems at this time of writing. An exception is an interesting recent book by Poster (1990) who counterposes various influential post-modern writers such as Foucault, Derrida, and Lyotard against areas in contemporary society such as databases, electronic writing, and the discipline of computer science. He basically explores the theme that people are constituted or made in acts and structures of communication, and he investigates some of the specific instances of the way that changes in contemporary communication patterns, utilizing new information technology and information systems, are involved in changing the nature of people and society.

The book you are reading is not a 'post-modern' work, and little direct reference will be made to post-modern writers in what follows. Nevertheless, the interesting and controversial ideas of Derrida on the nature of language as 'undecidable' and 'upon which meaning has to be imposed' (Cooper 1989) have influenced the author's thinking about the interpretation of language. In addition, the subtle views of Foucault (1979) concerning disciplinary power will be returned to later in the book. The position which this author takes on post-modernism is that it is a fertile field of ideas, and one does not need to take everything on board, including the dismissal of all modernist writers, but can pick and choose interesting concepts to be woven in with some of the other theoretical strands discussed above.

CASE STUDIES

The stated approach of this book involves broadly interpretive methods of research, aimed at an understanding of the context of the information system and the process over time of mutual influence between the system and its context. The type of theories discussed above provide guidelines and frameworks for conducting such research, and also provide ways of encapsulating the findings from the work. The main thrust of this section is to justify the view that the most appropriate method for conducting empirical research in the interpretive tradition is the in-depth case study. Such case studies will often be carried out longitudinally, namely over a reasonably long period with the opportunity to directly observe the unfolding of events over time. Longitudinal research is often supplemented by detailed historical reconstruction of earlier periods. In addition, the method frequently involves the use of two or more case studies for comparison purposes. Pettigrew (1990) justifies this as follows:

> The longitudinal comparative case method provides the opportunity to examine continuous processes in context and to draw in the significance of various interconnected levels of analysis. Thus there is scope to reveal the multiple sources and loops of causation and connectivity so crucial in identifying and explaining patterns in the process of change. (p. 271)

Criticisms of the in-depth case study method for empirical research tend to focus on the non-representativeness and lack of statistical generalizability arising from the work. This is sometimes excused on the grounds that the case study is being used as an exploratory method of analysis prior to, or in addition to, more detailed large sample work. This is not the argument in favour of the case study method being used in this book. The main argument here, as discussed by Craig Smith (1989), is that epistemology, the basis of one's claims to knowledge, and research methods are interrelated. If one adopts a positivist epistemological stance, then statistical generalizability is the key goal. However, from an interpretive position, the validity of an extrapolation from an individual case or cases depends not on the representativeness of such cases in a statistical sense, but on the plausibility and cogency of the logical reasoning used in describing the results from the cases, and in drawing conclusions from them.

The above discussion relates to the use of case studies in empirical research in general, but a similar point is made in the specific context of information systems by Orlikowski and Baroudi (1989) when they argue in favour of the use of case studies for information systems research:

> The argument of non-generalizability is often raised against studies conducted in the interpretive tradition. It is necessary first to make an important distinction between the positivist sense of generalization (of causal relationships from a sample to a population), and a second mode of generalization that is 'the extension from the micro-context to the totality that shaped it' [Burawoy 1985]. In the latter view every particular social relation is the product of generative forces or mechanisms operating at a more global level, and hence the interpretive analysis is an induction (guided and couched within a theoretical framework) from the concrete situation to the social totality beyond the individual case. (pp. 13–14)

A second article in the information systems literature which addresses the topic of the case research method is that by Benbasat, Goldstein and Mead (1987). They rightly argue that it is encumbent on case study researchers to be more explicit about their research goals and methods, and they provide a critique of some published work which could have been improved in these respects. They maintain that case research is particularly appropriate for 'sticky, practice-based problems', and this could be taken to include all aspects of information systems in an organizational context. However, the authors also consider that case studies are suitable for problems where 'research and theory are at their early, formative stages', without drawing an explicit link between this statement and their positivist stance on knowledge accrual, which in their view consists of hypothesis generation and testing leading to confirmation or disconfirmation. This is not a criticism of their positivist views *per se*, but is a good illustration of the link between the authors' epistemological stance and their opinions of the appropriateness of the case research method.

A major proportion of the book, namely Parts II and III, will be devoted to in-depth case studies and the implications which can be drawn from them. As an introduction to this later material, the view discussed above that case studies provide the main vehicle for research in the interpretive tradition will now be briefly illustrated using some particular studies from the literature. The case studies were carried out within the broad spirit of the interpretive approach discussed in this chapter, and can be used to show how generalizable results can be obtained from such work.

Systems Design Case Study

This case study concerned the experience of systems design from the perspective of a systems analyst employed by a credit company and, in particular, her work on a loan application system (Boland and Day 1989). The underlying theory which is used in this case derives from phenomenology and hermeneutics as discussed earlier in the chapter. The authors neatly sum up their epistemological stance as follows:

> The truth value of the statements that result from a phenomenological hermeneutic study is determined only by the way they are incorporated and made use of in the field of discourse on organizations and information systems, not by a failure to disconfirm them. (p. 92)

The study was a single-site longitudinal case study over a two-year period, and the data collection method was primarily in-depth discussions with the systems analyst herself. The purpose was to describe the phenomena of designing computer systems applications as she experienced them, and to attempt to distil the basic structures of meaning which she identified as making her experiences meaningful. The aim of the research was to explore these deeper structures with a view to their generalizability to other design settings, even though they were developed from the experience of a single case setting.

The results from the research suggested three structures of meaning which were valuable to her. The first concerned her experience of moving through organizational space understood as her location in relation to bi-polar opposites. One such set of opposites involved the tension between a focus on the core activities of the business consisting of disbursements and loan payments and associated with the operations manager of the company, and the opposing perspective where the emphasis was on activities peripheral to the core, involving new applications, and associated with the marketing manager. A second set of opposites concerned two different attitudes to control within the company. The first was linked with the operations manager again, who saw control as being concerned with carrying out set tasks well and being accountable for them. The opposing perspective saw control as a sense of freedom to exercise authority across the whole range of activities of the company, emphasizing the importance of flexibility and change. This latter perspective was linked with the president of the company.

A second structure of meaning for the systems analyst was her experience of interacting with others, particularly users, as a problem of interpenetrating with them through language, without intruding on them. Problems of interpenetration included the need to generate commitment on the part of the users, the difficulty for the users to conceptualize aspects of the proposed new systems without having had experience of them, and the lack of immediacy about the systems design task from their perspective when compared to current tasks. The dilemmas of intrusion were that interpenetration can be pressed too far, resulting in the users feeling that they were being asked to do the systems analyst's job, that the designer might be going outside the bounds of what was proper for her to enquire about the users' jobs in order to do her own job, and that the systems analyst could make the users 'feel small' when discussing technical aspects of which she had greater mastery.

The third structure of meaning was her experience of moral choice as to what constituted an improvement in the system, as well as a choice as to what general responsibility she had for the system in terms of such aspects as 'selling' the system to others in the company. With respect to moral choices concerning systems improvement, an interesting example is given where user-friendly systems, as experienced by the designer, became a code word for systems which allowed lower paid, less able people to be hired to replace higher paid, more able people. This question was interwoven with the issue of organizational power, where user-friendly systems implied increased power for select members of the management group. Whether this constitutes system betterment is experienced as a moral dilemma by the designer.

The results from this work have been given in some detail to illustrate the type of generalizations which can be derived from a single case study using interpretive methods. The results could be explored and used in other design settings, not with the aim of producing the final truth about the experience of being a systems designer and developer, but with a view to deepening our knowledge of how individuals make such experience meaningful to themselves, and thus also to ourselves. One final point which relates to this is that the case was a form of action research which changed the attitudes and structures of meaning of both the researched and the researchers. The authors point out, referring to the systems analyst, that this increased knowledge 'if anything, burdens and complicates her action with deeper levels of reflexivity and responsibility'. However, the same applies to the researchers themselves, and is the consequence of any serious intellectual endeavour.

Informating Case Studies

A second set of case studies illustrative of an interpretive approach are described in the book by Zuboff (1988). This book has been widely cited in the literature as an insightful and well-researched piece of work on the current and possible future implications of the widespread use of information technology in modern society. Zuboff comments interestingly on her epistemological stance:

> Behind every method lies a belief. Researchers must have a theory of reality and of how reality might surrender itself to their knowledge-seeking efforts. These epistemological fundamentals are subject to debate but not to ultimate proof. Each epistemology implies a set of methods uniquely suited to it . . . My own commitment to understanding social phenomena has been fundamentally shaped by the study of phenomenology and, in particular, its application to sociology and psychology. (p. 423)

Thus Zuboff's work has its philosophical roots in phenomenology, as with that of Boland. Her style of research on the meaning of individual experience, and her sense of how these experiences can be brought together to provide a broader picture is captured as follows:

> I want to understand the dialectical interchange between human responsiveness (feeling, perceiving, behaving) and what philosophers call the 'life-world' . . . on the one hand, the human body and its responsiveness actively structures the world, but that world in turn shapes and selects forms of human responsiveness . . . The interior, preconceptual, felt texture of human responsiveness is an immensely rich source of critical insight into a situation that a person is living. While this level of responsiveness provides for individual variation, the constellation of commonly felt meanings can be a powerful critique of a shared situation. (p. 423)

The field work which formed the empirical basis for the book involved eight in-depth case studies, which included both manufacturing and service industries and encompassed blue-collar workers, clerical employees, managers and professionals. Sites were selected where one or more of these worker groups had experienced a fundamental reorganization of their tasks as a result of computer-based technology. Data gathering methods used the principle of triangulation, which involves the collection of data on particular issues or phenomena from distinct sources, and particular techniques included small-group discussions, individual interviews, participant observation, and the use of files, reports and other forms of documentation. Interviews were conducted using a 'non-judgemental form of listening', drawing on the work of Gendlin (1978) amongst others. The analytical method for data analysis is described as 'inductive', which relates directly to the ideas discussed earlier concerning generalizations from case studies.

The results from the work are discussed fully in Zuboff's book, but some key ideas and concepts will now be briefly outlined. Zuboff coined a new word 'informate' to describe the process, seen in her case studies, whereby information technology not only automates procedures and approaches but, simultaneously, produces new information. Activities and events are made more visible when a technology informates as well as automates. Zuboff hypothesizes that informating requires more widespread intellectual skills to be developed and used, but that this is inconsistent with traditional aspects of power and authority in organizations. The conclusion is that the informating process sets knowledge and authority on a collision course, and that new organizational strategies and approaches are needed to deal effectively with the changed world which has been enabled by the developments of the 'smart machine'.

Zuboff discusses new strategic approaches in the later parts of the book. She is highly critical of organizations which adopt a strategy towards information technology which emphasizes automation. She argues for more flexible organization structures and a new division of labour, requiring the development of intellectual skills at all levels seen as a continuous learning process for all employees. This new 'division of learning' requires another vocabulary—one of colleagues and co-learners, of exploration, experimentation and innovation. Four domains of managerial activity are suggested involving intellectual skill development, technology development, strategy development, and social system development. This latter activity includes a major collective effort to create and communicate meaning, linked to people's capacity to sustain the high levels of internal commitment and motivation that are demanded by the abstraction of work. Zuboff does not see the effects of information technology as automatic and inevitable, but as a matter of social choice. She ends the book with an appeal that society should not waste human potential by relegating people to roles which involve no use of knowledge and skill, and no opportunity for growth and development. The use of information technology to its full potential means using human beings to their full potential.

Zuboff's work is a good illustration of the potential value of interpretive research, and the possibilities for generalization from empirical results derived from in-depth case studies. Of course, the research can be criticized; for example, it can be argued that the case studies are not representative of the broader picture which is forming within society at large. Indeed, the case studies were deliberately selected to be non-representative, by, for example, choosing cases where information technology had already had a major impact. However, the book provides good field data on a variety of organizations and an in-depth discussion, in these field settings, of the changes in work and work roles enabled to date by information technology. The distinction between automating and informating is simplistic as all such dichotomies are, but useful nevertheless. There is a valuable discussion of the effects of informating on power in organizations, and one does not have to agree with all the conclusions from the work to find the discussion interesting and stimulating. The speculation on future choices and dilemmas provides an agenda for debate, and the book is surely essential reading for anyone seriously interested in information technology in modern organizations and society.

Implementation Case Study

The final illustration of the interpretive approach is a classic case study by Markus (1983) on resistance to the implementation of a financial information system, which had significant effects on both divisional and centralized accounting functions and was the source of major conflict between them. Markus uses the case study to examine the relative merits of various theories regarding resistance to change in the context of new information systems.

Unlike the case study work discussed earlier in this section, Markus gives no explanation of her underlying philosophy. Nevertheless, the hints which are given concerning her methodology suggest an early version of the more developed approaches of Boland and Zuboff. For example, the purpose is to evaluate the various theories of resistance 'using logic and the limited data of a single case'. The unit of analysis for this research was the organizational subunit and the work involved the single case outlined above. No reasons are given as to why this particular research site was selected. With respect to data collection methods, some brief detail is given in the published work. Extensive interviews with designers and users were carried out, and documentary evidence included corporate annual reports, organizational charts, systems training manuals and design documents, and internal correspondence about the systems. One assumes implicitly that triangulation was a part of the research design, involving the collection of views from different participants on the same issues.

The results from the work suggested an explanation that people resist information systems because of the interaction of specific design features with aspects of the organizational context of system use. This 'interaction theory' was found to be a more powerful explanation of resistance than simpler theories based solely on the characteristics of users or the system itself. The political variant of interaction theory concentrates on the distribution of power within the organizational context, and the ways in which this is affected by the new information system. This version of the theory was found particularly useful for the case situation, and it is hypothesized more generally that the political variant of interaction theory is likely to be most appropriate when organizational participants disagree about the nature of the 'problem', when there is uncertainty about the proposed solution, and when the information systems cut across several diverse organizational subunits.

The research is also used to develop some more prescriptive guidelines for those concerned with implementing information systems. One of these is a warning against the naïve view that user participation in the design process is a panacea for implementation. Markus notes that:

> User participation in the design process . . . is clearly contraindicated in cases where powerful authorities have decided that a specific change, unpopular with users, will take place . . . In such situations, users are likely to resent strongly

a tactic that is meant to make them feel as though they have some say in the matter, when they obviously do not. (p. 441)

A second important implication from the research is that the best prescriptions for an implementation strategy will follow from a thorough diagnosis of the organizational setting in which the system will be used. This is of course a major rationale for the current book.

The research described by Markus and the subsequent conclusions are still relevant today, but have a rather dated air about them. In addition, there is little available concerning the philosophical underpinning of the work, and some elements such as the rationale and approach to data collection and analysis are only briefly outlined. The reason for including the case here is that, *for its time*, this was an outstanding piece of work in the interpretive tradition. We have moved on in our knowledge of information systems since the days of the late 1970s when the initial research was carried out, but the case was widely cited in the literature throughout the 1980s and undoubtedly made a significant contribution to knowledge arising out of the insights from a single case study.

THE RESEARCH PERSPECTIVE

An outline of the research perspective taken in the rest of this book can now be given, based on the introductory material presented so far. The topic of the book is computer-based information systems and the focal level of analysis is organizations rather than individuals or groups, or society in general. The overarching premise is that explicit social theory is of high value both to inform analyses and to encapsulate the conclusions from research and practice concerning information systems. The epistemology can be viewed as broadly interpretive, seeing the pursuit of meaning and understanding as subjective and knowledge as a social construction. The methodological approach is focused on explorations of the multi-level context of a computer-based information system, and the process of organizational change within which the information system is one element. The research method used involves in-depth case studies. These elements of the chosen research perspective are summarized diagrammatically in Figure 1.1.

The main body of the book is divided into three parts which provide the substance to support and develop the research perspective outlined above. Part I develops the theoretical foundation which has been discussed briefly in this introduction. Chapter 2, on organizational metaphors, argues that the mechanistic and organismic metaphors of organization which are commonly used in the literature are limiting; the case is developed for the use of combinations of alternative metaphorical approaches, and in particular the metaphors of organizations as cultures and organizations as political systems

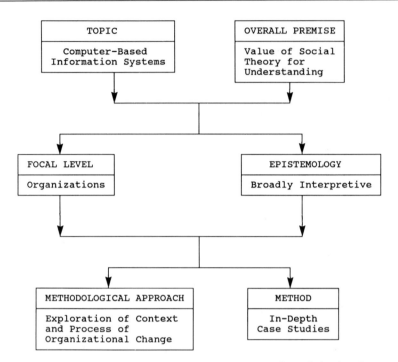

FIGURE 1.1 Outline of the research perspective of the book

are developed in some depth. Chapter 3 discusses an approach to understanding based on analyses of the content, context and process of organizational change associated with a particular information system. Theoretical models of value here include web models of context, cultural and political perspectives on the process of change, and structuration theory as a way of conceptualizing links between context and process. A synthesized analytical framework is generated, designed as a basis for an understanding of organizational change associated with computer-based information systems.

Three major case studies are described in Part II and are explored using the analytical framework developed in Part I. The first case study, discussed in Chapter 4, concerns the introduction of a material requirements planning system into a manufacturing company. The implementation of this system was unsuccessful in many respects, and the reasons for this failure are analysed in detail. Chapter 5 describes a case study of the information systems developed during the 1980s in a medium-sized UK building society, which was very successful in financial terms during this period. The role of the information systems is discussed and related to contextual elements in both the organizational and wider context within which the company was operating. A change in leadership towards the end of the research period involved a substantial shift in management style, and some difficulties which were encountered in this transition are also analysed. Chapter 6 describes the history over a decade of computer-based information systems developed by a central government agency in a Third World country for the purpose of integrating the planning and control of development projects. Two of the systems were implemented in technical terms but were not extensively used, and the reasons for this lack of organizational implementation are analysed in the chapter.

The understanding and insights arising from the theory and empirical work described in Parts I and II are used to explore four major information systems issues in Part III. These issues are strategy, evaluation, design and development, and implementation; they are discussed in turn in Chapters 7 to 10. For each of these issues, relevant literature is surveyed and themes from the case studies are discussed. A new synthesized perspective or interpretation of the issue is developed, and this is used to explore some areas for debate and action in any particular practical context. The final chapter, Chapter 11, synthesizes a perspective on information systems in organizations arising from Part III, relates this perspective to the broader relationship between IS and society, and draws implications from the whole book for future IS research, education and practice.

REFERENCES

Benbasat, I., Goldstein, D. K., and Mead, M. (1987) 'The case research strategy in studies of information systems', *MIS Quarterly*, **11**, No.3, 369–386.
Boland, R. J. (1979) 'Control, causality and information system requirements', *Accounting, Organizations and Society*, **4**, No. 4, 259–272.
Boland, R. J. (1985) 'Phenomenology: a preferred approach to research on information systems', in *Research Methods in Information Systems* (eds E. Mumford, R. Hirschheim, G. Fitzgerald and T. Wood-Harper), North-Holland, New York.
Boland, R. J., and Day, W. F. (1989) 'The experience of system design: a hermeneutic of organizational action', *Scandinavian Journal of Management*, **5**, No. 2, 87–104.
Brancheau, J. C., and Wetherbe, J. C. (1987) 'Key issues in information systems management', *MIS Quarterly*, **11**, No. 1, 23–45.
Burawoy, M. (1985) *The Politics of Production: Factory Regimes Under Capitalism*, Verso Books, London.
Burrell, G., and Morgan, G. (1979) *Sociological Paradigms and Organisational Analysis*, Heinemann, London.
Checkland, P. (1981) *Systems Thinking, Systems Practice*, Wiley, Chichester.
Checkland, P. (1982) 'Soft systems methodology as process: a reply to M. C. Jackson', *Journal of Applied Systems Analysis*, **9**, 37–39.
Checkland, P., and Scholes, J. (1990) *Soft Systems Methodology in Action*, Wiley, Chichester.
Cooper, R. (1989) 'Modernism, post-modernism and organizational analysis 3: the contribution of Jacques Derrida', *Organization Studies*, **10**, No. 4, 479–502.
Craig Smith, N. (1989) 'The case study: a vital yet misunderstood research method for management', in *Frontiers of Management* (ed. R. Mansfield), Routledge, London.

Foucault, M. (1979) *Discipline and Punish*, Vintage Books, New York.
Gadamer, H.-G. (1975) *Truth and Method*, Sheed & Ward, London.
Gendlin, E. (1978) *Focusing*, Everest House, New York.
Giddens, A. (1977) 'Review essay: Habermas's social and political theory', *American Journal of Sociology*, **83**, No. 1, 198–212.
Habermas, J. (1972) *Knowledge and Human Interests*, Heinemann, London.
Heidegger, M. (1962) *Being and Time*, Harper & Row, New York.
Hirschheim, R., and Klein, H. K. (1989) 'Four paradigms of information systems development', *Communications of the ACM*, **32**, No. 10, 1199–1216.
Husserl, E. (1931) *Ideas: General Introduction to Pure Phenomenology*, Macmillan, New York.
Jackson, M. C. (1982) 'The nature of "soft" systems thinking: the work of Churchman, Ackoff and Checkland', *Journal of Applied Systems Analysis*, **9**, 17–29.
Jönsson, S. (1991) 'Action research', in *Information Systems Research: Contemporary Approaches and Emergent Traditions* (eds H.-E. Nissen, H. K. Klein and R. A. Hirschheim), North-Holland, Amsterdam.
Kraemer, K. L., and King, J. L. (1990), 'Social analysis in MIS: the Irvine School, 1970–1990', in *Proceedings of the Twenty-Third Annual Hawaii International Conference on System Sciences, Volume 3* (ed. J.F. Nunamaker), IEEE Computer Society Press, Los Alimitos, CA.
Lyotard, J.-F. (1984) *The Postmodern Condition: A Report on Knowledge*, Manchester University Press, Manchester.
Lyytinen, K. J., and Klein, H. K. (1985) 'The critical theory of Jurgen Habermas as a basis for a theory of information systems', in *Research Methods in Information Systems* (eds E. Mumford, R. Hirschheim, G. Fitzgerald and T. Wood-Harper), North-Holland, New York.
Markus, M. L. (1983) 'Power, politics and MIS implementation', *Communications of the ACM*, **26**, No. 6, 430–445.
Mingers, J., and Taylor, S. (1992) 'The use of soft systems methodology in practice', *Journal of the Operational Research Society*, **43**, No. 4, 321–332.
Orlikowski, W. J., and Baroudi, J. J. (1989) 'IS research paradigms: method versus substance', Sloan Working Paper No 3028–89-MS, *Massachusetts Institute of Technology*, Cambridge, Massachusetts.
Pettigrew, A. M. (1990) 'Longitudinal field research on change: theory and practice', *Organization Science*, **1**, No.3, 267–292.
Poster, M. (1990) *The Mode of Information: Poststructuralism and Social Context*, Polity Press, Cambridge.
Winograd, T., and Flores, F. (1986) *Understanding Computers and Cognition*, Ablex Publishing, Norwood.
Zuboff, S. (1988) *In the Age of the Smart Machine*, Basic Books, New York.

Part I
THEORY

Chapter 2
ORGANIZATIONAL METAPHORS

The previous chapter outlined the research perspective which forms the basis for this book. The interpretive epistemology of this perspective considers knowledge as a social construction, and the use, design and study of information systems in organizations is thought of as a hermeneutic process of reading and interpretation. A powerful and interesting approach to the 'reading' of organizations is provided by the use of metaphor, and this chapter will develop this theme in some detail. A metaphor is defined as the 'application of (a) name or descriptive term or phrase to an object or action to which it is not literally applicable' (*Concise Oxford Dictionary*, 1976).

Metaphors can be thought of, at one level, as ways of livening up speech and writing. For example, when we say that 'the takeover bid was a pitched battle', we conjure up a vivid image of armed and deliberate conflict, using the pointed metaphor of physical conflict between armies for the social and psychological conflict of opposing sides in a takeover bid. The reader may have spotted the use of a further metaphor in this description where the verb 'conjure' is used to imply a 'magical' means of producing the required image; metaphor can be an unexpected and creative device for evoking new images of known situations, although metaphors such as the one above become blunted in their impact by frequent use.

Although metaphors can certainly be thought of as decorative devices for our speech and writing, their use can be considered more important and fundamental than this. Lakoff and Johnson (1980) summarize this as follows:

> In all aspects of life, not just in politics or love, we define our reality in terms of metaphors and then proceed to act on the basis of the metaphors. We draw inferences, set goals, make commitments, and execute plans, all on the basis of how we in part structure our experience, consciously and unconsciously, by means of metaphor. (p. 158)

In the context of the study of organizations, the widely-cited book by Morgan (1986) is based on viewing organizations through a process of metaphorical enquiry. He says the following:

> Metaphor is often just regarded as a device for embellishing discourse, but its significance is much greater than this. For the use of metaphor implies a *way of*

thinking and a *way of seeing* that pervade how we understand our world generally . . . It is easy to see how this kind of thinking has relevance for understanding organization and management. For organizations are complex and paradoxical phenomena that can be understood in many different ways. Many of our taken-for-granted ideas about organizations are metaphorical, even though we may not recognize them as such. (pp. 12–13)

In a similar vein, when discussing the use of metaphors in the context of accounting systems in organizations, Boland (1989a) argues that metaphors are not just colourful ways of expressing ourselves, but underlie the ways in which we think and act, and thus we 'cannot not use metaphors'. Boland (1989b) also warns information systems researchers to be wary of the 'metaphorical trap' of assuming that metaphors can be used as tools in an instrumental way; researchers are themselves caught up in the medium of language and thus the medium of metaphor:

> The multi-vocal, ambiguous nature of language and the way metaphors evoke nested complexes of symbolic meanings which, in turn, evoke a reverberating set of others make it impossible to just pick one out and use it in any clear, precise way. Language is not a tool and is not something we can step outside of. (p. 282)

Mangham and Overington (1987) argue that metaphors can provide fresh images and insights, but they emphasize the point mentioned above that the absorption of metaphors into everyday speech and writing largely removes the power of insight. This implies the need to consider alternative metaphors and to regard the search for metaphorical insight as a continuous process, rather than seeing it as a goal-oriented search for the 'best' metaphors. Bowles (1990), following ideas from Krefting and Frost (1985), connects the use of metaphors with the tapping of unconscious material in the human mind. He argues that this can be a creative approach to analysing organizational life, which is 'locked into deep patterns that underpin our existence'.

This chapter concentrates on metaphor as a way of thinking *about* organizations, although some mention is made in what follows about metaphors used *in* organizations. The next section reviews a variety of organizational metaphors and explores their relationship to the study of information systems. This review is followed by sections which develop two particular metaphors in some depth, namely those of organizations as cultures and as political systems. The chapter then concludes with a synthesis of the theoretical approach which has been developed, based on a pluralist and process perspective on organizational metaphors.

METAPHORS AND INFORMATION SYSTEMS

The first part of this review section draws on the eight organizational metaphors of Morgan (1986) and the discussion of their linkage to information systems in Walsham (1991). Morgan considers a wide range of different approaches to the study of organizations, and uses insights from a variety of disciplines including organizational behaviour, sociology, cybernetics, management theory, political science, social psychology, and biology. His eight images view organizations as machines, organisms, brains, cultures, political systems, psychic prisons, flux and transformation, and instruments of domination.

Organizations as Machines

The metaphor of organizations as machines is very powerful and pervasive in contemporary industrialized societies. The 'scientific management' approach to work originally developed by Taylor (1911) is strongly linked to the machine metaphor. Taylor's concern was to develop this approach to its logical conclusion to enable the creation of perfect productive machines from the raw ingredients of people and material resources. His approach has been widely criticized for the last 50 years, but his ideas have been profoundly influential on the management of organizations, and the ways in which we talk about organizational life. For example, such phrases as optimizing performance and maximizing efficiency imply the possibility of creating an organization which behaves in a routinized, predictable and totally controllable way.

With reference to information systems, a useful contribution to the discussion of mechanistic metaphors has been made by Kling (1987). He describes one way in which computer-based technologies and systems are conceptualized as 'discrete-entity models'. These focus on explicit economic, physical or information processing features of the technology, and the social context in which the technology is developed and used is limited to a few formal relationships or is ignored. Organizational behaviour is best described by the formal goals, procedures, and administrative arrangements of the acting units.

The discrete-entity approach to information systems development and the related mechanistic view of organization form the theoretical underpinning, albeit normally implicitly, of much of the technical literature on computer-based information systems. For example, the concept of a 'complete and correct set of requirements' (Davis and Olson 1984, p. 474) for an information systems development sweeps away the multiple perspectives and ambiguities of organizational life and hides them under the carpet of the mechanistic metaphor. A systems analyst who approaches the task of specifying an information systems design based on such a naïve view of organizations is unlikely to be successful in any sense of that term. A mechanistic approach to information systems development tends to create rigid and inflexible systems which are ill-suited to the need for adaptation to changing circumstances. In addition, a neglect of the subtleties of the social context of an information system is likely to have negative consequences in terms of human needs and aspirations, and from a more managerial perspective, to lack of motivation, poor productivity and resistance to change.

Organizations as Organisms

Whilst the mechanistic view of organization formed the early foundation of modern management, the image of organizations as organisms has arguably been the most influential metaphor for management practice over the last few decades. The organismic view sees organizations as analogous to living systems, existing in a wider environment on which they depend for the satisfaction of various needs. The origins of this approach can be traced back to the Hawthorne studies in the 1920s in Chicago (Mayo 1933), which demonstrated the importance of social needs and human factors in work activities and organizational effectiveness. The later work of Maslow (1943) then emphasized that management must concern itself with personal growth and development of its employees rather than confining itself to the lower level needs of money and security.

Developments from this early work include the socio-technical systems approach (see, for example, Trist 1982), which focuses on the interdependence of the social and technical aspects of work. In the literature on information systems, the socio-technical view has been drawn on to develop methods for the determination of information systems requirements and procedures for systems design (Mumford and Weir 1979). Both technical and social alternatives for job redesign are identified and a participative approach is then followed aimed at producing a systems design which improves both task efficiency and job satisfaction.

A second major school of thought based on the organismic metaphor is the contingency approach to organizations, pioneered by a number of writers (for example: Burns and Stalker 1961, Lawrence and Lorsch 1967). The essence of this approach is that organizations are open systems which need to satisfy internal needs and adapt to environmental circumstances, and that management should be centrally concerned with achieving good fits between organizational forms and the task or environment with which they are dealing. The achievement of good fits in practice is one of the main focuses of the field of organizational development.

With respect to information systems, much of the current management literature and consultancy prescription is linked to the organismic view of organization and, in particular, to the contingency approach. A standard textbook on management information systems (Davis and Olson 1984) describes the details of contingency approaches to the choice of application development strategies, the determination of application level requirements, the determination of organizational requirements, and the management of IS projects. Other well-known models and approaches are based on contingency theory, such as the stage theory of information systems development (Gibson and Nolan 1974) and the strategic grid for information systems planning (McFarlan and McKenney 1983).

The prescriptions arising from this literature often have value as frameworks for thinking about issues, but are rather simplistic when one attempts to apply them in specific organizations, which seem to resist the categorizations which are endemic to approaches such as contingency theory. Organizations which appear similar in terms of their task, structures and environment exhibit disturbingly different characteristics. For example, Barley (1986) describes the introduction of new technology into two 'similar' hospital radiological departments with totally different consequences. More generally, Attewell and Rule (1984) examined the literature on the effects of computing in organizations in such areas as centralization/decentralization, changes in quality of work, and impacts on power and authority. They concluded that these effects are more complicated and diverse than has traditionally been assumed. Human beings and organizations are more complex and problematic than is implied by approaches such as contingency theory. For example, the cultural and socially constructed view of organizations is not readily categorizable by measurable variables.

A second major weakness of the organismic metaphor is the stress on the unity of an organization on an analogous basis with the human organism itself. However, organizations are looser couplings than is implied by this metaphor, and conflict, politics and power struggles are potential forces of disunity. For example, the socio-technical design approach to information systems presumes it is possible to design systems which simultaneously satisfy technology needs and the human desires and aspirations of various interest groups. Little is said about circumstances where it is not possible to resolve these potentially divergent needs, and where political action is critical.

Other Metaphorical Approaches

The *machine* and *organismic* metaphors have been considered in some detail in this review section because of their important influence on the literature and practice of the management of organizations in general, and information systems in particular. Other metaphors discussed by Morgan include organizations as *cultures, political systems* and *instruments of domination*. We will explore these metaphors in some depth later in the chapter. The metaphors of organizations as *brains* and *psychic prisons* have some interest, but will not be discussed further here; their links to information systems are briefly discussed in Walsham (1991).

A further metaphor which Morgan describes is that of organizations as *flux and transformation*. Various strands are included but one of particular interest to the study of information systems is the autopoietic metaphor. The term autopoiesis was coined by Maturana and Varela (1980) to describe the self-referential nature of living systems, such as human beings, and the 'circular organisation' which they display. The autopoietic view sees an organism as organizationally closed and a system's interaction with its 'environment' is really a reflection and part of its own organization. Thus, according to Maturana and Varela, the question 'How does the organism obtain information about its environment?' should be changed to 'How does it happen that the organism has the structure that permits it to operate adequately in the medium in which it exists?'.

The above work was concerned with living organisms but provides an interesting extension of the organismic metaphor of organizations. The ideas are relevant to information systems, since contemporary organizations use these systems as a primary way to view both their internal and external environment. The key insight from autopoiesis is that the information collected reflects the way in which the organization is structured to view the world rather than the way the world 'is'. The practical implication for the design, development and use of information systems is the need for constant reflection on the adequacy of the structure of those systems rather than a unique concentration on the 'information' which the systems yield.

The metaphors in Morgan's book have been used as a basis for this review section because of their range and quality of development, but many other metaphors of organization can be considered. For example, Mangham and Overington (1987) offer the metaphor of organizations as theatre, which 'permits a humanistic, artistic and creatively playful approach to organizations' and contrasts, in their view, with the 'heavy-handed models of systematic rationality'. They also point out the interesting transitive property of this metaphor, with the ideas of 'life as theatre' and 'theatre as life' both being the subjects of debate over the centuries.

The discussion of metaphors in the information systems literature is mainly implicit, in the sense that authors have normally not spelt out what image of organization they are drawing on in their work. A partial exception is the paper by Hirschheim and Klein (1989) in which their alternative views of the role of a systems analyst as expert, facilitator, labour partisan, or emancipator, is a metaphorical approach to analysis. Madsen (1989) makes explicit use of metaphors and suggests that they can be used consciously to 'break down' the unreflected being of the human participants in the information systems design process, as a means of liberating new ideas. The concepts are developed on the theoretical basis of Winograd and Flores' use of Heidegger's concepts of breakdown, discussed in Chapter 1. Madsen's work is an attempt to operationalize the theoretical ideas, although in its suggestion of the instrumental use of metaphors alien to a user group, it is in danger of falling into one of Boland's metaphorical traps of assuming that researchers can remain 'above' the use of metaphors themselves, but utilize them as tools.

The discussion to date has concentrated on the use of metaphors as a way of thinking about organizations, but one paper in the information systems domain considers metaphors used in organizations. Kendall and Kendall (1992) conducted extensive interviews of people in user groups concerned with the development of a particular information system. They extracted nine metaphors of organization which they believed to represent common threads in their empirical data. These conceive the process of system development as a journey, game or war and the organization itself as a machine, organism, society, family, zoo or jungle. This type of empirical research has interesting potential for insight, although the work reported here contains no details on such important issues as who was using which metaphors and for what purpose, which would have required in-depth study of particular organizations.

ORGANIZATIONS AS CULTURES

The first metaphor chosen for detailed discussion, which falls centrally within the interpretive spirit of the book, is the view of organizations as cultures. A valuable paper by Smircich (1983) pointed out that the culture concept has been borrowed from anthropology, where there is no consensus on its meaning. She considered five different streams of research on culture, linking the first two, which see culture as an organizational variable, to mechanical and organismic views of organization. The other three streams of work use the concept of culture as a root metaphor for conceptualizing organization, and derive from cognitive, symbolic and structural anthropology. In these three traditions, culture is viewed respectively as shared knowledge, a system of shared meaning, and an expression of the mind's unconscious operation.

In this section, the primary view taken will be that of culture as shared meaning, linked to symbolic anthropology (Geertz 1973). When this perspective is applied to organizational analysis, culture is conceived of as a pattern of symbolic discourse. It thus needs interpreting, reading, or deciphering. The research agenda is to document the creation and maintenance of organization through symbolic action. Smircich (1983) provides a cogent summary of this perspective as follows:

> Symbolic organization theorists are concerned with interpreting or deciphering the patterns of symbolic action that create and maintain a sense of organization. They recognize that symbolic modes, such as language, facilitate shared realities, yet these realities are fleeting, always open to reinterpretation and renegotiation. Thus, for them, the very concept of organization is problematic. (p. 354)

Morgan (1986) addressed the metaphor of organizations as cultures largely from this symbolic perspective. He considered that, in talking about culture, we are really talking about a process of reality construction that allows people to see and understand particular events, actions and utterances in distinctive ways. Culture should not be viewed as a set of variables that societies possess, but as an active, living phenomenon through which people create and recreate the worlds in which they live. In trying to understand the process of 'reality construction', Morgan draws on the work of Weick (1969) on the enactment process. Weick emphasizes the selectivity of our view of reality and the subjective way in which we draw meaning from previous lived experiences and thus determine our attitudes to ongoing activity. Weick describes this as follows:

> The sequence whereby some portions of the elapsed experience are made meaningful can be viewed as removing some of the equivocality that is inherent in a flow of experience . . . It is these primitive meanings, these bits of enacted information, that constitute the informational input for subsequent processes . . . The meaning of the enacted information is not fixed, but fluid. It is fluid precisely because its interpretation varies as a function of the temporal distance from which it is viewed. Second, any enacted meaning . . . can fixate either on the completed deed, on the stages by which the deed was accomplished, or on both . . . Third, any specific interpretation that emerges from a reflective glance never tells it all. (p. 69)

In an organizational context, the enactment of meaning is a collective activity, at least in a partial sense, and thus cultural 'structures' or structures of shared meaning are created within the organization. These structures condition the enactment process at later points in time, but in view of the fluid and changing nature of the process, structures become modified and recreated during enactment. The complex link between action and structure has been explored by Giddens (1984) in his structuration theory. This theory emphasizes that action, which has strongly routinized aspects, is both conditioned by existing cultural structures and also creates and recreates those structures through the enactment process. Thus the creation and recreation of culture is a dynamic process linking action and social structure. This theory is developed in more detail in the following chapter.

Although computer-based information systems clearly have a key role in the processes of enactment and reality construction in contemporary organizations, the cultural metaphor in its symbolic form has received relatively little attention in the IS literature. A notable early exception was an article by Feldman and March (1981) which viewed the use of information in organizations as embedded in social norms that make it highly symbolic. Thus, for example, the requesting of information is not simply a basis for taking action, but is symbolic of competence and social virtue in contemporary Western civilization where the concept of intelligent choice is a central ideology. A related aspect of information use as symbolic is the concept of ritual, and Robey and Markus (1984) argue that elements of the system design process can be interpreted as rituals which enable actors to remain overtly rational while negotiating to achieve private interests. A recent paper by Hirschheim and Newman (1991) explores symbolism in IS development and the roles of myths, metaphors and magic; they argue that these concepts offer considerable scope in interpreting social action in the IS domain. A further set of work is that of Boland (1979, 1985), referred to in Chapter 1, where information systems are viewed as an environment of symbols within which a sense-making process takes place. He suggests a cultural approach to information systems requirements, including a dialogue on the problems and processes currently felt to be 'appropriate' for the organization. Finally, Lyytinen (1985, 1987) sees information systems as language-based systems and their use as involving communicative acts which can be studied as a linguistic process. Lyytinen discusses five alternative language views which are used, normally implicitly, as the theoretical underpinnings of particular information systems methodologies and applications.

The sense-making and linguistic perspectives on information systems, related to the symbolic cultural metaphor of organization, are a potentially fruitful area for further work. Two further aspects of the metaphor of organizations as cultures are discussed in the subsections below. Firstly, culture is not a monolithic concept within an organization, and the cultural metaphor is further developed by describing some theoretical approaches to the understanding of subcultures and their interaction. Secondly, a major issue regarding the culture concept is whether and how it can be used by management in an organization. This issue is discussed in its relationship to the prescriptive management literature on organizational culture.

Subcultures and Multiple Meanings

The term subculture is a broad description of a phenomenon with which we are all familiar, namely the existence of subgroups within a broader social unit, such as an organization, who share sets of meanings which perpetuate their distinctive character within the unit as a whole. In an organizational context, this definition of a subculture raises a whole range of theoretical and practical issues concerning how such subcultures are created and maintained, the interaction at the boundaries between subcultures, and the management of subcultures within the context of the organizational culture as a whole. Some work which has addressed these issues is now described.

Young (1989) criticizes much of the literature on organizational culture as suggesting either a view of organization as a single culture which ignores the existence of subgroups with different interests, or as a collection of sectional groups who basically strive for their own gain. This latter perspective recognizes the existence of subgroups, but Young points out that it often assumes that events have a single interpretation which then becomes a point of dispute between the subgroups dependent on how they assess their gain regarding the issue under consideration. This approach ignores the extent to which events and social relationships are capable of being invested with multiple meanings by their participative actors.

Young illustrates the above ideas on subcultures using a case study of a manufacturing company, where management perceived certain events, such as the wearing of roses on St George's Day by the shop floor machinists, as representing a common team spirit or culture amongst the machinists. However, two distinct subgroups within the machinists invested the same event with different meanings. Indeed this highly visible event was a vehicle for expressing the differences between the two production lines, who organized the collection of money and the distribution of the flowers in distinctive ways. Young uses this simple example amongst others to draw the conclusion that the social relationships between subgroups or subcultures is an integral element of the organizational culture as a whole, and that these relationships often involve the attribution of multiple meanings to seemingly simple events, actions and statements. He concludes that the tension between fragmentation, implied by distinctive subcultures, and unity, necessitated by the need for co-operative action, *is* the organizational culture (p. 204, italics in the original).

An earlier theoretical paper by Morgan (1981) developed the idea of a schismatic metaphor for organization which relates to the final conclusion of the work above. The schismatic metaphor assumes a fundamental tendency within organizations towards disintegration as a result of endogenously generated change. This tendency to schism is considered to arise from the striving of groups or subcultures for functional autonomy on the one hand, and from the positive feedback that can arise from the interaction between subgroups resulting in a point being reached at which relationships can no longer be sustained. Management can adopt various counterstrategies against these tendencies for subculture autonomy and intergroup conflict. Viewed in these terms, social systems, and in particular organizations, 'appear as networks of strains and tensions generated through the adoption of strategies and counterstrategies concerned with the development and constraint of the autonomy of systems elements' (Morgan 1981, p. 29).

This theme of the 'natural' state of schism is explored by Cooper and Fox (1989), where they put forward a post-modernist view that we tend to give precedence to (or 'privilege') organizational features such as unity, identity, structure, and permanence over 'anti-organizational' processes such as dissonance, separation, plurality and change. They suggest an approach to organizational analysis based on the interdependence of the nomadic mode of organization, characterized by flux, change, and contradiction, and the control mode, characterized by rationality, coherence and identity. Cooper and Fox see the disorder of the nomadic mode as the 'natural' state of the world and the control mode as needing to be 'constructed' out of this to serve the aims of those doing the construction. They draw a parallel between the disorder of organizations and the orderly writing about them, and the disorder of the process of scientific discovery compared to the carefully ordered accounts in the literature of science.

A radical reading of this post-modernist perspective would see any attempt to write about cultures and subcultures, including the section here, as a means of creating artificial order out of 'natural' chaos, motivated by the interests of the writer. Taken to its extreme, this seems to exclude the possibility of the value of any writing, and this author would not go that far! A less radical perspective would see the post-modernists as reminding us of the need to consider the agenda of the writer and, in the context of the discussion regarding subcultures, to ask what features of order are being used to justify the use of the term subculture.

A summary of the analysis in this subsection suggests the need to consider what features characterize subcultures and the processes whereby subcultures maintain their distinctive character. In addition, we need to study how subcultures interact with each other, including analyses of the multiple interpretations of particular events and actions, and how the natural tension between the tendency to fragmentation due to the autonomy of subcultures and the need for co-operative action changes over time.

With respect to information systems, there is little work in the current literature which specifically addresses the issue of subcultures, and the few exceptions (see, for example, Kendall, Buffington and Kendall (1987)) normally contain no analysis of the process of the maintenance and change of subcultures. There is, however, a significant literature on the political interaction and conflict between different interest groups in the context of the design and development of information systems. This literature will be discussed later in the chapter, but it is worth noting at this point that such work normally takes the interest groups as 'given', with little reference to how they are maintained and changed over time, and with no account of the multiple interpretation of events as described earlier. In other words, such literature normally takes a political stance, with the cultural metaphor being largely absent.

Management and Culture

The concept of culture has received considerable attention in the management literature. Much of this work is prescriptive; for example, the popular book by Peters and Waterman (1982) described eight desirable attributes which were possessed, and by implication should be possessed, by 'successful' companies. The book's findings are controversial since, apart from questions as to whether the measures of success were too narrowly chosen at the time, some of the companies have been noticeably unsuccessful since the publication of the book, even using narrow financial criteria. Nevertheless, the book can be considered of value in popularizing the issue of culture in the management context, in contrast to a narrow focus on, for example, finance or technology. A considerable amount of work has followed in the latter half of the 1980s concerned with 'managing' culture.

The discussion of culture in the previous few pages should make us somewhat wary concerning simple prescriptions, and in particular sceptical regarding the ability to 'manage' culture in any direct sense. Organizational culture and related concepts such as subculture are problematic in definitional terms, and embody subtle, complex and rather nebulous characteristics. Culture cannot be managed through a set of levers which are pulled to 'bring people into line'. Turner (1986) makes a similar point when he disagrees with the principles expressed by the 'pop culture magicians', who sell the belief that corporate culture can be controlled, changed and manipulated from the top down in ways which meet managerial needs for cost effectiveness and productivity gains.

On a more positive note, what can usefully be said about management and organizational culture which might be relevant to the study of information systems? From the symbolic perspective on culture which has been described, Morgan (1986) argues that managers can influence the evolution of culture by being aware of the symbolic consequences of their actions and by attempting to foster desired values. For example, a manager of a systems design process can talk and act as if different perspectives on the final design are acceptable and indeed desirable, and the role of the systems analyst should be to try to understand some of the natural desires for autonomy of the different subcultures and to be trying to create a system which balances the tension between autonomy and the need for co-ordinated action. Such an attitude on the part of the management of a systems design project should influence members of the design team towards an approach which does not see an information system as imposing a new way of working on different groups, and 'resistance' as a phenomenon that needs to be 'overcome'.

A similar argument is made by Smircich (1985) when she discusses the complexities and heterogeneity within the concept of organizational culture, and argues that we should take a positive view of multiple realities, instead of treating different interpretations as 'communications problems'. We should thus think of managing *for* multiple realities, instead of managing in spite of multiple realities. Decision-making and problem-solving activities thus become acts of consciousness raising designed to facilitate more enlightened action. This could sound rather idealistic and perhaps impractical, but many information systems in the decade of the 1980s have failed to be accepted and used effectively by organizational participants, and in the future we need better approaches in areas such as systems design that genuinely address the existence of multiple realities and symbolic meaning within the organizational culture.

ORGANIZATIONS AS POLITICAL SYSTEMS

The second metaphor of organizations chosen for detailed discussion is that of organizations as political systems. The political metaphor, according to Morgan (1986), encourages us to see organizations as loose networks of people with divergent interests who gather together for the sake of expediency. The political aspects of organizations have been alluded to during the previous discussion of organizations viewed as cultures, for example when considering the schismatic perspective. It is clear that the cultural and political metaphors are closely intertwined, but their interconnection will be discussed in detail in the final section of the chapter, whereas we will focus on the political metaphor itself in this section.

A crucial concept for the political metaphor is power, which is the medium through which conflicts of interest are resolved. Despite the common usage which is made of the word power, it remains an elusive and problematic concept, and our discussion starts with some theoretical ideas which underpin the usage of the term in this book. A number of writers have emphasized that power should not necessarily be viewed negatively but is inherent in all human purposeful action. Giddens (1984) says the following:

> Power is the capacity to achieve outcomes; whether or not these are connected to purely sectional interests is not germane to its definition. Power is not, as such, an obstacle to freedom or emancipation but is their very medium— although it would be foolish, of course, to ignore its constraining properties. (p. 257)

Another influential writer on the subject of power is Foucault (1976, 1979). He emphasizes, amongst other aspects, the local nature of the exercise of power and the way in which such local elements may form a wider chain or system of power:

> Power must be understood in the first instance as the multiplicity of force relations imminent in the sphere in which they operate and which constitute their own organization; as the process which, through ceaseless struggles and confrontations, transforms, strengthens, or reverses them; as the support which these force relations find in one another, thus forming a chain or system, or on the contrary, the disjunctions and contradictions which isolate them from one another; and lastly, as the strategies in which they take effect, whose general design or institutional crystallization is embodied in the state apparatus, in the formulation of the law, in the various social hegemonies. (1976, pp. 92–93)

The last part of Foucault's passage above is referring to the power structures of the nation state, but applies equally well to the institutionalized aspects of power in the context of a business organization.

So what do we learn about power from writers such as Giddens and Foucault which is of relevance to organizational analysis in general? The main messages are that power and its use in political activity pervade all action and discourse in organizations, that the exercise of power is a continuous process that has subtle local properties, and that local actions are linked in a complex way to more general networks and institutional frameworks. The implication for research and practice in organizations is that political action and the exercise of power are of major significance but are complex and difficult to understand, and thus require detailed and in-depth attention, particularly in contexts where issues are regarded as important and where individual interests diverge.

This leads naturally to computer-based information systems in contemporary organizations, since they frequently satisfy the above criteria for contexts where the study of power and political action is important. Information systems are implicated in major changes in work and work roles, on issues such as the centralization or decentralization of control, on the relationships between different groups within organizations, and on aspects such as surveillance and individual freedom of action. Divergent interests and perspectives are normally present in such contexts, and thus information systems are arguably one of the key areas for political action in contemporary organizations.

The importance of power and political action has received significant attention in the information systems literature. An early article by Keen (1981) pointed out the importance of the politics of organizational change related to computer-based information systems. A classic case study by Markus (1983), discussed in Chapter 1, described power and political action over an extended period of several years in the introduction of a financial information system which had significant effects on both divisional and centralized accounting functions and was the source of a major conflict between them. Kling and Iacono (1984) described the post-implementation politics related to a material requirements planning system and discussed how key actors used the language of efficiency to help push the information system development in a direction which increased their own capacities for control in the organization. Markus and Bjorn-Andersen (1987) discussed how information systems 'professionals', such as systems analysts and developers, can exercise power over information systems users in a variety of ways, including the use of technical knowledge and procedures and the symbolic shaping of users' desires and values. It is interesting to note that the authors' use of the term 'professionals' is itself an example of such symbolism, implying that professional knowledge is something beyond and above that possessed by or accessible to the users themselves. Waema and Walsham (1990) describe political actions and the exercise of power in the formulation and implementation of information systems strategy in a UK building society.

Despite the interest reflected above, it is relevant to question why the literature in this area is not more extensive, bearing in mind the undoubted importance of political action in the broad arena of organizational activity involved with computer-based information systems. A related point is that the prescriptive literature, aimed at practising managers or information systems specialists, frequently makes little or no mention of political and power elements. A significant attempt to explain these phenomena would occupy more space than is available here, but two broad points can be made. Firstly, it has been noted that the process of the exercise of power and the taking of political action is highly complex, both in theoretical terms and in attempting to observe it in practice. With respect to this latter point, people often attempt to conceal their motives for political action in order to protect what they perceive as their self-interest. Thus, researchers addressing such issues need to spend large amounts of time in specific organizations in order to gather field data, and such data will remain problematic and subject to conflicting interpretations even after such effort. There are simpler forms of research (and ways of producing published articles!) than such in-depth and time-consuming work.

With respect to the literature aimed at practitioners, a similar problem arises in terms of the difficulty in producing good 'prescriptions' in the complex area of political action. However, a second reason can be put forward as to why politics and power are rarely mentioned, related to the myth of rationality in contemporary business organizations. It has been noted earlier that the concept of rational choice is a central ideology in Western society, and that managers therefore demonstrate their adherence to this, and thus their social virtue, by being seen to behave in the 'rational' interest; ideas of power and the taking of political action are ever present in the world in which they live, but such things are not to be spoken about, or particularly written about, too openly. A further explanation of this taboo is that managers legitimize their formal authority over the rest of the workforce and their own subordinates by being seen to behave 'rationally' and, by implication, in everyone's self-interest in the longer term. This legitimation is undermined by an emphasis on political action and the divergent interests of different individuals and groups within an organizational context.

This section on the political metaphor of organization started with a view of power as intrinsic to all human affairs, and thus the conclusion that power should not necessarily be viewed negatively. However, the process of the exercise of power, or the taking of political action, is not exempt from moral judgements and the above discussion on the legitimacy of managerial authority is an example of such a concern. The relationship between politics and ethics, or moral philosophy, is of relevance to a concern about the individual, organizational and societal implications of information systems and is discussed in more detail in the subsection below. This section on the political metaphor is then concluded by a discussion of the relationship between management and political action within the theme of autonomy and control.

Morality and Political Action

Political action can involve the mobilizing of racist groups such as the Ku-Klux-Klan to intimidate and abuse black people, or can involve the activities of individuals and agencies seeking to help the world's poor to help themselves. Most people would make relatively clear moral judgements on these activities at the opposite ends of the spectrum, but much human political activity is in a greyer area where moral judgements are harder to make. Morgan (1986) looks at the darker side of the spectrum when he considers the organizational metaphor of instruments of domination whereby 'certain people acquire and sustain a commanding influence over others, often through subtle processes of socialization and belief'. Morgan notes that domination can be exercised in a variety of ways including the exploitation of employees within organizations, institutionalized discrimination in societies, and the abuse of power through the medium of the international economy.

Information is an extremely important aspect of the dominance metaphor. Cooper (1986) notes that information, which excludes certain alternatives, is a form of social power which involves the forcible transformation of undecidability into decidability. This condensed statement carries some valuable ideas concerning information. Firstly, that any piece of information is based on the division of a whole into parts, for example designating a person as a man or woman, and the choice of the boundary for the division excludes other alternatives. Secondly, that the person making the division is exercising a form of social power in choosing that particular boundary. Thirdly, that the infinite variety of life is essentially undecidable and that our boundaries and differences, our 'information', forcibly transform the undecidable into something concrete and decidable.

An illustration of the relevance of these theoretical ideas to computer-based information systems is in the area of accounting systems, which provide 'information' on the past performance of the business, current operating conditions and future projections. They are used as a basis for setting targets, for monitoring performance and for identifying and correcting deviances. However, they are only one way of looking at the world which institutionalizes certain boundaries and ascribes a privileged position to particular numeric data. This is a concept of practical relevance; for example, an undue emphasis on the narrow perception of accounting systems diverts attention away from other organizational perspectives such as the cultural aspects discussed earlier.

Thus, accounting systems, and their privileging of certain types of information, can be thought of as instruments of domination. Control over the behaviour of individuals is attempted through the use of financial targets and other accounting measures of performance. This is not necessarily to ascribe a malevolent role to accounting systems but, used as the primary way of viewing the world, they can be seen as institutionalizing the dominance of financial information, which may be to the detriment in human terms both of individuals and of the organizations and societies within which they work and live.

A related concern with respect to computer-based information systems is the theme of surveillance. Zuboff (1988) coined the term 'informate' to describe the way in which such systems produce new information which makes activities, events and objects, and thus people, more visible. The positive side of this capability is the additional insights on the workings of the organization which arise from the informating process. The negative side concerns the potentiality for increased surveillance and domination which the visibility of human work makes possible. One vision of information technology for surveillance in a centrally controlled society was the novel *Nineteen Eighty-Four* by Orwell (1949). Zuboff refers to the architectural plan for a 'panopticon' conceived by Bentham in the eighteenth century (Harrison 1983) and 'consisting of a twelve-sided polygon formed in iron and sheathed in glass in order to create the effect of what Bentham called "universal transparency"'. Foucault (1979) saw the panopticon as a metaphor for modern society, and Zuboff applies this to the concept of an 'information panopticon' whereby information systems may have the potential to make human behaviour in organizations universally transparent. Zuboff does not, however, take a technologically determinist position, and argues that the degree to which we move towards such a vision of centralized dominance through information systems is a matter for social choice.

A final illustration of the link between information systems and the moral aspects of the political metaphor can be given with respect to the so-called 'developing' countries. The very term itself is an illustration of the use of the language of domination since it implies the supremacy of the so-called 'developed' countries. Much debate has taken place over the last few decades concerning the structure of the world economic order and its role, via such organizations as the multinationals, in perpetuating the dependence of the poor countries on the rich countries. The role of information and communication systems is increasingly important here since the dominance and control of global organizations is greatly facilitated, at least in principle, by advances in the capabilities of information technology and international communication. Stover (1984) notes that:

> Criticism of the communication order has been persistent and sustained, dealing with three basic problems: the imbalance of world information flows, the

dominance of Third World culture through film and television program exports from Europe and the United States, and the dominance of advanced countries in the development and transfer of information technology. (p. 43)

A related issue to the international communication order concerns the role of information and communication systems within a developing country itself, where government can use such systems as a means of increasing centralized dominance and control. Alternatively, one can see information systems as an enabling mechanism for development of decentralized localities, by the provision for example of improved information systems for the planning and implementation of rural development projects.

This subsection has concentrated on some ethical aspects of the political metaphor of organizations and, in particular, the view of organizations as instruments of domination. However, with respect to information systems, we have seen that dominance is not an inevitable consequence of the characteristics of such systems, and that social choice determines the degree to which the dominance of particular people or groups is increased or reduced in the future. A further element to note is that total dominance is not possible in human society, since individuals retain their ability to fight back even under the most adverse of conditions, and any repressive system carries the seeds of its own destruction within it. This latter point is explored further below where the taking of political action by management is discussed within the theme of autonomy and control.

Autonomy and Control

It has been argued in this section that power is intrinsic to all human activity, that information systems are a key area in contemporary organizations, and that the exercise of power and the taking of political action have moral implications. These ideas are valuable, but they raise the issue of how to translate them into management action. This subsection discusses the issue by arguing that a key area is the balance between management control and individual and group autonomy within the organization.

Feldman (1989) considers that much of the management literature is misguided in seeing control and autonomy as alternatives, whereas they should be viewed as inseparable aspects of managerial action. In this view, autonomous work activity in organizations is a meaningless concept unless it is related to a context of management control; otherwise, the question 'autonomous from what?' has no answer. Feldman illustrates these ideas with a particular case study where the major management control activity was financial, which had the effect of limiting available resources. Within these resource constraints, the autonomous behaviour of groups was generally given free rein, resulting in destructive levels of autonomy in terms of the effective co-ordination of organizational action as a whole. The paper concludes that a key area for action is the management of the interactive relation between autonomy and control.

The above article addressed the topic of the management of innovation, but the conclusions are highly relevant to the management of the design, development and use of information systems. For example, Kling and Iacono (1984) discuss the way in which computer-based information systems provide an increased potential for social control:

> Control is exercised by many actors in a complex social fabric rather than simply through vertical management control or through lateral work relationships. Participation in a larger institutionalized world of computer use defines work activities, and it subjects users, regardless of their position in the hierarchy, to tighter social controls. (p. 77)

It is important to note that, in line with Feldman, Kling and Iacono do not see heightened control as necessarily negative, for example in terms of the degradation of jobs. Thus the control framework provided by a computer-based system can be associated with considerable autonomy within particular work groups, dependent on the way in which the balance between control and autonomy is managed.

The above discussion leads to the view that control is a necessary part of management action but that this needs to be managed in a sensitive way in order to gain the benefits of the creativity and energy which arise from autonomous activity on the part of individuals and groups. This could be taken to imply that total control is a possibility, but should be rejected on the pragmatic grounds of decreased overall benefit. It is important to note that total control, in any case, is an infeasible option. Symons (1990) notes that control involves rules and procedures, which are never free of surplus or ambiguous meaning. Where rules are invoked, there must be discretion in their application, which empowers individuals to exercise autonomy. From this arises the tacit and taken-for-granted basis of organizationally negotiated order and, on occasion, its fragility and instability.

We have seen earlier that more radical analyses of control and autonomy place even less emphasis on control and stability as natural features of organizations. The schismatic metaphor of Morgan (1981) assumes a fundamental tendency within organizations towards disintegration, arising from the striving of groups towards functional autonomy and their interaction with other groups with different interests. The post-modernist view of Cooper and Fox (1989) sees disorder as the 'natural' state of the world and the control mode characterized by rationality, coherence and identity as an artificial construction designed to serve particular self-interests. These radical perspectives on management control can be taken, on the one hand, as a nihilist rejection of the established social order. An alternative view, favoured in this book, sees such work as a healthy antidote to the view of organizations as controlled hierarchies. In addition, there is a very positive side to the view that control is not the natural state, since it implies that repressive organizations and societies governed and dominated by self-seeking autocrats will be inevitably undermined in the longer term by the natural processes of flux, change and contradiction.

This final subsection of the political metaphor of organizations has developed the concept of autonomy and control as inseparable aspects of management action. Political action geared to total control will fail, and a key task for management is to attempt to intervene in a positive way in the precarious balance between autonomy and control. Subtle choices need to be made on appropriate approaches to control at all organizational levels and both within and between all organizational groups; excessive control, or the concentration on one aspect of control such as financial performance, is likely to stifle the creativity and motivation which arises from the exercise of personal and group autonomy. A radical view would see all this as a form of management coercion; there are dangers here, it is true, and the writings of the critical social theorists and the post-modernists should be encouraged in order to explore these concerns. Nevertheless, management in contemporary organizations needs to continue to act in what they see as positive ways, and the theme of autonomy and control will be developed in the remainder of the book with a view to providing some useful guidelines for the management of computer-based information systems.

A CULTURAL/POLITICAL PERSPECTIVE ON ORGANIZATIONS

The underlying premise of this chapter is that metaphors provide interesting ways of 'reading' organizations as part of an interpretive epistemology. They are pervasive in the way we think about, and make sense of, the world in which we live. Metaphors can provide fresh images of organizations, and thus be capable of enabling new insights. However, the search for metaphorical insight is a continuous process, and should not be seen as the one-off task of finding the 'best' metaphors.

With respect to the literature on computer-based information systems, the machine and organismic metaphors of organization have been dominant, and it was argued that there is benefit to be gained by exploring alternative images. This is not to say that the two dominant metaphors have no value. For example, an interesting new approach is provided by the autopoietic view of organization, which is an extension of the organismic metaphor, emphasizing organizational closure and the way that a system's interaction with its 'environment' is really a reflection and part of its own organization; this approach is certainly of relevance to computer-based IS.

This chapter has concentrated on and developed two metaphors of organization which have been less commonly referred to, explicitly or implicitly, in the information systems literature. The first of these was the image of *organizations as cultures*. A brief summary of some key elements of this metaphor is given in Table 2.1. The primary view taken is that of culture as shared meaning, linked to symbolic anthropology. Organizational culture is conceived of as a pattern of symbolic action and discourse which needs interpreting, reading or deciphering. Culture is an active, living phenomenon through which people create and re-create the worlds in which they live. Subcultures are an important concept for this metaphor, and there is a need to explore the ways in which they maintain their distinctive character and, for example, ascribe different meanings from other groups to the same events. Finally, a management perspective related to this metaphor is that culture cannot be controlled, but that management can influence the evolution of organizational culture by symbolic action, and needs to see its role as managing for multiple perspectives.

The second metaphor examined in some depth was that of *organizations as political systems*. A brief summary of some key elements of this metaphor is also given in Table 2.1. This image sees organizations as loose networks of people with divergent interests. These interests result in political action in which power is a key concept. Power is intrinsic to all human activity, and the exercise of power is a continuous process with subtle local properties. Morality is inevitably involved in the exercise of power, and this includes the negative possibilities for domination, although this is never total. Finally, a

TABLE 2.1 Some key elements of the cultural and political metaphors

	Cultural	Political
View of Organizations	Organizations as patterns of symbolic discourse and action	Organizations as loose networks of people with divergent interests
Some Key Ideas	Culture is an active, living phenomenon through which people create the world in which they live	Power is intrinsic to all human activity. Exercise of power is continuous, with subtle, local properties
	Subcultures maintain distinctive character and ascribe different meanings to same events	Morality is involved in exercise of power. Can include domination, but this is never total
Management	Cannot control culture, but can influence its evolution. Need to manage for multiple perspectives	Need to actively manage the precarious balance between autonomy and control at multiple levels

management perspective related to this metaphor concerns the need to aim for a balance between autonomy and control. Total control is neither desirable nor feasible, but the creation and maintenance of an appropriate balance between autonomy and control is a difficult task, necessitating choices at many organizational levels and involving different vested interests.

Whilst the images of organizations as cultures and political systems involve distinctly different concepts, they should not be seen as separate and non-overlapping; indeed, they are inextricably interlinked. For example, the use of language in discourse ascribes symbolic meaning to actions as captured in the cultural metaphor, but the same language use is also an exercise of power in commanding the listener's attention along the dimensions controlled by the speaker, and reflects power relations between the speaker and listener. Standards of morality or norms of behaviour provide meaning and significance to action, but also legitimate the exercise of power. An attempt to influence the evolution of organizational culture is concerned with the management of meaning, but is also a political action.

Particular metaphors, as they are used, focus on certain highlighted parts of a figure/ground relationship, and different elements are emphasized when the focus is shifted. A merging of different metaphorical perspectives thus has potential for synergy; the use of a combination of the cultural and political metaphors together produces a richer mixture than the sum of the two perspectives viewed separately. Lakoff and Johnson (1980) describe the use of two metaphors in this way as a permissible mixed metaphor, where the metaphors are coherent when taken together, although not necessarily consistent with each other.

A fundamental aspect of both the cultural and the political metaphor is their emphasis on the processes of creation and re-creation taking place in the organizational context. Culture is viewed as an active living phenomenon and the exercise of power is seen as a continuous process. Another way of expressing this emphasis is to say that organization is an accomplishment and we need to investigate how this is achieved. In order to do this, there is a need for theoretical models of organizational process in context which can be used as a basis for empirical investigation. Such models are the subject of the next chapter.

REFERENCES

Attewell, P., and Rule, J. (1984) 'Computing and organizations: what we know and what we don't know', *Communications of the ACM*, **27**, No. 12, 1184–1192.

Barley, S. R. (1986) 'Technology as an occasion for structuring: evidence from observations of CT scanners and the social order of radiology departments', *Administrative Science Quarterly*, **31**, No. 1, 78–108.

Boland, R. J. (1979) 'Control, causality and information systems requirements', *Accounting, Organizations and Society*, **4**, No. 4, 259–272.

Boland, R. J. (1985) 'Phenomenology: a preferred approach to research on information systems', in *Research Methods in Information Systems* (eds E. Mumford, R. Hirschheim, G. Fitzgerald and T. Wood-Harper), North-Holland, New York.

Boland, R.J. (1989a) 'Beyond the objectivist and subjectivist: learning to read accounting as text', *Accounting, Organizations and Society*, **14**, No. 5/6, 591–604.

Boland, R. J. (1989b) 'Metaphorical traps in developing information systems for human progress', in *Systems Development for Human Progress* (eds H. K. Klein and K. Kumar), North-Holland, Amsterdam.

Bowles, M. L. (1990) 'Recognizing deep structures in organizations', *Organization Studies*, **11**, No. 3, 395–412.

Burns, T., and Stalker, G. M. (1961) *The Management of Innovation*, Tavistock, London.

Cooper, R. (1986) 'Organization/disorganization', *Social Science Information*, **25**, No. 2, 299–335.

Cooper, R., and Fox, S. (1989) 'Two modes of organisation', in *Frontiers of Management* (ed. R. Mansfield), Routledge, London.

Davis, G. B., and Olson, M. H. (1984) *Management Information Systems: Conceptual Foundations, Structure and Development*, McGraw-Hill, New York.

Feldman, M. S., and March, J. G. (1981) 'Information in organizations as signal and symbol', *Administrative Science Quarterly*, **26**, No. 2, 171–186.

Feldman, S. P. (1989) 'The broken wheel: the inseparability of autonomy and control in innovation within organizations', *Journal of Management Studies*, **26**, No. 2, 83–102.

Foucault, M. (1976) *The History of Sexuality, Volume 1: An Introduction*, Allen Lane, London.

Foucault, M. (1979) *Discipline and Punish*, Vintage Books, New York.

Geertz, C. (1973) *The Interpretation of Cultures*, Basic Books, New York.

Gibson, C. F., and Nolan, R. L. (1974) 'Managing the four stages of EDP growth', *Harvard Business Review*, Jan–Feb, 76–88.

Giddens, A. (1984) *The Constitution of Society*, Polity Press, Cambridge.

Harrison, R. (1983) *Bentham*, Routledge & Kegan Paul, London.

Hirschheim, R., and Klein, H. K. (1989) 'Four paradigms of information systems development', *Communications of the ACM*, **32**, No. 10, 1199–1216.

Hirschheim, R., and Newman, M. (1991) 'Symbolism and information systems development: myth, metaphor and magic', *Information Systems Research*, **2**, No. 1, 29–62.

Keen, P. G. W. (1981) 'Information systems and organizational change', *Communications of the ACM*, **24**, No. 1, 24–32.

Kendall, J. E., and Kendall, K. E. (1992) 'Metaphors and methodologies: living beyond the systems machine', Research Paper No. 20/92, Management Studies Group, University of Cambridge.

Kendall, K. E., Buffington, J. R., and Kendall, J. E. (1987) 'The relationship of organizational subcultures to DSS user satisfaction', *Human Systems Management*, **7**, 31–39.

Kling, R. (1987) 'Defining the boundaries of computing across complex organizations', in *Critical Issues in Information Systems Research* (eds R. Boland and R. Hirschheim), Wiley, New York.

Kling, R., and Iacono, S. (1984) 'The control of information systems developments after implementation', *Communications of the ACM*, **27**, No. 12, 1218–1226.

Krefting, L.A., and Frost, P.J. (1985) 'Untangling webs, surfing waves, and wildcatting: a multiple-metaphor perspective on managing organisation culture', in *Organizational Culture* (eds P. J. Frost, L. F. Moore, M. R. Louis, C. C. Lundberg and J. Martin), Sage, Beverly Hills.

Lakoff, G., and Johnson, M. (1980) *Metaphors We Live By*, University of Chicago Press, Chicago.

Lawrence, P. R., and Lorsch, J. W. (1967) 'Differentiation and integration in complex organizations', *Administrative Science Quarterly*, **12**, No. 1, 1–47.

Lyytinen, K. J. (1985) 'Implications of theories of language for information systems', *MIS Quarterly*, **9**, No. 1, 61–74.

Lyytinen, K. J. (1987) 'Different perspectives on information systems: problems and solutions', *ACM Computing Surveys*, **19**, No. 1, 5–46.

Madsen, K. H. (1989) 'Breakthrough by breakdown: metaphors and structured domains', in *Systems Development for Human Progress* (eds H.K. Klein and K. Kumar), North-Holland, Amsterdam.

Mangham, I. L., and Overington, M. A. (1987) *Organizations as Theatre: A Social Psychology of Dramatic Appearances*, Wiley, Chichester.

Markus, M. L. (1983) 'Power, politics and MIS implementation', *Communications of the ACM*, **26**, No. 6, 430–445.

Markus, M. L., and Bjorn-Andersen, N. (1987) 'Power over users: its exercise by system professionals', *Communications of the ACM*, **30**, No. 6, 498–504.

Maslow, A. H. (1943) 'A theory of human motivation', *Psychological Review*, **50**, 370–396.

Maturana, H. R., and Varela, F. J. (1980) *Autopoesis and Cognition*, Reidel, Dordrecht.

Mayo, E. (1933) *The Human Problems of an Industrial Civilization*, Macmillan, New York.

McFarlan, F. W., and McKenney, J. L. (1983) *Corporate Information Systems Management: The Issues Facing Senior Executives*, Irwin, Homewood.

Morgan, G. (1981) 'The schismatic metaphor and its implications for organizational analysis', *Organization Studies*, **2**, No. 1, 23–44.

Morgan, G. (1986) *Images of Organization*, Sage, Beverly Hills.

Mumford, E., and Weir, M. (1979) *Computer Systems in Work Design: The ETHICS Method*, Wiley, New York.

Orwell, G. (1949) *Nineteen Eighty-Four*, Harcourt-Brace, New York.

Peters, T. J., and Waterman, R. H. (1982) *In Search of Excellence*, Harper & Row, New York.

Robey, D., and Markus, M. L. (1984) 'Rituals in information systems design', *MIS Quarterly*, **8**, No. 1, 5–15.

Smircich, L. (1983) 'Concepts of culture and organizational analysis', *Administrative Science Quarterly*, **28**, No. 3, 339–358.

Smircich, L. (1985) 'Is the concept of culture a paradigm for understanding organizations and ourselves?', in *Organizational Culture* (eds P. J. Frost, L. F. Moore, M. R. Louis, C. C. Lundberg and J. Martin), Sage, Beverly Hills.

Stover, W. J. (1984) *Information Technology in the Third World*, Westview, Boulder.

Symons, V. J. (1990) *Evaluation of Information Systems: Multiple Perspectives*, unpublished PhD thesis, University of Cambridge.

Taylor, F. W. (1911) *Principles of Scientific Management*, Harper & Row, New York.

Trist, E. L. (1982) 'The evolution of sociotechnical systems as a conceptual framework and as an action research program', in *Perspectives on Organization Design and Behaviour* (eds A. H. Van de Ven and W. F. Joyce), Wiley, New York.

Turner, B. A. (1986) 'Sociological aspects of organizational symbolism', *Organization Studies*, **7**, No. 2, 101–115.

Waema, T. M., and Walsham, G. (1990) 'Information systems strategy formulation', *Information and Management*, **18**, No. 1, 29–39.

Walsham, G. (1991) 'Organizational metaphors and information systems research', *European Journal of Information Systems*, **1**, No. 2, 83–94.

Weick, K. E. (1969) *The Social Psychology of Organizing*, Addison-Wesley, Reading, Massachusetts.

Young, E. (1989) 'On the naming of the rose: interests and multiple meanings as elements of organizational culture', *Organization Studies*, **10**, No. 2, 187–206.

Zuboff, S. (1988) *In the Age of the Smart Machine*, Basic Books, New York.

Chapter 3
ORGANIZATIONAL CHANGE: CONTEXT AND PROCESS

In the previous chapter, various images of organizations were discussed and the cultural and political metaphors, taken together, were considered to offer new insights for the study of information systems. The chapter identified the process of organizational change as of key importance in understanding how and why political action takes place and how cultural attitudes and values are maintained and changed over time. Chapter 3 incorporates these ideas, but builds on them to provide a more detailed practical framework for analysis of the process of organizational change associated with a computer-based information system. This framework is then used as a basis for the analysis of the major case studies in Part II.

The main premise underlying this chapter is that much previous work on information systems has concentrated mainly on the content of change, and has given insufficient emphasis to the process of change and its links with intraorganizational and broader contexts. For example, we think of change as involving the use of a new decision support system to aid the monitoring of regional sales performance, or the introduction of a new stock control system for a production facility. The focus here is on the content of the decision support or stock control system itself. However, the process of introduction of such systems normally involves significant changes to the way in which people are expected to work and interact. This change process takes place within the evolving subtleties of the current organizational context and often cuts across a number of different groups or subcultures. The wider socio-economic context of the organization is also important in the change process. For example, the Thatcher years in the United Kingdom of the 1980s provided a radically different socio-economic environment for UK organizations, with an emphasis for example on privatization and competition, when compared to the previous decade.

The framework developed in this chapter is concerned with the context and process of organizational change in addition to its content. The first main section below develops a basis for *context/process analysis*, drawing on recent work on strategic change in organizations. This basis is expanded and developed in the following section on *context/process in information systems*, which uses web models of context and political and cultural perspectives on the change process. The third section describes a conceptualization of the *linking of context and process via structuration theory*. A view of *structuration theory applied to information systems* is then developed. Finally, the last section of the chapter brings the theoretical ideas together in the form of a *synthesized framework for analysis*. The case examples used in this chapter to illustrate the theories are drawn from interesting work in both the IS area and the more general management literature.

CONTEXT/PROCESS ANALYSIS

A starting point for the analysis of the context and process of organizational change is the research carried out by Pettigrew (1985, 1987, 1990) and others at the University of Warwick in the UK. This work has involved the development of theory, and the carrying out of an extensive programme of field work in both the public and private sectors taking the form of longitudinal case studies. The research has resulted in detailed descriptions of the case studies, which have then been used as a basis for prescriptions in such areas as leadership and the management of strategic change.

The main thrust of the work is that theoretically sound and practically useful research on organizational change should involve the continuous interplay between ideas about the context of change, the process of change and the content of change. It is important to see organizational change as linked to both intraorganizational and broader contexts, and not to try to understand projects as episodes divorced from the historical, organizational or economic circumstances from which they emerge. The management of organizational change is not seen as a straightforward, rational process but as a jointly analytical, educational and political process. Power, chance and opportunism are as influential in shaping outcomes as are design, negotiated agreements and master-plans. It is also noted that implementation of a change programme cannot be separated from its formulation, and that these processes should not be viewed as discrete or chronological but as interactive and muddled. In short, organizational change and its implementation is viewed as a complex, messy process inseparable from its intraorganizational and broader contexts.

Pettigrew (1987) describes the key features which are needed for what he terms a 'contextualist' analysis, identifying vertical and horizontal levels of analysis and the interconnections between those levels through time. The vertical level refers to the interdependencies between levels of analysis based upon phenomena at a further level; for example, elements of interest-group behaviour within an organizational context may be impacted by a changing societal context. The horizontal level of analysis involves the connection between phenomena in historical, present and future time. Thus a wholly contextualist analysis has four major characteristics. Firstly, a clearly delineated *set of levels of analysis.* Secondly, a description of the *processes under examination.* Thirdly, a *model of human behaviour* underlying the research. Finally, the *linkage between context and process* is a crucial aspect of the analysis. Processes are viewed as both constrained by structures and involved in shaping structures, either by maintaining them or altering them.

Case Study of ICI

An outline of the above elements of a contextualist analysis is now given with respect to a major research programme conducted over a 9-year period in the UK-based chemical company ICI (Pettigrew 1985). The *levels of analysis* in the study included various levels within the organization itself, but also the higher levels of the UK chemical industry and its economic and political context over a 20-year period from the early 1960s. The *processes under examination* included the birth and development of groups of internal and external organization development consultants, and more generally the strategic change activities of the main boards of the ICI company. The *model of human behaviour* in the research incorporated both political and cultural elements, seeing leadership, for example, as requiring the understanding and skill to intervene in the organization's structure, culture, and political processes. The *linkage between context and process* was explored by examining elements of context which were drawn on in cultural and political processes and thus how these contexts were reinforced or changed. For example, it was noted in Pettigrew (1987) that mobilization of the context of economic difficulties the firm was facing provided, at various times, the legitimacy and justification for change. This, in turn, created new economic and cultural contexts for ICI.

With respect to the conclusions which have arisen from this extensive research programme, it is not possible to do justice to them here. However, to provide a flavour to the results, two brief illustrations are now given. Firstly, a key element of strategic change is seen as the changing of core beliefs, and this is viewed as a long-term conditioning or political learning process, influenced by the interest and, above all, the persistence of visionary leaders. An example of core beliefs is the new ideology of the 1980s, associated with the leadership of the Chief Executive, John Harvey-Jones. This emphasized a sharpening of market focus, a greater entrepreneurial approach from more decentralized units, and a change in mode and style of operation of the main ICI Board. A second illustration of results from the research is that the ICI study corroborated earlier work which sees strategic change over long time periods as characterized by radical periods of change interspersed with periods of incremental adjustments.

The contextualist approach to research outlined above provides detailed observation over a long time period of the events which occurred in the organization, gives explanations of trends and events in terms of historical, cultural and political processes in the firm, and leads to insightful ways of viewing leadership and strategic change. However, some qualifications have been noted in the literature. Murray (1989) argues that the approach is good at describing how events take place, but is less clear as to why they occur in the first place, and whether the events in the single firm are typical and representative of broader sociological or economic trends. Murray considers that the contextualist approach is a significant development in organization studies, but that the focus on a single organization leads to an overemphasis on managerial action at the expense of structural constraints on that action which arise from the broader socio-economic context.

CONTEXT/PROCESS IN INFORMATION SYSTEMS

A major strength of the contextualist approach in understanding organizational change is its clear emphasis on multi-level contexts, on process, and on the links between process and context. Computer-based information systems in contemporary organizations involve significant organizational change and thus the concepts of the contextualist approach are highly relevant. In this section, the study of context and process is considered with specific reference to information systems. The study of context/process links will be examined in detail later in the chapter.

Models of Context

A valuable approach to the study of context in the domain of information systems is provided by work on 'web models' (Kling and Scacchi 1982; Kling 1987). Web models draw broad boundaries around the focal computer system and examine how its use depends upon a social context of complex social actions. The models define this social context by taking into account the *social relations* between the set of participants concerned with the information system, the *infrastructure* available for its support, and the previous *history* within the organization of commitments made in developing and operating related computer-based technologies.

With respect to social relations as considered in web models, it is important to note that participants include users, system developers, the senior management of the company, and any other individuals or groups who are affected by the computer-based information system. Kling (1987) notes that computing developments will be attractive to some organizational participants because they provide leverage such as increasing control, speed, and discretion over work, or in increasing their bargaining capabilities. Fear of losing control or bargaining leverage will lead some participants to oppose particular computing arrangements, and to propose alternatives that better serve their interests.

Infrastructural resources with respect to computing systems are conceptualized in web models to include relatively concrete elements such as documentation manuals or skilled programmers, but also the capabilities to produce these on demand, such as the ability to hire or train programmers, or to write new documentation. Key infrastructural resources are identified by following a chain of equipment, consumers and providers which form a 'production lattice' for the focal computing resource; the interdependencies in this network form the 'web' from which the approach derives its name. Kling (1987) notes some ways to trace the production lattice, which involve following the chain of social and technical interactions of the various suppliers of basic resources and skills, or including those inputs or resources whose alterations yield large improvements, or whose failures yield significant reductions, in the quality of output provided by the computing resource.

The final element of web models concerns a historical perspective, where it is argued that computing systems are typically developed and extended over a long time period of years, and it is important to gain understanding of the various procedures, structures and commitments which have been made in the past. Later work (Kling and Iacono 1989) looks more broadly at the organizational context of computerized information systems, and emphasizes how such systems and related organizational structures can become institutionalized and difficult to change, constraining further information systems development.

The Printco Case Study

An illustration of the application of web models and the later institutional analysis is provided by the Printco case study (Kling and Iacono 1984, 1989). Printco was a medium-sized manufacturing firm whose business involved the design, production and marketing of dot-matrix printers for use with mini and micro computers. The case describes the introduction, development and use of a material requirements planning (MRP) system, aimed initially at reducing inventory costs. The system was successful in the first instance, but growth and diversification in the company's business produced the need for more sophisticated MRP software which could handle problems such as capacity planning, and the tracking of multiple revisions to the same product.

A decision was taken to convert to a new system on different hardware, and the conversion was planned to take one year of elapsed time. After 18 months, the data processing (DP) staff had not completed the conversion, and the project had many problems including lack of skilled programmers, poor vendor support, and inadequate documentation of the existing MRP system. In due course, a new DP manager was hired who terminated the conversion project. However, conflict then ensued between the new DP manager and the DP steering committee; the former concentrated his energies on trying to mobilize support for the purchase of better hardware whereas the steering committee were keen on upgrading the MRP system on existing hardware. After 10 months, the steering committee fired the new DP manager. An internal manager of engineering services was promoted to the job of DP manager and an upgrade to MRP ll on a larger IBM machine was then set in train. In the meantime, user departments other than manufacturing had been largely neglected by data processing, and had taken their own steps to purchase equipment and software to serve their specific needs.

The Printco case can be used to illustrate three key concepts in web models, namely the social relations between participants, infrastructural support and historical analysis. Firstly, however, in terms of the network of participants who were interviewed, Kling and Iacono (1984) note that 44 interviews were conducted with 40 respondents over an 18-month period, and interviewing was stopped when no other people who had significant interactions with or influence on the system were mentioned. The respondents were either users or resource controllers of the MRP system, which was the core module of the manufacturing division's inventory control system.

With respect to social relations, Kling and Iacono focus essentially on a political model. They note that key actors at Printco discussed the development and use of the MRP system in terms of increasing efficiency and productivity, yet they deployed it to increase their own control. For example, the senior vice-president of manufacturing played a critical role in the original MRP implementation and in its later development and use. He had no formal authority over DP staff, but was able to convince his peers that the MRP system was vital to the organization's goals, and therefore that DP resources should be focused in this area. This resulted in the meeting of manufacturing's needs and the relative neglect of the computing preferences of other areas of the firm.

The example above illustrates how the vice-president was able to mobilize infrastructural support, in terms of data processing resources, to achieve his own aims. A second example of the concept and role of infrastructure involves the failure of the first conversion project. The reasons given include inadequacies in documentation, vendor support, and programming skills, which are concrete examples of critical infrastructural elements which were missing at this stage of the MRP system development.

Finally, with respect to the importance of historical analysis, we see in outline how each successive stage was conditioned and influenced by the previous events and actions which had occurred. Kling and Iacono (1989) discuss this in terms of institutionalization, and they note how intangible dimensions of the social context of computing can become highly organized and constrain subsequent attempts at substantial change. For example, they include elements such as the work prioritization of support staff, and illustrate this by noting that the conversion from the original MRP system to a more sophisticated one was a novel effort which did not fit the routine established work patterns of this small DP shop. A second example given concerns the skills of the computing staff, where the original programmers worked with one software language, but were required to learn a completely new language for the conversion project. Their learning curve was slow, and it proved very difficult to locate and hire new programmers with skills in both languages.

Models of Process

Web models have been used as an example of a rich analysis of context in information systems, and the concepts have been briefly illustrated using the Printco case. It is less easy to find good models of process in the information systems literature. Any research based on longitudinal case studies implies some focus on process, and this includes the Printco case itself. Other examples include the work of Boland and Day (1989), Zuboff (1988) and Markus (1983) discussed in Chapter 1. These studies all contain elements of processual analysis, but the detail is normally limited and we see only a sketch of processual highlights. Of course, a detailed description of the process of unfolding of events and actions over time would occupy a large amount of space, and thus we tend to read condensed and truncated versions of the researcher's own understanding of process. This is inevitable to some extent, but the thesis put forward below is that some richer analyses of process may be possible without an excessive increase in pages of text.

The approach here refers back to the material in Chapter 2 by proposing that models of process can be linked to the cultural and political metaphors of organization discussed in that chapter and outlined in Table 2.1. It was noted that the cultural and political metaphors both emphasize the processes of creation and re-creation taking place in the organizational context. Culture was viewed as an active, living and changing phenomenon and the exercise of power and the taking of political action were seen as an endemic and continuous process. Some elements for analysis of the cultural and political metaphors were identified in the previous discussion, and the Printco case is now used to illustrate these ideas, by giving examples of further analysis which would provide a fuller processual model of the case.

With respect to the cultural metaphor, a key concept discussed previously was that of subcultures, and in the Printco case we can see possible groups as the DP staff, the manufacturing division, other divisions in the company, or possibly subsets of these categories. The interesting question from a processual perspective is how these subcultures maintained and changed themselves over time. For example, how did the DP staff culture change in the periods of the different managers, and what were important events or actions which were linked to any transformation process?

A second possible area for investigation concerns the interaction at the boundaries between the subcultures. For example, how did the interaction between manufacturing and data processing take place over time, and how did the relationships between these groups change? A similar question can be posed regarding the relationship between data processing and other divisions in the company. Some aspects of these questions are referred to and discussed in Kling and Iacono (1989). For example, the role of the data processing steering committee as a way of attempting to control DP activity from outside the group is mentioned. Nevertheless, a fuller analysis along the above lines would be an interesting extension.

Two further elements of an extended cultural analysis can be put forward. Firstly, the 'story' of the case is told from one perspective, namely that of the researchers producing a synthesized version from their work. It is certain that different individuals and groups would have perceived the same events in different ways. For example, the failure of the conversion project was no doubt viewed very differently from the perspective of the manufacturing vice-president, the current data processing manager, and a member of another division within the company. The ascribing of multiple meanings to the same events is a fundamental aspect of the behaviour of subcultures, and an analysis of such multiple perspectives provides a richer cultural picture.

A final point on the cultural metaphor concerns the attitude to the relationship between management action and culture of the various managers involved in the information systems project. It was noted in Chapter 2 that culture cannot be controlled and managed in any direct sense, but managers should be aware of the symbolic consequences of their actions and its influence on culture. For example, how was the firing of the new DP manager by the steering committee perceived by various groups, and how did that influence their future behaviour? A more basic question is whether the various managers involved had any conception of the need to influence cultural attitudes.

The political metaphor of organization is explicitly and extensively used in the published analysis of the Printco case, and therefore less needs to be said concerning the merits of this approach. Nevertheless, there are two further elements worth mentioning. Firstly, with reference to the discussion in the earlier chapter concerning the abuse of power and attempts at domination, what impacts did the various political actions taken have on the quality of the work life of the participants in the process at various stages, and were there any attempts by individuals to dominate others in an excessive way? More generally, what moral judgements can be made concerning the rights and wrongs of particular events, such as the replacement of the various DP managers? How did members of the various subcultures perceive the morality of the actions taken?

A second aspect of the political metaphor, as discussed in the previous chapter, involved a management perspective on the need to actively manage the precarious balance between autonomy and control. The Printco case would be an interesting case in which to explore this perspective, since elements of such an analysis are visible in the published work and appear to be important aspects of the case. For example, Kling and Iacono (1989) describe a 'laissez-faire' attitude towards data processing staff and resources on the part of key organizational actors during the period of the conversion project, implying an excessive degree of autonomy on the part of the data processing group as a whole. The later attempt at control of this group via the DP steering committee was a failure, due apparently to the autonomous action of the new DP manager who pursued his own course towards hardware upgrade. The autonomy/control model of management action provides a theoretical construct for further exploration of the political process in this case.

LINKING CONTEXT AND PROCESS VIA STRUCTURATION THEORY

This chapter so far has emphasized the value of models of context and process in understanding organizational change and, with respect to information systems, has proposed web models of context and cultural and political models of process. The contextualist analysis (Pettigrew 1985) which was the starting point for the chapter noted that a crucial aspect of the analysis was the linkage between context and process. This linkage is of key importance for understanding the impact of computer-based information systems in organizations, which are both constrained by the context in which they are developed and, in turn, are a factor in maintaining or altering that context.

In this section, the sociological model of structuration theory will be described as a theoretical approach to conceptualizing the linkage between context and process in social systems; some applications of this theory in management research will also be outlined. The relevance of structuration theory to the specific domain of information systems will then be discussed and illustrated in the subsequent section. The theory is a subtle and intricate approach to the interpretation of social systems. A reader unfamiliar with the theory will gain only a first impression in this chapter. The structurational analysis of the cases in Part II of the book should provide a deeper understanding. The description of structuration theory and its applications in this chapter draws extensively from Walsham and Han (1991).

Structuration Theory

Structuration theory is the work of the British sociologist Anthony Giddens (1979, 1984). One of the principal aims of the theory is to resolve the debate between those social theories which place their emphasis at the level of human agents and human action, and alternative theories which focus on the structure of social systems. In terms of the previous discussion, these two streams of work can be broadly thought of as emphasizing process and context respectively.

This agency/structure debate is resolved by Giddens into a duality of structure, whereby agents and structures are not two independently given sets of phenomena, but represent a duality whereby structure is drawn on in human interactions but, in so doing, social structures are produced and reproduced.

This fundamental concept of structuration theory can be illustrated by a schematic chart of the analytical dimensions of the duality of structure as shown in Figure 3.1. In this diagram, both social structure and human interaction are broken down into three dimensions and are then interlinked by three modalities as shown. Firstly, human communication involves the use of interpretative schemes which are stocks of knowledge that human actors draw upon in order to make sense of their own and others' actions. They thereby produce and reproduce structures of meaning which are termed structures of signification. Secondly, human agents utilize power in interaction by drawing on facilities such as the ability to allocate material and human resources; in so doing, they create, reinforce or change structures of domination. Finally, human agents sanction their actions by drawing on norms or standards of morality, and thus maintain or modify social structures of legitimation. It is important to note that the separation of structure and interaction into three dimensions is merely a helpful analytical device since the dimensions are inextricably interlinked. For example, although signification is structured through language, language use also expresses aspects of domination and has normative force.

The above description implies that social action can not only reproduce existing social structure but also produce new structure. The model of human agency in the theory views human beings as monitoring their own conduct and its results in a reflexive way which, together with an emphasis in the theory on the unintended consequences of intentional human conduct, implies that all action carries within it the seeds of change. Social structure in the theory is regarded as rules and resources which exist only as memory traces

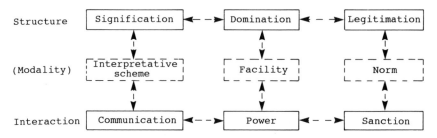

FIGURE 3.1 Structuration theory: analytical dimensions of duality of structure. Reproduced by permission of Basil Blackwell Ltd from A. Giddens The Constitution of Society, *Polity Press, Cambridge © 1984 A. Giddens*

in human minds and are made manifest only in the instances when they are drawn on in social action and interaction.

To complete this outline of some key elements of structuration theory, two further aspects of Giddens' view of human agency should be mentioned. Firstly, he distinguishes between practical consciousness, or the ability to act in a knowledgeable way, and discursive consciousness, which is concerned with being able to explicitly describe actions and motivations. The view of human agency in structuration theory emphasizes the former, since human beings are viewed as being more knowledgeable than 'what they can say'. A second and related idea is the concept of routinization of most social activities, which is of major significance in explaining the 'fixity' of much social conduct and the corresponding stability of institutions.

Structuration Theory in Management Research

A small number of researchers working in the general field of management and organizations have recognized the insights which can be gained from structuration theory, and three examples are outlined in this subsection to illustrate some applications of the ideas in the theory. Riley (1983) applied the theory in an investigation of political culture. Her symbolic perspective on organizational culture and emphasis on culture as a system of disparate but integrated subcultures is closely linked to the discussion on the cultural metaphor in the previous chapter. The article describes empirical analysis, in two companies, of the symbols that embody political intentions or display the trappings of political power. These include verbal symbols such as metaphors, myths and jokes; action symbols such as the controlling of information flow and the use of personal authority for self-interest; and material symbols such as cars and other perks. Riley discusses how the use of these symbols at the level of action maintains structures of signification, legitimation, and domination, which form the political culture of the organization. The article is a useful illustration of the value of structuration theory as a way of conceptualizing the links between symbolic action and social structure but does not, however, include any analysis of how these structures, or the organizational culture, are transformed over time.

A second area where structuration theory has been applied is that of accounting. Roberts (1990) describes a case study of the takeover and management of Electric Light Bulbs Ltd (ELB) by a large conglomerate group of companies, Conglom Inc. The article uses the theoretical basis of structuration theory to illuminate the dynamics of the structuring of relationships both between Conglom and ELB senior management, and within ELB itself. In contrast to the paper by Riley discussed above, we see elements of the way in which the social structures change over time. Prior to the takeover, ELB exhibited a dominance of a production culture over purely financial concerns. Although this culture was strong, the seeds of change were present at the lower levels within ELB, where there was awareness of such issues as the need for cost control and the threats of emerging competition. After the takeover, external consultants were used by Conglom to audit the ELB business and identify loss-making areas, leading to their sale or closure. Thus by drawing on new structures of signification based on accounting concepts, the dominance of the production culture was instantly supplanted by the dominance of a purely financial logic. Roberts notes that this latter approach can enable corporate financial success to be realized, but sometimes at the expense of the long-term strategic positioning of individual unit companies. The article uses structuration theory in a largely implicit way, but the dynamics of the structuring processes are made visible and yield some interesting insights.

A further article which utilizes structuration theory in the area of accounting research is that by Macintosh and Scapens (1990). The authors conceptualize management accounting systems as representing *modalities* of structuration in each of the three dimensions of the theory. Accounting systems provide interpretative schemes which managers use to interpret past results, take actions and make plans; they are a facility which management at all levels can use to co-ordinate and control other participants; and they communicate a set of values or norms about what is approved and what is disapproved. The article then illustrates the application of these ideas, using a case study of the way in which the University of Wisconsin budgeting system was drawn on in the structuring of relations between the university and the state. The case analysis using structuration theory is a re-interpretation of the earlier case work reported by Covaleski and Dirsmith (1988); as such, it can be criticized as distanced from the source material, but nevertheless the article can be used to illustrate some elements of structuration theory.

The traditional budgeting system used by the university and state in connection with state financing for the university's activities drew upon long-standing meaning structures such as an ideology of 'impersonal expertise' on the part of university professors. In order to maintain a 'distance' between the politicians at the state level and the 'neutral experts' within the university, an enrolment funding formula (EFF) was used to determine the amount of funding allocated to the university. The EFF demonstrated publicly that the university was accountable and it provided the rationale for the state to adopt a 'hands-off' policy regarding the allocation of funds within the university. In terms of structuration theory, the budgeting discourse drew on a signification structure which contained notions of the neutrality of the expert and budgeting as a rational and efficient allocation process.

During the 1970s financial pressures on state resources meant that funds available for higher education began to shrink, at least in real terms, and the state used the EFF to reduce the funds allocated to the university. In response, the university attempted to exercise power over the state by drawing on resources such as recourse to the media and the lobbying of elected representatives. A new strategic approach to budgeting was developed, based on the need for funds in three broad budget categories concerning the modernization of equipment in high-technology areas, the expansion of programmes, and library and information resources. The university was drawing on signification and legitimation structures such as the role of the university in state-wide economic recovery in order to attempt to replace one interpretative scheme, the EFF, with another more favourable to them. The Governor and the State Department of Administration reacted by refusing to recognize the separate budget categories, but agreed to fund most of the actual budget requests in the new system. However, an unintended consequence was that the Governor subsequently vetoed a major pay rise for the academics. In structurational terms, the Governor drew on the signification structure of the old budget discourse to argue that the university's new procedure lacked rationality; he used his authoritative resources to combine the three budget categories into one, and he used his allocative resources to withhold salary increases. The university President resigned and for the next budget the state and university returned to the traditional budget discourse.

This case analysis has been outlined in some detail since it provides an example of the use of structuration theory as a way of explaining the socially constructed nature of accounting practice. Macintosh and Scapens note that structuration theory is not a theory in the empiricist tradition, but an organized way of making sense of social life and a sensitizing device for researchers. The study of accounting systems, as discussed by both Roberts and Macintosh/Scapens, is strongly related to the study of computer-based IS, and we now turn to this area directly.

STRUCTURATION THEORY APPLIED TO INFORMATION SYSTEMS

A critical insight from structuration theory is that the modalities of interpretative schemes, facilities and norms provide a means to link action and structure. A theoretical view of computer-based information systems in contemporary organizations which arises from structuration theory is that they embody interpretative schemes, provide co-ordination and control facilities, and encapsulate norms. They are thus deeply implicated in the modalities that link social action and structure, and are drawn on in interaction, thus reinforcing or changing social structures of signification, domination, and legitimation. Three specific pieces of IS research are analysed in the following subsections in order to illustrate this conceptualization, and more generally the potential value of structuration theory in the information systems domain.

Introduction of New Technology

Barley (1986) describes the introduction of computer tomography (CT) scanners into the radiology departments of two different community hospitals in Massachusetts, USA. The technology provided an information system for the radiologists and technicians concerned with the scanning process. Structuration theory was used in the research as an analytic device for the exploration of how the actions of the technicians and radiologists and the institutionalized traditions or forms within the organizations influenced each other over time or 'how the institutional realm and the realm of action configure each other'. The introduction of the identical technology resulted in very different organizational outcomes in the two hospitals, resulting from the different social process or structuring which occurred in each case.

The article traces the relationship between action and structure over time and how the new technology, when introduced, disturbed the processes of routinization at the level of action which led to changed structure. The three dimensions of the duality of structure can be discerned in the case studies where Barley describes aspects of communication/signification, power/domination and sanction/legitimation, although neither these terms nor the associated modalities are used explicitly in the case descriptions. However, specific mention is made of another key concept in structuration theory, the unanticipated consequences of intended action; for example, Barley describes how a group of radiologists withdrew from the CT scanning process during one period of time in order to discourage the dependence of the technicians, but the effect was the reverse of that intended, resulting in an increase in dependence.

The paper is a concrete application of structuration theory in the broad area of information systems, but two qualifications can be put forward. Firstly, as noted above, the paper uses a rather limited version of the theory in its empirical analysis, with no explicit mention of such key aspects as the three analytical dimensions. A second and related qualification, of major importance for empirical analysis, is that Barley does not use the modalities in structuration theory as the links between action and structure, but uses instead the concept of scripts as a linkage device. Scripts are:

> outlines of recurrent patterns of interaction that define, in observable and behavioural terms, the essence of actors' roles . . . actors' identities are replaced by the positions they play, their behaviours and speech are reduced to generic form and content, and the action's unfolding is charted as a sequence of turns composed of typical acts. (Barley 1986, p. 83)

Giddens (1984, p. 84) characterized the use of scripts as a dramaturgical viewpoint that emphasizes the 'given' character of roles. He suggests a broader link between structure and action based on an analysis of 'social position' of which social roles are a specific subset involving face-to-face encounters, well-defined entities and normative definitions of 'expected' behaviour. Giddens argues that broader contexts such as the positioning of individuals with respect to home, workplace, city, nation-state and world systems increasingly relate to the incidental details of daily life; thus analysis of the linkages between action and structure in a focal system should not be restricted to the boundaries of that system.

The above discussion should not be taken to mean that analysis of roles is of no significance. Such analysis in the Barley case studies focused on the interaction of the radiologists and technicians in the focal setting of the CT scanning areas. However, action in the focal setting is conditioned by, and in turn conditions, social structure which extends beyond the focal setting. Empirical work is needed which takes account of these broader contexts, in order to provide richer descriptions of social behaviour.

Information Technology and the Structuring of Organizations

Some recent work by Orlikowski and Robey (1991) contains an interesting use of structuration theory as a model for understanding the nature of information technology and its role in the structuring of organizations. Technology is viewed both as constructed and enacted by human agents and as having institutional properties which constrain and enable human action. One comment on this, as noted by Garnsey (1992), is that it may be misleading to treat technology as a structural property without emphasizing the contrast between such physical structures and Giddens' social structures which are memory traces in the human mind. Orlikowski and Robey (1991) also discuss the way in which information technology and information systems are implicated in the modalities of structuration theory, in a very similar way to that outlined at the start of this section.

Orlikowski (1992) illustrates the theoretical perspectives discussed above using a case study of the development and use of CASE (Computer-Aided Software Engineering) tools designed to increase productivity in a software consulting firm. The research involved an ethnographic study over an eight-month duration. The history of the case is broken down into three stages. Stage 1 involved the initial development of the technology, where technical consultants within the company were required by management to create an 'official and comprehensive systems development methodology' based on standardized tools. In Stage 2, software consultants were expected to use the tools, and they became in that sense institutionalized. Stage 3 describes the ongoing interaction with the technology of the tools and notes that, in some cases, efforts were made by consultants to undermine these institutional tendencies, which were viewed as too restrictive; in one particular project, access to the computer system was manipulated in order to bypass the tools.

The technical consultants' action in Stage 1 was influenced by existing institutional knowledge and norms with respect to the software development process, related to structures of signification and legitimation, and the intentions of management to exert greater control over the process, related to structures of domination. In Stage 2, we see how the new tools were implicated in the modalities of structuration, whereby the actions of the consultants in using the tools were mediated by the assumptions, options and demands built into them. Finally, in Stage 3, we see how institutionalization can sometimes be undermined by knowledgeable human actors who monitor their actions and consequences in a reflexive way, and thus the seeds of change are always present.

The case study provides a fascinating glimpse into the history of CASE tools in this organization and is of interest in this area alone. In addition, the illustrations of the analytic power of structuration theory in the information systems domain are valuable. A fuller description of the case study from a structurational perspective would be a helpful future contribution, since the limited space devoted to the case study in the cited paper means that the dynamics of the process of change, and the ways in which action and structure were linked, are only briefly outlined.

Institutional Character of Information Systems

In addition to specific empirical applications such as that by Orlikowski above, structuration theory can be used as a meta-theory within which to discuss and locate research on action and social structure in the information systems field which does not itself make explicit mention of the theory. This approach is illustrated here by further reference to the work on web models and the institutional character of information systems discussed earlier in the chapter (Kling 1987; Kling and Iacono 1989).

Looking first at the level of *action*, we see that, in the original formulation of web models, resource dependency was a key explanatory variable for action taken with respect to the development and use of computerized information systems. This corresponds quite closely to the power/domination dimension in structuration theory and the associated modality of facilities to control and co-ordinate material and human resources. Less attention is given to the other two aspects of social practice, namely communication and sanction. As an illustration of this, emphasis is placed in web models on the rules associated with standard operating procedures, but equal importance attaches in practice to the values and norms which are implicitly embedded in standard operating procedures, and to agents' mutual knowledge regarding the procedures.

With respect to *structure*, Kling and Iacono (1989) view institutions as constraints and, whilst this is a valid perspective, the conceptualization of institutions in structuration theory sees them as inevitable and views them as enabling as well as constraining. The earlier comments in the discussion of the work of Barley, regarding the need to consider wider contexts extending outside the organization, also apply to some extent to the Kling–Iacono article, with respect to their use of the social organization of computing as their defining boundary; although it should be noted that a major contribution of the earlier web models was the enlargement of the contextual boundaries being studied when considering a focal information system.

The main contribution of structuration theory is not in its conception of either action or structure, but in its reconciliation of the two levels in the *duality of structure*, and its use of modalities as a linkage device. As discussed previously, the Printco case certainly addresses context and some aspects of process, but the mutual unfolding and two-way link between action and structure, which is central to structuration theory, is not examined in detail. The above critique should not be seen as a fundamental criticism of the action-in-context orientation of web models or the later institutional analysis. The argument being made is that structuration theory can be used to locate and illuminate this work from a broad theoretical perspective, and to suggest avenues for further empirical analysis.

SYNTHESIZED FRAMEWORK FOR ANALYSIS

This final section pulls together the theoretical approaches discussed in the chapter and synthesizes them into a broad framework for analysis, designed as a basis for an understanding of organizational change associated with computer-based information systems. The key components of the framework and associated conceptual elements are shown in Table 3.1. The elements of the framework have been discussed in detail in the chapter, but a brief summary of each of the main components is given below.

Firstly, the *content* of any organizational change programme related to information systems is clearly important. With respect to the organization, this can involve changes to products, processes and systems, and associated changes in the computer-based information systems involve computer hardware, software, operating systems and related technologies. These aspects have not been emphasized in the theoretical development in the current chapter, but this reflects the view that substantive content is already well covered by the existing literature in the information systems field.

The second main component in the analytical framework is *social context*. The approach taken in the chapter has drawn, firstly, from the concepts of web models as a way of identifying and tracing the social context of a computer-based information system. Elements of this approach include the social relations between participants concerned with the information system, the social infrastructure available or necessary for its support, and the history of previous commitments made in connection with computer-based systems. In addition to web models, the importance of broader social contexts has been

TABLE 3.1 Organizational change and IS: synthesized analytical framework

Key Components of Change Framework	Associated Conceptual Elements
Content	Organization—products/processes/systems Information systems—hardware/software/systems
Social Context	Web models—social relations/infrastructure/history Multi-level contexts
Social Process	Culture—subcultures/multiple meanings Politics—control and autonomy/morality

Context/Process Linkage	Structuration theory—action and structure duality
	IS and modalities—embody interpretative schemes
	    —provide co-ordination and control facilities
	    —encapsulate norms

discussed in the chapter. These contexts for the individual include the home, city, or nation-state. It is impossible to include all such contexts in the social analysis of a particular situation but, on the other hand, it is desirable to try to incorporate elements of these broader contexts where feasible since they contribute to a richer social analysis.

The third component of the framework is concerned with *social process*, and involves taking both a cultural and a political perspective on the organizational change associated with an information system. The first of these emphasizes how the information system is related to the maintenance and change of subcultures, the interaction at the boundaries between subcultures, and the multiple meanings ascribed by different groups to the same events and actions. The political perspective on the organizational change process emphasizes the information system as involved in the processes of control and domination, as being implicated in moral issues such as the quality of work life, and having a part to play in the dynamics of the management of the balance between autonomy and control in organizations.

The final component in the analytical framework concerns the *linkage between social context and social process*, and structuration theory has been put forward as a sophisticated conceptual approach in this area. Information systems are deeply involved in the modalities which link social context and social process in contemporary organizations. Computer-based IS embody interpretative schemes, provide co-ordination and control facilities, and encapsulate norms. They are drawn on in the social processes which take place in organizations, and in so doing social structures are reinforced or changed. Empirical investigations based on the theory are concerned with tracing these structuring processes over time.

Structuration theory offers a subtle and detailed view of the constitution of social life, but the analytic dimensions of the duality of structure and its associated modalities could be considered as too detailed and complex for empirical analysis in some instances. The relationship of the models of context and process developed earlier in the chapter to structuration theory is that the former can be considered to be simpler models which nevertheless relate to elements of the latter. For example, cultural and political models of process can be thought of as mapping on to the three interlinked dimensions of action in structuration theory, where the cultural model emphasizes shared and contested norms and interpretative schemes and the political model focuses on the exercise of power and the use of facilities. The choice between a simpler or more complex model to explain a particular empirical example is a matter for the researcher's judgement, depending on the view taken concerning the additional depth of insight to be gained by using the more complex theory.

Limitations of the Framework

The comment in the last sentence above leads directly to a qualification on the value of analytical frameworks in general, and the above framework in particular. A simple way of expressing this qualification is to say that a researcher should have an analytical framework, but should retain a degree of scepticism concerning its value. It was noted in Chapter 1 that theory is both a way of seeing and a way of not-seeing, since the use of a particular theory excludes other ways of viewing the same events. The framework described above is best conceptualized as a learning device, whereby the exploration of events using the theory should lead to insight on the substantive topics under investigation, but one should also reflect on the limitations of the theory leading to its future revision. Some further observations on theory will be offered in the final chapter, after its relevance to empirical analysis and major information systems issues has been explored in the coming chapters.

A second qualification is needed concerning the value of any theoretical framework as a basis for empirical research. The framework is of no value in aiding the social process of the research itself. This process requires social skills and social awareness which are practical in nature. The point is perhaps obvious, but too rigid an adherence to a theoretical framework can be an inhibitor to the social process taking place between researcher and interviewee. This might be convenient in terms of obtaining responses which relate directly to the framework, but much of the variety of human life will be ignored, and the interpretation of events and actions is likely to be correspondingly impoverished. A good framework should not be regarded as a rigid structure, but as a valuable guide to empirical research.

REFERENCES

Barley, S. R. (1986) 'Technology as an occasion for structuring: evidence from observations of CT scanners and the social order of radiology departments', *Administrative Science Quarterly*, **31**, No. 1, 78–108.
Boland, R. J., and Day, W. F. (1989) 'The experience of system design: a hermeneutic of organizational action', *Scandinavian Journal of Management*, **5**, No. 2, 87–104.
Covaleski, M. A., and Dirsmith, M. W. (1988) 'The use of budgetary symbols in the political arena: an historically informed field study', *Accounting, Organizations and Society*, **13**, No. 1, 1–24.
Garnsey, E. W. (1992) 'In defence of systems thinking: constitutive processes and dynamic social systems', unpublished paper, Management Studies Group, University of Cambridge.
Giddens, A. (1979) *Central Problems in Social Theory*, Macmillan, London.
Giddens, A. (1984) *The Constitution of Society*, Polity Press, Cambridge.
Kling, R. (1987) 'Defining the boundaries of computing across complex organizations', in *Critical Issues in Information Systems Research* (eds R. Boland and R. Hirschheim), Wiley, New York.
Kling, R., and Iacono, S. (1984) 'The control of information systems developments after implementation', *Communications of the ACM*, **27**, No. 12, 1218–1226.
Kling, R., and Iacono, S. (1989) 'The institutional character of computerized information systems', *Office, Technology and People*, **5**, No. 1, 7–28.
Kling, R., and Scacchi, W. (1982) 'The web of computing: computer technology as social organization', *Advances in Computers*, **21**, 1–90.
Macintosh, N. B., and Scapens, R. W. (1990) 'Structuration theory in management accounting', *Accounting, Organizations and Society*, **15**, No. 5, 455–477.
Markus, M.L. (1983) 'Power, politics and MIS implementation', *Communications of the ACM*, **26**, No. 6, 430–445.
Murray, F. (1989) 'The organizational politics of information technology: studies from the UK financial services industry', *Technology Analysis and Strategic Management*, **1**, No. 3, 285–298.
Orlikowski, W. J. (1992) 'The duality of technology: rethinking the concept of technology in organizations', *Organization Science*, **3**, No. 3, 398–427.
Orlikowski, W. J., and Robey, D. (1991) 'Information technology and the structuring of organizations', *Information Systems Research*, **2**, No. 2, 143–169.
Pettigrew, A. M. (1985) *The Awakening Giant: Continuity and Change in ICI*, Basil Blackwell, Oxford.
Pettigrew, A. M. (1987) 'Context and action in the transformation of the firm', *Journal of Management Studies*, **24**, No. 6, 649–670.
Pettigrew, A. M. (1990) 'Longitudinal field research on change: theory and practice', *Organization Science*, **1**, No. 3, 267–292.
Riley, P. (1983) 'A structurationist account of political culture', *Administrative Science Quarterly*, **28**, No. 3, 414–437.
Roberts, J. (1990) 'Strategy and accounting in a UK conglomerate', *Accounting, Organizations and Society*, **15**, No. 1/2, 107–126.
Walsham, G., and Han, C-K. (1991) 'Structuration theory and information systems research', *Journal of Applied Systems Analysis*, **17**, 77–85.
Zuboff, S. (1988) *In the Age of the Smart Machine*, Basic Books, New York.

Part II
CASE STUDIES

Chapter 4

THE PROCESSING COMPANY

The case study described in this chapter concerns the introduction of a new computer-based information system into a UK manufacturing company. The planned system was complex, impacted all areas of the company, and at the time when the research was started it was known that many problems had been encountered. Indeed, the case study was selected for in-depth work largely because of such factors. It should not therefore be thought of as a typical or representative case but, as argued in the first chapter, the validity of any extrapolation from this case, and those described in the two following chapters, depends on the plausibility and cogency of the logical reasoning used in analysing results from the case and drawing conclusions from it. The case is described in detail in Symons (1990a), and the description of the case in this chapter and some of the subsequent analysis draws extensively from that source. The topic of the original research was 'the evaluation of information systems' (Symons 1990b), but the case is used in this chapter to explore a wider range of information systems issues.

The research employed historical reconstruction and a longitudinal approach, involving contact with the company over an 18-month period up to the end of 1989. Multiple methods of data collection were employed including interviews, company documents, archival records, and direct observation. However, the principal research method involved semi-structured interviews, and the following was noted regarding the techniques employed:

> I attach high priority to careful interview technique. Several issues are important: to build up a degree of trust between interviewer and interviewee; to ask informants for their personal accounts of the situation, being open to whatever is 'on their mind'; to try not to prejudice responses by using too structured an interview technique; to help in reconstruction of past events by leading up to them with questions about the present. I found it helpful to do several open-ended interviews over a period of time with the more candid, articulate individuals. I took verbatim notes during interviews, and was meticulous about recording data as soon as possible after collection so as not to forget the details. (Symons 1990a, p. 110)

The main purpose of this chapter is to give a detailed analysis of the case study, using the framework developed in Chapter 3. The next section provides a brief case history as an introduction, and this is followed by three sections which analyse the case with respect to the key components of social context, social process, and context/process linkage. The fourth component of the framework, concerning the organizational and information systems content of the change programme, is not treated as a separate section, but elements of content are presented and discussed throughout the other sections. The final section of the chapter draws some conclusions from the preceding analysis with respect to a range of information systems issues.

OUTLINE CASE HISTORY

The Processing Company was a wholly-owned subsidiary of a large international manufacturing organization; in the early 1980s it had about 450 employees and a turnover of £25 million. Its original area of business was the manufacture of a product for which the market had gradually shrunk since the 1970s with the entry of newer, technically superior products manufactured by multinational firms. Increasing competition therefore forced the Processing Company to switch from making to buying in base material, and to diversify into the expanding market for converted products which, by 1986, accounted for about half of total sales. Traditionally the Processing Company had had a small range of products with few customers and a limited number of large orders; lead times were long and no stocks were held without an order. By the early 1980s, the situation was radically different; there were about 2000 converted products of which approximately half were manufactured for stock and half to customer order. The number of customers had increased dramatically and orders had become smaller and more numerous, with shorter lead times.

In the 1970s, information systems for business control included manual card systems, a minicomputer and associated software for the control of stocks of manufactured base material, and an accounts and statistics package run on an IBM mainframe at Divisional Headquarters located over 50 miles away from the manufacturing site itself. By the early 1980s, it had become clear that the existing information systems for converted products were inadequate. Unacceptably large differences between book and physical stock showed that the business was not in effective control of finished product stocks and work-in-progress; the same applied to stocks of packaging materials, and there was no effective system of work measurement. Customer service was slipping and delivery dates were not being met on the majority of orders. Management decided that improved computer-based information systems were needed to increase their control over the business and, in particular, started the process of looking for a material requirements planning (MRP) system suited to their needs.

After an initial unsuccessful search for a suitable system within the holding company, the management consultancy branch of the company's auditors were then employed as consultants and drew up an Invitation to Tender

(ITT) in conjunction with the Project Leader seconded from business control. It was proposed to introduce systems in the areas of sales order processing, production planning, shop floor production control, finished goods stock control, packaging stock control, purchasing, and production statistics. In December 1984 the ITT was sent to five systems houses, including IBM which was one of the two preferred suppliers of the holding company. IBM in fact decided that their own software was not appropriate to the company's requirements, and so only four proposals were received. The consultants evaluated the proposals according to the criteria of equipment, applications programs, costs, and the supplier's experience and support available. The main choice in the end was between a proposal from Systems House for Prosys software running on Data General equipment and a package requiring significant bespoke development running on IBM hardware. The former was felt to be a less risky option, having a standard package already developed and a wider user base, and the consultants recommended this proposal, subject to software modifications which were to be agreed. A further evaluation stage was then gone through at the insistence of the holding company, involving an alternative package at a different IBM-based systems house, but finally, in August 1985, it was reluctantly agreed by the holding company that the contract could be awarded to Systems House.

The contract was signed in September 1985, and installation of the Data General hardware and transfer of existing systems were completed two months later. Work had already started on drawing up specification documents for modifications to the standard Prosys modules. The departments involved were identified and a 'key user' was appointed in each to represent the users in discussions on modifications, train users, and assist with implementation. The sales order processing module was to be implemented first, followed by purchasing and manufacturing, with the aim of completing the project by the end of 1986. The specification work for sales order processing and purchasing continued over several months as many more modifications were required than had originally been envisaged. Software began to come in from Systems House in May 1986, and over the summer the internal Project Team were extremely pressured in trying to simultaneously test software, set up the database and revise procedures. One major change involved the replacement of the old 4-digit part numbering system with a precise 13-digit one; attempts to explain the importance of this met with considerable resistance.

Pressure from management to implement the system was building up, and in October 1986 the sales order processing department started dual running. This proved extremely difficult, since the workload involved in using old and new procedures in parallel was excessive, and sales clerks made errors due to their lack of understanding of how to use the new part number codes. In addition, the Project Team had not finished testing the software and they were not satisfied that the system was robust enough. Management decided, however, that the switch-over to the new system should not be delayed any longer, and this was carried out in December 1986 for home orders and January 1987 for exports. The following period saw 'total chaos' in order processing and despatch; hundreds of orders were late and much business was lost.

Repetitive training in the importance of the system, and continual stock takes to improve the accuracy of the records, gradually increased staff familiarity and confidence, until by April 1987 error rates were down to a manageable level and use of the system had settled into a routine. At this stage, work was resumed on specification for the manufacturing modules, and the Project Team and senior management attended a three-day MRP workshop run by Systems House personnel. It was then that they began to understand the new systems as involving not simply hardware and software but 'a whole new philosophy of working'.

Management was now concerned that the company did not have the experience, skills and resources required to undertake full system implementation even within a new extended timescale. The consultants were brought in again and, in early 1988, produced reports on a revised organizational structure, an implementation plan, and an education and training programme. Soon after this, the Processing Company was merged with another subsidiary, the Managing Director retired, the board members were replaced, and a new strengthened senior management structure was imposed. A re-evaluation was started on the computer-based information systems for both finance and manufacturing.

SOCIAL CONTEXT

The analytical framework developed in the previous chapter used the concepts of web models as a way of tracing the social context of a computer-based information system. Elements of this approach were identified as the social relations between participants, social infrastructure, and the history of previous commitments. In addition to web models, the importance of broader contexts was emphasized, both in terms of socio-economic contexts within which the organization was located and the broader social contexts of the individual, including such aspects as the home situation or city within which the person was located. The discussion of social context below draws on this framework and the analysis is organized under the headings of history, social relations and infrastructure; some elements of the discussion are summarized in Table 4.1.

TABLE 4.1 Processing Company: some elements of social context

Historical Context

- Underinvestment in personnel and equipment/changing market
- Low morale of workforce
- Poor quality management

Social Relations

- Senior management team rather cosy and complacent
- Chief Accountant and Commercial Manager 'did not get on'
- Works Manager not significantly involved

Infrastructure

- Poor management co-ordination/commitment
- Senior management inexperienced in computerization
- Inadequate skills/experience in computer project team
- 'Key users' badly chosen/not adequately involved

Historical Context of the Processing Company

The Processing Company was founded in 1946 and was originally a small family-owned firm. The holding company obtained a part-share and then full ownership in the late 1960s, although the subsidiary, being a downstream operation, was allowed to remain fairly autonomous. The Processing Company was thus never brought fully into the structure of the holding company and had its own managing director and set of accounts. One consequence of this hands-off approach by the holding company was an underinvestment in personnel and equipment in the Processing Company relative to the rest of the holding company. By the 1980s, morale was low in the company, aggravated by problems due to the changing market and a 20% reduction in personnel with the closure of the original manufacturing plant. According to one of the new management team of the late 1980s:

> The business is rather tired and sad, suffering from underinvestment and a changing market. There were 100 redundancies when the manufacturing business was cut out—that's 500 down to 400 employees. That also loses some business that was marginal before, and some more is now under threat. It's a downward spiral when you cut away marginal business—you transfer the fixed costs to the rest and another part becomes marginal.

The hands-off approach of the holding company also applied to the senior management of the Processing Company, who were largely left to their own devices. This was described by the manager quoted above as follows:

The management was poor quality. I wouldn't say sloppy, but demotivated—there's a whole raft of factors involved. The business had been pushed into a dusty corner and largely ignored. Management became jaded—they tried some motivation programmes but there was no incentive to make any significant change; and when they did try and met with the type of hurdles (resistance to change) you normally get, they weren't expecting them.

Thus the broad historical context of the Processing Company contained many negative features at the time when the new MRP system was first considered. These features were an important influence on the direction of events as will be seen in the later sections on social process and context/process linkage.

Social Relations

The senior management context of the case study can be further illuminated by a consideration of the social relations between various key actors. The Managing Director came to the Processing Company in 1984 from another subsidiary of the holding company, and three of his five senior managers came with him. The management team was regarded by other managers in the same Division of the holding company as being rather cosy and complacent. Line managers, many of whom had been at the Processing Company for years, were viewed as similarly parochial and uninterested in the relationship of their departments within the overall business.

The Computer Services Manager reported to the Chief Accountant, who was responsible for computer-based information systems in the Processing Company but had no practical experience in them. It was the Commercial Manager who was the main motivating force behind the MRP project, but again he had no experience of computers. His business control manager, interested in the improved product information which would come from the computer system and enthusiastically promoting the project, was seconded to a position as Project Leader of the implementation team. The Computer Services Manager, despite his greater experience of computer systems, was involved only in hardware installation, and routine system operation and maintenance. This was partly for personality reasons, but also because the Chief Accountant and Commercial Manager, his own boss and that of the implementation Project Leader respectively, did not get on. The Works Manager was not significantly involved in the computing project, except in appointing his Management Services Manager to assist in implementation, even though much of the effort of the project was directed within his department.

Infrastructure

The social relations described above imply a social infrastructure for the computing project of poor management co-ordination and general lack of management commitment and support. The board members were keen to have the system in place, but were not themselves experienced with computers and, crucially, did not understand the organizational problems involved in introducing a new system. They viewed the project as just one among a number of initiatives going on in the company at the time, and did not appreciate the scale of resource it required.

A further element of infrastructure concerns the computing skills and experience of the project team. The Project Leader had significant experience of computers but his team did not; they comprised a deputy seconded from business control, an ex-machine operator who had been injured in a works accident, a temporary employee from purchasing, and two sandwich students. There was a serious shortage of resource to undertake data collection; the company appointed whoever was available, rather than the users or staff with skills and experience.

Management's lack of recognition of the need to provide appropriate infrastructural resources for the computing project is again evident in the area of user participation and involvement. Although 'key users' were appointed in each of the departments involved in the project, the Project Team were unable to obtain adequate participation and senior management did not intervene when this state of affairs was unfolding. The key user appointed in the critical area of sales order processing was new to the job, was not computer literate, and had recently been suddenly bereaved. This latter aspect is an example of the broader social context of the individual influencing the social context at the workplace. It was not until six months after implementation that this person began to use the computer system, and thus was totally unable to provide support and advice to other sales order processing staff during the disastrous phase after switch-over to the new system.

SOCIAL PROCESS

The previous section has provided an analysis of elements of the social context of computerization and this section describes a complementary analysis of social process. This analysis is based on the framework developed in Chapter 3, and involves cultural and political perspectives on the process of organizational change associated with the computer-based information system; some elements of the analysis are summarized in Table 4.2.

TABLE 4.2 Processing Company: some elements of social process

Cultural Perspective

- Incompatible perspectives of subcultures of computing project team and sales order processing staff during development process
- Distrust and differing views between Commercial and Works Departments, leading for example to an ineffective pilot trial
- Management insufficiently aware of need to influence cultural change

Political Perspective

- Conflict avoidance with respect to sales order processing resulted in no effective participation during crucial design phase
- Open conflict occurred regarding autonomy/control in the warehouse
- Management showed lack of understanding of need to manage autonomy/control balance

Cultural Perspective

This case study provides a range of examples to support the concept of subcultures and the importance of their multiple perspectives on the same events. Groups which may be classed as subcultures include the sales order processing staff, the computing project team, the warehousemen, and the senior management of the company. One caveat is needed before embarking on an analysis of process viewed through the subculture metaphor. Within each of these groups there was no doubt the subtle variety of view which any collection of human beings includes, and it is necessarily simplistic to group them together as a homogeneous unit. The unfolding of events is often influenced by the internal variety of the subcultures as well as their external interaction. Thus the analysis which follows should be viewed as a relatively crude generalization of human behaviour, which it is hoped, nevertheless, provides some interesting ideas on how and why various actions and events occurred.

A first example of the different perspectives of two subcultures, and the way in which this influenced events, is the contrast between the views of the computing project team and the sales order processing staff during the phase prior to switch-over to the new system. The computing project team regarded the users as having no experience of computers, being rather apprehensive about them, and not being prepared to invest the time and effort in learning how to use the new system until they were forced to do so after the switch-over. However, from the perspective of the sales order processing staff, the computer project was 'an enforced change for no particularly clear reason from a system they were reasonably happy with'. In their view, consultation and communication about the project were virtually non-existent. There was little attempt to improve basic disciplines and procedures before the switch-over. Training was minimal, consisting of a single seminar which was too long and technical; documentation was inadequate.

The process of interaction between the subcultures of the sales order processing staff and the computer project team involved a clash of perspectives and no serious attempt to achieve a common purpose; it is clear that this was a major contributory factor to the disastrous state of affairs immediately after the switch-over. The project team were aware to some extent of the need for better user involvement but, with inadequate resourcing and senior management pressure to meet deadlines arising from the contextual elements discussed previously, users were largely neglected. A mention can be made here about the role of the outside consultants to the project. They were retained during the development phase for advice and assistance, and their brief included, amongst other areas, implementation and training. However, the consultants were called to the site only infrequently, and always with the Project Leader acting as the interface between them and users. They were not involved in project implementation in any depth, and it is thus an open question as to whether things would have been better if they had been intimately involved.

A second example of the effect of the interaction of subcultures on process is provided by the different perspectives of the Commercial and Works Departments. These departments were at physically opposite ends of the company site and seemed equally remote in terms of trust and knowledge of each other's problems and priorities. Commercial management viewed the company as having been too dominated by the priorities of production, whereas works management held very different views. For example, the business control function was responsible for balancing the priorities of the Customer Service Department on the commercial side, involving supplying customers with the right order within the agreed lead time, with the priorities of production involving such aspects as making long production runs and maximizing output. However, business control reported to the Commercial Manager and was regarded by works management as having no understanding of production constraints.

The process of the computer project prior to and following switch-over can be seen to have been influenced by this climate of mutual lack of understanding between the commercial and production subcultures. The computing Project Leader and his assistant reported to the Commercial Manager while working full-time on the computer project, and were no doubt perceived less favourably by production on account of this. An example of lack of co-operation, related to this context, concerns a pilot trial of the order processing system prior to switch-over, based on a few home orders. The trial orders were raised by Customer Services, but not picked up by the warehouse, so the system was never fully tested. The Project Leader pointed out to management that the users were not relying on the system, but no management action was taken.

When the old systems were removed after switch-over, it was immediately discovered that the lot-number control of the new system was incompatible with the existing method of physical product storage, where one lot of material was split between several pallets. A major modification to the software was required, which was expensive and took several months to implement.

The illustrations of the impact of the perspectives of different subcultures on the process of the computer project given above lead to the question, identified as important in Chapter 3, as to what extent management were aware of such cultural issues. Although culture cannot be controlled in any direct sense, managers do influence cultural attitudes and need to be aware of the symbolic consequences of their actions. The answer to the question in this case study, particularly prior to switch-over, is clear; senior management were not sufficiently aware of the importance of cultural attitudes and the need to influence organizational change as an integral and essential part of the computer project.

A number of points can be put forward to substantiate this assertion concerning the attitude of senior management. One of the consultants commented that the new system was conceived by management as preserving the status quo:

> Introduction of the system wasn't seen as being a major change ... The Processing Company hadn't got a timescale, had no specific objectives, and the project was not management driven. It's drifted on because they've allowed it to do so, haven't brought in sufficient resources.

The Works Manager, who certainly shared responsibility for the project, commented that:

> I don't think our Managing Director fully understood the concept and what is involved—as a result none of us (the senior management team) really threw our weight behind it.

A slow realization of the implications of the project and the need for significant organizational and cultural change developed following the disaster of switch-over. It was noted earlier in the outline case history that management finally began to understand that the new systems involved not simply hardware and software, but a whole new philosophy of working. The senior management at the time of switch-over were not, however, allowed the opportunity to manage this newly identified task of cultural change, since they were subsequently replaced *en bloc* by the holding company.

Political Perspective

The different views and attitudes of the various subcultures involved in the computing project, and their lack of resolution into a common purpose, were undoubtedly key factors in the problems of the computing project. The political process whereby the various groups interacted is intertwined with the cultural change process and the description of events above has thus implicitly involved a political perspective. It is worth noting that a clash of subcultures does not always result in the political process being characterized by open conflict. The lack of common goals can equally well result in an avoidance of conflict, but the cost of this can be that important issues are neglected. An example of this in the case study was the need for user participation of the sales order processing during the phase prior to switch-over; an unwillingness to tackle this issue on the part of senior management avoided conflict in the short term but contributed significantly to the later disaster after switch-over.

One area where differing views resulted in open conflict concerned the company warehouse. The new MRP system took away some of the previous responsibility of the warehousemen for home transport arrangements and for making optimal use of the scarce warehousing space. However, the ware-housemen could see improvements in these areas which would save money for the company, so they found ways of working around the formal system. They were reproved by management for their 'bad attitude', and yet many of the employees in this area had long experience in the Processing Company, of around 20 years, and were keen for the company to do well in order to protect their own jobs and those of others in the local community. They regarded the new system as involving some unnecessarily wasteful rules and procedures, and interpreted the reduction of their discretion as management 'not trusting' them. The warehousemen thus saw management action in this area as an abuse of power and their resistance, which took the form of working round the formal procedures, had a moral dimension from their perspective, in trying to protect the interests of the local community.

In addition to the moral dimension of political action, a further key aspect of the political metaphor, identified in the framework of Chapter 3, is the need for management action to maintain an appropriate balance between autonomy and control. The warehouse in the Processing Company provides a good illustration in this area, where senior management viewed the new information system as a tool by which to increase their control of what was happening in the warehouse and to eliminate 'informal' procedures. This increased regulation turned out, however, to be anti-functional, because when the new system was implemented its multitudinous small problems and inflexibilities necessitated unofficial manual fixes. Indeed, due to inefficiencies in the operation of the system, the warehousemen were in the end allowed discretion in some areas, such as the despatch of urgent orders.

The above description of events in the warehouse is only one example of senior management's lack of understanding of their key role in balancing the desire for autonomy on the part of work groups with the need for appropriate levels of management control and, crucially with respect to the computing project, their lack of appreciation of the impact of computer-based information systems in this area of the autonomy/control balance. They saw computerization as the automation and formalization of existing procedures and, in political terms, saw the computer project as an opportunity to exercise much tighter control on the activities of work groups. This attempt to exert rigid control using the rules and procedures of the new computer system backfired in the case of the warehouse. More generally, the view that any area of significant human activity can be totally formalized is wrong, and informal procedures will always shadow the formal system, whether computerized or not.

CONTEXT/PROCESS LINKAGE

The chapter to date has provided an outline of the history of the case study, followed by a more analytic look at the events and actions in terms of models of social context and cultural and political perspectives on social process. Some examples have been provided of the way in which contextual elements influenced social process. Less emphasis has been placed on the way in which social process either reinforces or changes contextual elements. In this section, the formal model of structuration theory, as discussed in Chapter 3, is used to describe the way in which context and process are inextricably interlinked, and structuring processes take place over time in which social action, influenced by social structure, reinforces or modifies that structure.

The analysis of the case study in this section is broken down into three time periods, consisting of the initial strategy and choice of system hardware and software, the development of the customized system for sales order processing, and the period after the switch-over. The analysis aims to highlight some key elements in the structuring processes over time, and thus to provide a meta-level framework for understanding the case study. The description draws on the detailed analysis of context and process presented earlier, and should be seen as complementary to the earlier analysis rather than a replacement for it; some elements of the description are summarized in Table 4.3.

Stage 1: Strategy and Choice of System

The proposal for a new computer-based information system originated from the senior management of the Processing Company. They legitimated their proposal for change by appeals to the norms of good customer service, which was not being achieved, and financial viability of the company, which was being compromised by excessively high stock levels. Their initiation of the proposal and the ability to push it forward resulted from their perceived power to act, arising from the structures of domination inherent in the management/labour relationship. However, it is worth noting that a primary

---

TABLE 4.3 Processing Company: some elements of context/process linkage

---

Stage 1: Strategy and Choice of System

- Legitimation of need for new system by norms of good customer service and financial viability
- Primary purpose for senior management was exertion of closer control
- Holding company exercised power to include IBM systems in evaluation
- Key element in system choice involved interpretative scheme of ITT
- Routinization of work of sales order processing/warehouse staff not disrupted in this stage

- -

Stage 2: System Development

- Signification structure of computer-based IS as tools for automation and control reproduced by drawing on interpretative scheme of ITT
- Attempt to 'enforce' participation failed
- Senior management exercised power over project team to insist on switch-over date

- -

Stage 3: After the Switch-Over

- Stages 1 and 2 largely reproduced existing social structures
- Disastrous switch-over reflexively monitored by all interested parties resulting in changed actions/structures
- New management team started to actively intervene to attempt to create shared structures of meaning

---

purpose of local senior management in moving towards further computerization was to alter the structures of domination and enable them to exert closer control over the workforce.

The actions of the holding company management concerning the choice of the new computer system largely involved exerting power over local management to compel them to look very carefully at IBM equipment. This resulted in the inclusion of both IBM and an IBM-recommended systems house amongst the list of suppliers invited to tender, and subsequently forced a second evaluation stage of the chosen system against a further IBM-based supplier. The exercise of power by the holding company management reflected structures of domination in the relations of subsidiary and holding companies, and was legitimated by the holding company using appeals to the norm of group compatibility in computing systems.

So how was it that local management succeeded in getting their own way with respect to the choice of system hardware and software, despite the considerable opposition of the holding company to non-IBM equipment? Local management can always appeal to the norm of desirable levels of local autonomy, and no doubt this was a factor in the case study. However, a key element in the choice of system was the Invitation to Tender (ITT). Local management legitimated the choice of Data General equipment and the related software by using the interpretative scheme of the ITT, which focused almost exclusively on the functionality of procedures, and reflected local management's structure of signification concerning a computer-based information system, as a way of automating existing procedures and exerting tighter control over work in the company. The holding company did not challenge this structure of signification, or the related interpretative scheme of the ITT. Thus the discourse on IS strategy and evaluation was conducted in the language favoured by senior management of the Processing Company, and in the end the holding company 'reluctantly agreed' with the choice of local management.

The staff of the Processing Company, such as the sales order processing clerks and the warehousemen, were not involved at all in this stage of strategic initiation and choice of system hardware and software. The routinization of their activities was not disrupted and their conceptions of their role, their structures of signification regarding their work and its place in the company, were not touched. Thus there was no preparation for the later major changes associated with the move to the new computer-based system. The key subcultures of the commercial and production departments, involving radically different structures of signification and legitimation, reflected an unresolved, if largely tacit, struggle for domination by these two groups. This was a further negative contextual element in the subsequent stages, where co-operation between the groups was a necessary condition for the success of the new system.

Stage 2: System Development

The 15-month period which followed strategic initiation and choice of the new system was concerned with installation of hardware, transfer of existing systems, and customization of the Prosys software. In theory, the period also involved the training of users and all other necessary preparations for implementation, although this was largely neglected. A key role during this period of system development was that of the project team, and it is interesting to note that the evaluation stage, in drawing on the interpretative scheme of the functionally-based ITT, reproduced for the project team and local senior management the structure of signification concerning the nature and purpose of computer-based information systems as tools for automation and control.

In trying to obtain the co-operation and involvement of the sales order processing and warehouse staff during the system development period, the project team could not appeal to the above structure of signification, which was certainly not subscribed to by these staff. Attempts to legitimate the new system to staff revolved around exhortation, rather than any genuine communication based on shared structures of signification and common norms. After failing to obtain co-operation by these means, the project team attempted to draw on the resource of senior management and use their power, related to the structure of domination of their perceived 'right to manage', to enforce user participation and training. A number of reasons can be given as to why this was not successful. Senior management lacked a sense of common purpose in general terms, related to competing structures of signification and legitimation referred to earlier, and their shared view on computer systems, reproduced by the evaluation process, did not emphasize or even seriously address the social, cultural and organizational aspects which should have been of central concern during the systems development stage.

Senior management did, however, utilize their power in another way to insist to the project team that the switch-over to the new system for home and export orders should be carried out by particular dates. It has been noted that senior management failed to use the power of their 'right to manage' to bring together different subcultures and influence structures of signification, in order to achieve a common purpose with respect to the computing project. It is ironic that this failure was compounded by the decisive use of their power to insist on early switch-over dates, which magnified the disaster at that time.

Stage 3: After the Switch-Over

In Stages 1 and 2, the human actors involved in the introduction of the new computer system drew on existing structures of signification, domination, and legitimation and therefore these structures were largely reproduced rather than being changed in any fundamental way. However, the chaos and problems which occurred after the switch-over to the new sales order processing system were visible to everyone in the Processing Company as well as to the holding company, and provided the opportunity for vigorous social action and changed social structures. The key norms of good customer service and financial viability, which were subscribed to by all parties and had provided the original legitimation for the project, were evidently not achieved by the use of the new system after switch-over. These events were monitored by all the human beings involved in a reflexive way, with a particular focus on the unintended consequences of disastrous performance in order processing and despatch following the intentional conduct of introducing the new system. Following this reappraisal, new activity was initiated, and a brief description is now given of the actions of the warehousemen, local senior management, and holding company management.

The new computer-based information system embodied an interpretative scheme regarding the warehouse which was challenged by the warehousemen on the basis of their practical knowledge or consciousness of such areas as

transport arrangements and the utilization of warehousing space. Drawing on
the accepted norms of good customer service and efficient cost control, they
were able to sanction their scope for autonomous action in areas such as the
despatch of urgent orders. The warehousemen were thus able to subvert the
attempted imposition by senior management of a new structure of domination,
involving complete automation of procedures and total control. Nevertheless,
the new system undoubtedly facilitated a greater degree of management
control and thus a changed structure of domination.

Senior management of the Processing Company, following the monitoring
of events after switch-over, started to modify their structures of signification
regarding computer-based information systems and to see them as involving
significant changes in work style and philosophy, rather than as ways of
automating existing procedures. As described earlier, they commissioned a
new consultancy report which emphasized the inadequacies of the existing
organizational structure and made proposals for ways of enabling communication and bringing together of the different subcultures to create new and
shared structures of signification. Senior management accepted the consultants'
recommendations in principle, but in practice took little action to carry them
out, perhaps due to being 'demotivated' as discussed earlier, and thus unwilling
to initiate a process of radical organizational change.

In the meantime, the holding company had been monitoring events, and
now used its power over its subsidiary to sack the whole board of the
Processing Company and to replace it with people largely from outside the
existing company. The events surrounding the computing project were not
the only issue, since we have seen that they can be thought of partly as an
effect of existing deficiencies rather than a cause, but nevertheless the disaster
of the sales order processing system provided legitimation to the action of the
holding company since the target norms of good customer service and sound
financial performance were so poorly achieved in the period following switch-
over. The new management team started the processes of communication
designed to create shared structures of signification concerning future computer-
based systems for the company. One of the new team, directly responsible for
computing systems, captured this as follows:

> I want an integrated system covering the core areas of the business—order
> management, production management, scheduling and product costing ...
> There's a tendency for managers to be functional managers rather than managers
> with their share of responsibility for the totality of the business ... I want there
> to be a shift to functional groups with common ownership ... I have commitment
> from my general manager and the rest of the management team. With leadership
> and enunciation we can sell the message to the next level down, and below that
> we can certainly sell it.

We see here the deliberate attempt to use senior management power to communicate interpretative schemes embodying accepted norms, and thus to create shared structures of signification across the company.

It has been argued earlier that the perspective on computer-based information systems arising from structuration theory sees them as implicated in the modalities of social systems, and a summary of Stage 3 can be given from this theoretical viewpoint. The computer system in the Processing Company embodied an interpretative scheme for both sales order processing and order despatch, which was sanctioned on the basis of the norms of good customer service and efficient cost control, implied certain rules of action for the co-ordination of user staff in order processing and the warehouse, and provided staff with a facility to allocate material resources to carry out procedures within these rules. When the system was a major failure with respect to exactly the norms used to legitimate it, this provided the opportunity for various groups, including the warehousemen, senior management and the holding company, to legitimate changed action on their part resulting in due course in transformed social structures, and attempts to initiate the development of new computer systems to encapsulate these revised structures in changed modalities.

CONCLUSIONS

The purpose of this final section is to draw some conclusions, deriving from the preceding analysis of the case study, with respect to a range of major information systems issues. The conclusions are grouped under the headings of strategy, evaluation, design and development, and implementation; however, it should not be assumed that these topics form a sequence or are independent, since they are inextricably interconnected. The issues themselves are only touched on here and the focus is on specific conclusions from the case study. A full discussion of each of the major issues, drawing on the existing literature and all the case study material, will be given in Part III.

Strategy

The first point to note is that the broad historical context of the Processing Company contained many negative features at the time when strategy for the new computer system was first considered. The holding company's hands-off approach had not been successful since, although it had allowed considerable autonomy on the part of local management, a combination of changing markets coupled with low levels of investment and a reduced workforce had resulted in senior management being largely demotivated. The holding company were clearly responsible in part for this state of affairs, although the lack of shared commitment on the part of local management can also be seen as a failure in the leadership provided by the Managing Director of the Processing Company, and a certain complacency on the part of local senior management in general.

The strategy with respect to computerization focused on a material requirements planning system to be implemented in stages. It is interesting to note, in view of the later failures, that the core content of this strategy was sensible, namely that improved computerized systems were needed to handle the expanded product range and other changed market conditions within which the company was operating. A major problem with the discourse on information systems strategy which took place was the focus on automation and control as the main goal, which is too narrow a view of computerized systems and normally leads to strong resistance. Information systems should be seen as a key element in management strategy, but a major strategic role of senior management is to actively manage the balance between autonomy and control implied by new systems. Senior management of the Processing Company failed on both these dimensions by underestimating the importance of the new systems and by seeing them largely as a control mechanism.

A related deficiency in senior management's approach to the computer system was their lack of a strategic view with respect to the process of cultural change. MRP systems as described in the case study involve all staff in new ways of working and in new perceptions with respect to the place of their work within the company as a whole. Senior management need to facilitate desirable change in this area by sensitive management of the process of change, such as encouragement of the extensive dialogue needed between interested parties. The lack of intervention by the senior management of the Processing Company during the development phase when user participation was failing is an example of poor management of the change process, and reflected a lack of strategic understanding by senior management of the need for political intervention on their part to influence the process of cultural change implied by the move to the new computer system.

Evaluation

The initial evaluation of which computer system to purchase involved some conflict between the holding company and the Processing Company over the choice of non-IBM hardware. This was largely resolved through the interpretative scheme of the ITT, which reflected a formal-rational perspective on computer-based information systems, viewing them as being largely concerned with the functionality of formal procedures to achieve shared 'rational' goals. The second evaluation stage was seen by senior management of the Processing Company largely as a ritual which had to be performed to convince the holding company management to allow the purchase of the Prosys system. The goals of local senior management implicit in the evaluation process focused on automation and control and were not shared by all parties. The ITT was a reflection of management's narrow view of computerization and the 'successful' use of the ITT during the evaluation process reinforced this conception of the purpose and value of computer-based systems.

Thus formal evaluation carried the day in the initial phase, but formal procedures such as the use of the ITT in the case study are always shadowed by the informal evaluations carried out by individuals, reflecting their own views and interests and those of any subcultures to which they are linked. For example, the sales order processing staff saw the proposed system as something which was not needed and which was being imposed on them. Such informal evaluations of interested parties are crucial, since a group forming a negative view of the proposed change can subvert the 'agreed' outcome of the formal evaluation as was the case in the Processing Company, where the sales order processing staff made little effort to become involved prior to switch-over. A similar state of affairs applied in the warehouse, where the warehousemen informally evaluated the merits of the new system and drew a number of negative conclusions concerning its effectiveness in utilizing scarce warehouse space and reducing transport costs. Their informal evaluations forced, in time, a re-evaluation of the scope of the new system, and resulted in autonomy for the warehousemen in certain important areas such as urgent orders.

After the chaos of the switch-over, all the interested parties re-evaluated their positions, resulting, for example, in a shift for senior management towards a rather different strategic conception of computer-based information systems emphasizing some of the organizational issues which they had previously ignored. However, the holding company carried out its own re-evaluation of the management of its subsidiary, resulting in the sweeping away of the whole senior management tier. It can be seen from the above discussion that evaluation can be conceptualized as a continuous process, with both formal and informal elements, and that each stage of formal evaluation is shadowed by the informal assessments of different interest groups. Management should not see themselves as solely concerned with formal evaluation mechanisms, since informal evaluations are a crucial aspect of the unfolding implementation process.

Design and Development

During the system development phase prior to switch-over, the project team regarded their job as largely concerned with writing software and 'implementing' systems in a technical sense, with little emphasis on the need for active user involvement during this phase. The project team were a long way away from a more sophisticated view which sees the system design and development phase as a learning and cultural change process on the part of both the project team, user groups, and interested parties such as senior management and others in the organization who will be affected by the new computer system. As noted earlier, the reliance on the functionally-based ITT during the initial evaluation phase legitimated and reinforced a narrow conceptualization on the part of the project team of the purpose and likely impact of the new system.

There was some recognition on the part of members of the project team of deficiencies in 'training' users. This still reflects a limited view of new systems as requiring just training rather than more substantial interaction and learning on the part of both users and the project team, but nevertheless a more favourable outcome might have resulted if these training deficiencies had been actively pursued. Unfortunately, senior management inertia and lack of understanding of the seriousness of the situation meant that they contributed little support to the project team in their efforts to involve interested parties.

A related deficiency during the development phase was the shortage of adequate skills and experience in the project team itself. It is clearly highly desirable for a computer project team to have senior management's full support during systems development, but it is possible that a more successful result at the end of the phase could have been achieved by the project team alone if its members had had the necessary prior experience. However, management neglect was not localized to lack of support during the development phase, but was also reflected in the initial ad hoc and inadequate composition of the project team. The outside consultants could perhaps have helped to remedy some of these internal deficiencies, but they were kept at arm's length and did not get actively involved in the development process.

Implementation

The definition of 'successful' implementation is problematic, since success can be measured on different dimensions such as the meeting of senior management's objectives, carrying out a project within time and cost constraints, meeting the expectations of different interest groups, or achieving a high level of use for a new system (Walsham 1991). These goals are not always compatible, and thus one can debate the relative success of a system which meets some of the goals and not others. In the case of the Processing Company the situation is simpler, since the new system failed to achieve any of the above goals in the first instance, with the possible exception of the high level of use for the order processing system. This latter point can not, however, be regarded as a positive achievement, since use of the new system was enforced and resulted in chaos in order deliveries and substantial lost business for the company.

The Processing Company is thus a case study of implementation failure across a range of different measures. The reasons for this are interwoven with the processes already discussed. The strategic management context had many negative features, senior management were demotivated and lacked strategic and technical understanding of computer systems, the evaluation process emphasized formal procedures and reinforced the perspective of computerization as automation and control, and the development phase was notable for its lack of user involvement and primarily technical emphasis. Successful implementation requires, as a necessary condition, that the process of organizational change associated with a new computer system be actively managed in order to generate a shared commitment to the system and to the concomitant changes in work and its conceptualization by interested parties. In the case of the Processing Company, it is clear that responsibility for managing the process of change fell into a space between the project team and senior management, and thus no one took appropriate action.

No case study is ever one of total failure, since learning takes place. The disastrous switch-over acted as a release for the tensions which had built up during the first two stages of the project, and stimulated more vigorous efforts on the part of all the interested parties. In time the sales order processing system passed into routine use. In addition, senior management and the computer project team started to take a more thoughtful stance on the role and impact of computerized systems. However, there were major direct costs of the initial implementation failure such as the lost business, and indirect costs included negative feelings towards the computer system which still lingered even after its use had become routinized. The failure also resulted in a serious delay in the implementation of the rest of the MRP system, and discussions on how to proceed were still taking place over two years after the switch-over on the order processing system. The final word on the case study comes from the previously quoted member of the new management team responsible for computerization:

> The net benefit of Prosys has undoubtedly been negative—it's not gained us much and it's lost us a lot. That's not the fault of the package itself—it was the ambience of the business and the general approach.

REFERENCES

Symons, V. J. (1990a) *Evaluation of Information Systems: Multiple Perspectives*, unpublished PhD thesis, University of Cambridge.

Symons, V. J. (1990b) 'Evaluation of information systems: IS development in the Processing Company', *Journal of Information Technology*, **5**, 194–204.

Walsham, G. (1991) 'Problèmes d'implémentation dans l'évaluation des systèmes d'information', *Technologies de l'Information et Société*, **3**, No. 2, 69–85.

Chapter 5
SKY BUILDING SOCIETY

The case study in this chapter concerns the strategy, development and implementation of computer-based information systems in a medium-sized UK building society during the period 1981 to 1989. The case can be divided into two phases. The first phase took place over the period 1981 to 1987 and involved a dramatic improvement in the society's financial performance under the leadership of its Chief Executive, with IS being central to the changes which took place. The society was chosen for a case study partly in view of this IS-driven success, and access was negotiated via the Chief Executive. The second phase from 1987 to 1989 took place under a new Chief Executive, with a rather different management style based on participation; some difficulties were encountered and a reappraisal of management style was taking place by the end of the period. Elements of the case were described in Waema and Walsham (1990) and fuller detail is given in Waema (1990); the description of the case in this chapter draws extensively from these sources. The topic of the original research was 'IS strategy' but the case is used in this chapter to explore a wider range of information systems issues.

The field research for the case study was carried out during a period of about two years up to mid-1989; thus the research involved both an historical reconstruction of the period 1981–87 and a longitudinal study of the period 1987–89. The primary method of data collection was through in-depth interviews with a wide range of participants at all levels in the organization. Many of the interviews were tape-recorded and then subsequently transcribed. The interviews were tailored to each particular person and focused on their perceptions of what happened and why; on how decisions and actions were influenced, made, and conflicts resolved; on their particular role, attitude, and motivation; and on the consequences of previous actions in terms of organizational change and future actions. Other sources of data included documentary evidence from both primary and secondary sources. Some primary sources were minutes of meetings, strategy documents, internal memos and reports, and the organization's staff magazines. Secondary sources included articles in newspapers, and various financial services sector publications.

The description of the case in this chapter uses the broad framework developed in Chapter 3 and summarized in Table 3.1. The next section provides an outline case history as a general introduction, and this is followed by two sections which analyse the case, firstly in terms of social context and social process, and secondly using a structurational analysis of context/process linkage. The organizational and IS content of the change programme is addressed throughout, rather than being treated separately. The final section of the chapter draws some conclusions from the preceding analysis with respect to the information systems issues of strategy, evaluation, design and development, and implementation.

OUTLINE CASE HISTORY

In order to gain a better understanding of the broader context of the organizational events and actions described in the case study, it is necessary to locate the history of Sky Building Society in the 1980s within the context of the major changes in the UK financial services sector prior to and during that period. The first part of the section deals with this broader sectoral context. This is followed by a brief case history of Sky from 1981 to 1989, with the focal issue of the development and management of computer-based IS outlined within the wider organizational and management context over that period.

Building Societies and the Financial Services Sector in the UK

Building societies in the UK up to the end of the 1960s occupied a relatively comfortable market niche, dominating the market for the supply of mortgage loans for the purchase of private houses by owner occupiers, and raising their funds from the personal savings market. They enjoyed tax advantages over other financial institutions, investments with the societies were perceived to be highly liquid and secure, and the absence of intersociety price competition due to the Building Societies Association interest rates cartel provided a further element of a safe environment.

The comfortable position of the building societies started to change in the 1970s when other financial institutions such as the banks began to provide serious competition in the retail savings market. Competition intensified in the late 1970s and early 1980s, and by 1984 the societies no longer enjoyed favourable tax treatment, the interest rate cartel had been abolished, and the Conservative government's privatization programme provided a further major source of competition in the personal savings market. By the early 1980s, banks were also providing significant competition in the house loan market, enabled by the abandonment of government constraints on bank lending, and encouraged by the relatively safe nature for the banks of this form of lending compared, for example, with loans to Third World countries. From 1985 onwards, other financial institutions, notably foreign banks, entered the house loan lending market and both they, and the main UK banks, could undercut building societies in mortgage pricing funded from the cheaper wholesale money markets to which the building societies had little access.

The societies were thus under severe competitive pressure during the 1980s in their traditional market, but a series of legislative acts from 1986 onwards allowed the societies to diversify into new areas from which they had previously been excluded. These included retail banking with a full range of money transmission services such as cheque books and overdraft facilities; insurance brokerage; dealing in stocks and shares; and, in the housing area, estate agency and conveyancing services. Thus the 1980s for the building societies was a period of new opportunity as well as competitive threat.

The changes in the financial services sector outlined above, particularly over the decade of the 1980s, were intimately connected with information technology and its use in the sector. Advances in IT, notably reduced hardware costs, increased software capability, and greatly improved communications technology, gave rise to a range of product and process innovations in the sector. These included automated teller machines (ATMs), electronic funds transfer at the point of sale (EFTPOS), on-line real time systems rather than daily batch processing, and integrated customer database systems. The result was a greatly increased range and quality of financial products and services, a significant reduction in entry barriers, and a changed basis of competition in areas such as the provision of money transmission services via co-operative ATM and EFTPOS networks. Thus the use of IT and the development of computer-based information systems were central strategic issues for all financial services sector organizations in the 1980s, and the case of Sky Building Society can now be used to illustrate such issues in greater detail.

Sky Building Society

In the context of the financial services sector, Sky Building Society in the 1980s could be considered to be of medium size, with assets in the middle of the decade of something over one billion pounds sterling, over 250 branches and agencies, and over 400 employees. It had its head office in London and an administrative centre outside London. A new Chief Executive, who will be called Brown, was appointed in August 1981. Brown's previous job was the general manager in charge of marketing in one of the top five building societies. Prior to his appointment, Sky Building Society had stagnated for some time and its operations were considered to be very costly. Brown himself said that the society was 'high cost, low growth—essentially in a defensive and sinking position'.

In September 1981, very soon after his appointment, Brown made some major changes in the senior management structure. The new structure was characterized by a relatively 'thin' senior business management team with a wide span of control, and involved loosely defined job descriptions, flexible reporting arrangements, and informal communication channels. A notable aspect of Brown's personal style was a rather autocratic approach to decision-making at the senior level. In addition, he became personally involved in decision-making at all levels. He expressed his goals for the society in terms of a 'focus on profitability' and a 'customer-orientation'.

Brown was very knowledgeable about IT from experience in previous jobs, and he estimated that he spent up to 25% of his time on issues related to computerization and management information. He was again involved at all levels, even to the extent of taking a direct interest in screen design. Major new information systems were implemented during the time of his leadership. The first of these involved the decentralization of investment account processing from the mainframe system at the administrative centre to branch front counters in 1983. This was followed by a similar decentralization of mortgage applications processing in 1985. These two systems enabled improved customer service in terms of up-to-date account information and a much quicker turnaround for mortgage applications. Further benefits included the availability to management of an instant profile of the society's lending on a branch and regional basis. A further major change took place in 1985–86 when the society extended its retail banking services by offering cheque accounts and introducing ATMs.

Attempts to merge with a larger building society in 1986 fell through, and Brown resigned in early 1987 to become the managing director of a major UK financial institution. During the period of Brown's leadership, the society had been completely transformed. Its assets had multiplied by about four times, operating costs had gone down from over 1.7% to 1.0% of mean total assets, advances on mortgages had multiplied by about eight times, and the total number of employees had only increased by about 50 people. Sky had become one of the fastest growing and most profitable of all the 150 or so UK building societies.

In June 1987, Sky appointed a new Chief Executive, who will be called Taylor. Taylor had been an operations general manager in one of the top ten building societies. He brought into Sky a leadership style which was a significant departure from that of his predecessor Brown. The key feature of this new style was increased participation in decision-making at all levels, and the principal aim was to create a sense of 'ownership' and thereby commitment to organizational objectives. Various means were used to encourage this new level of participation, including quarterly management conferences involving group brainstorming sessions, a formal system of corporate planning, and widened participation at senior management levels.

With respect to computer-based IS, Taylor took a much less central role than Brown, and other senior managers, such as the Deputy Chief Executive and the Systems Development Manager, became important actors. An issue which had become dormant under the leadership of Brown now came to the forefront again. This was a proposal to bring together mortgage administration processing, which was being run under a central batch system, together with the investment and mortgage applications systems, to create a new decentralized and integrated customer-oriented system. A feasibility study was carried out which recommended going ahead with the proposed system using a 'formalized systems development approach'. A considerable amount of effort and time was then absorbed in using a particular structured methodology to derive a detailed specification for the system. However, by the time this was completed, attitudes had shifted, and senior management now took the view that the development of mortgage loan systems was of equal if not greater priority than an integrated customer-based system. Finally, in April 1989, a decision was reached that both loan systems and the customer-based system could be designed simultaneously, with a view to having the loan systems in place a year later, although doubts were expressed as to whether this deadline was realistic. In summary, no major new information systems were implemented in the two years following Taylor's appointment, although much resource had been devoted to IS strategy and planning and a new direction had been agreed, at least in principle.

It is not possible to form a definitive judgement on such issues as the society's financial performance under Taylor, or on the success of the experiments in participative decision-making. However, it is worth noting that, by the end of the research period in mid-1989, senior management themselves were expressing reservations. Taylor admitted that he had found it 'hard, time-consuming and expensive' to introduce an effective participative management style. With respect to computer-based information systems, senior business management expressed similar reservations about the utility of the participative and structured design approach for the strategy and planning of new IS, mainly in terms of the slow progress which had occurred using these methods and the dangers of 'designing systems for today with no awareness for tomorrow'.

SOCIAL CONTEXT AND PROCESS

The framework developed in Chapter 3 identified social context and process as key analytical components, and the analysis of the case study in this section explores some elements of these components. A brief discussion of the social context of Sky in 1981 is given below, and this is followed by an analysis of the process of organizational change over the two periods from 1981 to 1987, and 1987 to 1989, taken firstly from a cultural perspective and then a political perspective; some elements of these change processes are summarized in Tables 5.1 and 5.2.

The historical context of Sky prior to the arrival of Brown in 1981 was characterized by poor financial performance, low growth, and no significant innovation. This stagnation had continued during a time of change and turbulence in the financial services sector as a whole, and it was recognized in 1981 that further major sectoral changes were about to occur. Thus Brown was in a good position to introduce change and he was well aware of this favourable context as the following quote from him illustrates:

> It's not easy to change working practices, but it can be done. You can usually do it when times are difficult. Sky had its problems in 80/81 . . . That meant that people would respond to change because they knew it was needed and, therefore, you first have to have, I think, the right climate for change. This can be achieved by crisis; exploit a good crisis to get the changes that otherwise would take years, so I think that an opportunistic style of management is much required in most businesses.

The above passage could be taken to imply that Brown had a rather short-term view of the change process, but this is far from the case. Indeed, a key historical element is Brown's own history in the 1970s, where he was primarily concerned with customer needs and marketing, which helped to form his strategic vision for Sky in 1981. This vision was focused on a customer orientation which, if followed through to implementation, would provide high levels of both growth and profitability. A second key element of Brown's vision involved the use of decentralized computer-based IS to provide support for the staff at the branch offices to deliver better customer service, and in the process better information on performance for senior management monitoring and control purposes. The following quote from Brown illustrates key elements of his vision for IS in Sky and its link to customer service:

> So many management information systems I've seen have been corporately imposed downwards . . . They are not there to help run the business; they are designed to provide more figures for a centralized management . . . So the first thing we did . . . was to bring computer service right up to the customer interface for investors and subsequently in 1985 for mortgage lenders too . . . But you also of course get the spin-off of management information which comes from being able to capture information economically, in quantity, precisely, with an identified individual who did it . . . My objective was to keep it (a customer account) very simple, recognizing that the average person did not have filing systems . . . you do all the transactions and record it on the account, whether they are a saving/deposit transaction, a cheque withdrawal, a cash withdrawal from an ATM or whatever . . . Secondly, in the mortgage area, people want to leave an office with a mortgage offer. If you say 'Well, we'll have to send that off' to our processing office, or to head office, or whatever, you are offering inferior service.

TABLE 5.1 *Sky: some elements of social process 1981–87*

Cultural Perspective

- Initial conditions—supportive climate and clear vision for change
- Brown created and maintained dominance over senior management, although there were signs of covert resistance
- Symbolic commitment by direct involvement in work of IS subculture
- Strategic thrust was customer orientation via branch staff, with support to staff symbolized by major training programme

Political Perspective

- Brown limited power of senior staff by 'cutting out barons'/making little use of committees
- Brown's own ambitions thought by some staff to have led to short-term policies
- IS analysts saw their role enhanced and created no significant opposition
- More autonomy in their work for branch staff, but higher visibility and closer central surveillance

Cultural Perspective on Change 1981 to 1987

Brown's vision for change captured above and the supportive climate for change in Sky in 1981 can be regarded as favourable starting points. Nevertheless, the change process over the period 1981 to 1987 under Brown's leadership cannot be simply explained in terms of initial conditions. In this subsection, change over the six-year period is analysed from a cultural perspective. Brown was undoubtedly the key actor attempting to manage change during this time, and his relationship with particular subcultures and the approaches he used to influence and manage cultural change are now discussed.

With respect to the senior management group in Sky, Brown started the change process in a rather dramatic fashion by creating a new slimmed-down team with a wide span of control. Subsequent to this, Brown established and maintained a dominance over this group and an autocratic style of decision-making. This is illustrated by the following quote from a key member of the group:

> In Management Committee meetings, Brown tended mostly to state the things he had decided on. He would say 'I have decided on this and that and the other' . . . We tended perhaps not to go deeply into things as we ought to have done or we tended not to argue about them because really we thought there was very little to be gained by it. He was working in a very autocratic way.

Although Brown's style was overtly accepted by the senior management group, we see signs of covert resistance in the above quotation, and this was an important contextual element in the period immediately following Brown's resignation, as will be explored later.

A second important subculture in Sky was that of the IS developers, and Brown influenced their work and attitudes by being very directly involved himself in the details of IS strategy, design and development. One of the senior managers commented as follows:

> Brown would call the DP Department or come down here and meet them informally for lunch and tell them exactly what he wanted. He would then ask them to come up with a proposal. They would often say that it was not possible and he would then tell them what he wanted again until they said it was possible. He was perhaps in a good position in that he knew what computers could do and therefore would not take no for an answer.

This approach to creating and changing systems lacked a standard approach, according to a number of the IS analysts, and resulted in rather ad hoc systems development. In addition, the pressure from Brown for rapid change meant that staff had often to work very hard in meeting deadlines, including weekend work. The fact that staff in general were willing to do this was undoubtedly related to Brown's symbolic commitment to the importance of their work, expressed by his direct involvement in all their activities.

A third broad subculture in Sky comprised the management and staff of the 250 or so branches dealing directly with customers. Brown's strategic thrust towards a customer orientation was reflected directly in his approach to IS support for branch staff to provide better customer service. It is interesting to note his view on how to manage the process of delivery of systems which could provide appropriate support to branch staff:

> So what I did in Sky . . . was to introduce a half-baked system which was then modified by a lot of feedback (from branch staff)—trying it on and polishing it until it fits the business . . . The important thing is that you keep on evolving the system, and that enables you to keep it relevant. So at no point are people going to say 'this system is never going to work . . . let's ditch it' . . . That sort of responsiveness is very important, otherwise I think there is a view that 'this system is being imposed on us'. You must overcome that negative attitude developing.

Brown's attitude to the work of the branch staff, as with the IS staff, represented a commitment to their importance. This commitment was symbolized, and the process of cultural change was mediated, through a major and costly training programme. Brown described the rationale for this as follows:

> So staff training is important, communication, you do need to spend more . . . on continual training, monitoring. So that you go through a period when you

have a peak in costs, when you have costs associated with introducing a new system, and costs still associated with running and then running down the old system. This is always the time when confidence is lowest . . . That's the time when you have to be fairly tough and stick with it until it works. Then you come out into the Promised Land in that respect.

Aspects of social infrastructure of vital importance to IS development have previously been noted as including management commitment to provide adequate resources to produce well-trained staff, and it is clear that Brown provided such commitment in the case of Sky.

Political Perspective on Change 1981 to 1987

The dominance of Brown over the other members of the senior management group was a conscious political act on his part, at least if we accept the testimony of his own statements after the event. Brown commented on ways to limit the power of other senior staff by talking directly to staff at lower levels:

You can play the medieval game, you know, king will talk to the public and cut out the barons,

and by limiting the use of committees:

Committees are useful, like Royal Commissions, for killing things. I actually wanted the process of computerization to happen, positively, and so it was necessary to take a leading (role) . . . I don't think committees do anything more, really, than reflect the existing vested interests, nicely balanced, different veto groups, all chaired together to make sure nothing happens that upsets the existing balance of power. If you have a committee . . . that's all that's going to happen; a long detailed report professionally prepared as to why things can't be done . . . and I'm not too fond of committees as a result.

No significant overt resistance by other senior managers to Brown's approach appears to have manifested itself. Nevertheless, the personal motivations of Brown himself were undoubtedly assessed by others, as demonstrated by this quote from a member of the senior management group:

He (Brown) wanted to demonstrate to the outside world, as well as to the Directors, that he could turn the society round and make it much more profitable, reduce staff, reduce costs, become more efficient generally . . . obviously with the ultimate view of being taken on by somebody else to do the same thing in a bigger organization.

Support for this view is provided by the fact that this is what actually happened. In addition, merger talks between Sky and a larger building society took place in 1986 and their failure is thought by many to have been a key reason for Brown's resignation in 1987. The desire to run a bigger organization may, of course, be interpreted as the reasonable goal of an ambitious man. A rather less generous interpretation of the morality of Brown's approach, put forward by some staff, was that he only took actions which were likely to produce improved financial results in the relatively short term, which were not necessarily best for Sky in the longer term. Examples given were the piecemeal and ad hoc development of computer systems, and the stalling of the development of the customer-based system under Brown. These issues will be returned to again in the discussion of the developments of systems in the period after Brown's resignation.

A political perspective on the attitudes and actions of the IS analysts and managers, and the reasons for their general acceptance of Brown's approach, was commented on by Brown as follows:

> They (the computing people) saw it as a way of bringing computerization right into the front end. There wasn't much opposition at all from the established computer centre because they saw their role within the company enhanced; the computer manager previously had a rather low status, that was enhanced by bringing computerization right up.

A price which was paid for their increased status was undoubtedly a reduction of autonomy under Brown's strong control. A major shift in the autonomy/control balance also took place with respect to the work of the branch staff. On the one hand, much more responsibility and autonomy in their work was enabled by the new technology and systems, particularly with respect to providing direct customer service themselves with less reference to central control. On the other hand, Brown had a personal computer connected to the society's mainframe database, which he used to access local branch management information. Thus the performance of branches was monitored directly by Brown much more closely than had been the case previously, and this can be seen as tightening his personal control of the work at the branches. This central monitoring by Brown is also a good example of the informating aspects of computer-based information systems, and the influence of this in terms of increased visibility and surveillance.

Cultural Perspective on Change 1987 to 1989

Taylor's appointment as Chief Executive in 1987 started a new period in Sky where a conscious and explicit effort was made by senior management to effect significant cultural change. The key word in the new style was participation, and a variety of approaches and actions were initiated, designed to foster and develop a participative culture. A member of the senior management team under both Chief Executives justified his support for the

TABLE 5.2 *Sky: some elements of social process 1987–89*

Cultural Perspective

- Key word in new management style under Taylor was 'participation'
- Particular approaches included corporate planning, new style of management conferences, widened senior management group, and structured design methods for IS
- Reactions often negative including corporate plan as 'non-event', 'less informative' conferences, and 'time-consuming' IS approach

Political Perspective

- Suppression of personal interests under Brown created context for vigorous political activity under Taylor
- IS staff saw structured design as opportunity for increased control over their work/reversion to more 'normal' methods
- Deputy Chief Executive pressed case for customer-based systems, related to his own background and interests in retail banking
- By end of period, Taylor has doubts about participative style

change with the opinion that the old culture had resulted in 'passive apathy' because of its 'autocratic, top-down, non-participative, non-consultative' nature. In this subsection, some of the main approaches to the management of cultural change are outlined, together with a brief assessment of their impact.

An early step taken by Taylor to encourage participation was the introduction of a formal system of corporate planning. In some of the initial stages of the corporate planning process, over 30 people from most levels of the society were involved. Taylor argued that such widened participation was an important first step in 'changing the old culture'. However, the output from the new plan was not received enthusiastically by all managers in the society, and a middle-level manager summarized some commonly-held doubts about the speed and value of the whole activity as follows:

> The corporate plan was something we had heard about, it had taken more than a year to produce, it had involved some people . . . but effectively only a small percentage of the society was involved . . . Apart from heads of department level and above, it (the presentation of the plan to staff) was largely a non-event . . . It was presented very sleekly but I think the sleekness of the presentation was not what was wanted. What was wanted was a practical discussion . . .

Another method of encouraging participation was through a change of style in the quarterly management conferences. Under Brown, senior managers had communicated what was happening to middle and line management. Taylor changed these conferences into 'brainstorming' sessions in which groups discussed ideas drawn up by the Management Committee and presented their ideas back to the conference. One of the senior managers felt that this made them 'more relaxed, informal, and refreshing' than previously but admitted that they were 'less informative'. A more general comment on the change from Brown to Taylor's style, for which the management conferences provide one illustration, was made later by another senior manager:

> Brown's culture shock in 1981 was overnight and was accepted readily ... everything was 'big bang' ... Taylor has his foot off the pedal ... another cultural shock is when you are asked to be an innovative thinker when you are used to receiving instructions. Moreover, this management style has not produced many tangible results. The results so far have been in terms of crisis management.

A third way in which participation was promoted was by widening participation at senior management levels. A key action to promote this took place during 1988 when a series of promotions took place to Assistant General Manager level and these new appointees became members of the Management Committee. This was expressed by Taylor as 'a reinforcement of the family group if you like'. It effectively reversed the action taken by Brown in 1981 when he deliberately shrank the size of the senior management team and widened their responsibilities.

With respect to strategy and planning for computer-based IS, the participative style encouraged by Taylor was manifested in a number of ways, including a major move to a structured systems design method involving significant user and analyst participation at all stages. This new approach was very time-consuming, and a later comment by the Deputy Chief Executive expressed the view that it took too long to develop systems by this method and that user involvement was needed but 'in a controlled way'. By the end of two years under Taylor, no new systems had been implemented, although it could be argued that some progress had been made in new system specification.

Political Perspective on Change 1987 to 1989

The autocratic approach of Brown had the effect of suppressing much overt political action during the time when he was Chief Executive, but the lid on the political pot was lifted following his resignation, and legitimization of the open expression of the political interests of individuals and groups was further encouraged by Taylor's attitude to participation and his desire to stimulate, in his own words, 'a heated exchange of opinion'. In this subsection, some examples are given of political action by interested parties in this later period.

In the period under Brown, the status of the IS analysts and management had been raised, but they had largely been told what to do, and the approach to systems development had resulted in piecemeal and ad hoc extensions being made under severe time pressure. A climate of covert resistance had been created, and the arrival of Taylor provided an opportunity for the IS professionals to argue for a more standard approach to systems development involving greater levels of participation. Structured design was promoted by the Systems Development Manager with the support of the IS staff, and the approval of this by senior management thus provided the IS professionals with levels of autonomy not permitted under Brown. This can also be seen as an attempt to revert to more 'normal' methods of working, since IS staff are typically trained via formal and structured approaches.

Branch management and staff also expressed their views more forcibly in the changed climate. A senior manager described this as follows:

> A lot of branch managers are questioning decisions. They are referring decisions back through the regional managers. So senior managers are having to justify their decisions to people who would normally have accepted them.

A specific example of this involved overt resistance by branch managers and staff to some aspects of the corporate plan, and in particular the implied recentralization of some of the branch activities. A senior manager explained this as follows:

> Branch managers and staff are a bit worried some of the work they do will be taken away from them . . . We could get back to where we were 20 years ago— we had very small branches with girls sitting at the counter with nothing to do . . . Brown saw branch staff sitting there and he thought 'right, the work is going to these people' . . . And they suddenly became very busy. And although there were a lot of grumbles, I think they eventually preferred activity to inactivity.

A third group who expressed their political views in the new climate were the members of the senior management team themselves, and an illustration of this can be given involving the Deputy Chief Executive, who pressed the case for the development of integrated customer-based systems with vigour after the arrival of Taylor. The Deputy Chief Executive, who was an ex-banker, had been a strong supporter of diversification into retail banking services, and he believed that the customer-based system would provide support for a strategic change in this direction. It was noted earlier that Brown had not supported this development, and one view as to the reason for this was that it would not yield short-term financial gain, which was Brown's main personal objective. Brown himself, in the following comment given after his resignation, provided a more strategic rationale for his attitude:

> If you are a relatively small financial institution in the vast catchment market of the UK, then it is not a matter of intensively farming a small group of people for which an integrated database is essential. It is more a matter of skimming the profitable ones from a large pool.

It is interesting to note that, by the end of the research period in 1989, senior management seemed to be moving away from retail banking as a key strategic development, and it was still uncertain as to whether the customer-based database system would actually be implemented.

A summary of this subsection is to say that Taylor's approach stimulated political activity on all fronts. By the end of the period, he was expressing doubts about his attempts to introduce an effective participative style, although he still retained the view that it was needed. He was concerned about the time taken to implement change, and appeared to be adopting a stance that resistance needs to be overcome by the use of power:

> I think it is going to take a lot longer to bring about cultural change than I first thought . . . Not only is cultural change going to take longer, I realize now actually implementing some of the positive factors, such as open branch offices, is going to take a tremendous amount more effort than I thought. In other words, we are going to need a bit more muscle to put it through than I thought.

With respect to Taylor's approach to computer-based IS, his hands-off style was a factor in stimulating vigorous political activity on the part of all interested parties. This resulted in a long debate about direction for future IS, which had still not been fully resolved by the end of the research period.

CONTEXT/PROCESS LINKAGE

This section presents a formal analysis of some elements of the case study using structuration theory as a basis. The description shows how social structure and action are inextricably interlinked, and structuring processes take place over time in which action, influenced by structure, reinforces or modifies structure. As in the format of Chapter 4, this structurational analysis should be seen as complementary to the preceding analytical sections. The discussion is divided into the two periods under the different Chief Executives; some elements of the discussion are summarized in Table 5.3.

Period 1: Brown's Leadership from 1981 to 1987

The period immediately prior to 1981 was not a successful one for Sky, and Brown was able to initiate and legitimate change by appeals to the desirable norms of high profitability and growth which had not been achieved under the previous management. He drew on his facility to change formal management structures and thus created a new social structure of domination involving a tighter senior management group with a wider span of control. With respect to computer-based IS, Brown set about the process of communicating a key interpretative scheme of 'decentralized IS for good customer service', aimed at creating shared structures of signification based around this concept.

TABLE 5.3 Sky: some elements of context/process linkage

Period 1: 1981–87

- Brown legitimized change by appeal to norms of high profitability and growth, not achieved under previous management
- Key interpretative scheme was 'decentralized IS for good customer service'
- Spectacular achievement of growth/profitability norms reproduced legitimation structure and Brown's personal domination
- Brown's domination not total; reflexive monitoring by IS staff and senior management created contextual condition for change in next period

- -

Period 2: 1987–89

- Taylor attempted to create new structure of signification, based around participation and collectivity of action
- Period of struggle ensued to establish new structures of domination
- IS staff appealed to norm of well-planned systems development, to exert their own autonomy
- Key signification structure of business focus still missing at end of period

The above description indicates how Brown started the period of his leadership, but a critical question is to ask how he was able to maintain his tight hold on the business and the various interest groups throughout the subsequent six-year period. One element in the answer is to note that the norms of high profitability and growth, drawn on by Brown to sanction his initial actions, were seen to be achieved in a spectacular fashion in the succeeding years, thereby reproducing the structure of legitimation based around these norms and reinforcing Brown's personal domination.

With respect to specific interest groups, the interpretative scheme referred to above, based around decentralized IS, was a key element in creating a shared structure of signification between Brown and the IS staff regarding the increased importance with which he viewed their work compared to pre-1981. Similarly, a shared structure of signification was created between Brown and the branch staff regarding their centrality to the business; Brown used his facility to allocate resources in spending large sums of money on training programmes to further reinforce this signification structure for branch staff.

It should be noted that Brown's domination of staff was not total; for example, members of the computing staff reflexively monitored their actions and were concerned that the general approach to systems enhancement was rather ad hoc and incremental, and thus violated norms shared by computing staff concerning the importance of well-planned and coherent systems development. Nevertheless, Brown's domination was consistently reproduced during his leadership by Sky's high level of achievement of the key profitability and growth norms based on the information systems for which Brown had been the driving force, and thus computing staff were unable to mount any significant opposition at this stage. Nevertheless, as we have seen previously, this created a shared signification structure amongst the computing staff concerning the need for 'better planned' systems, which was an important contextual element in the period subsequent to Brown's departure.

Brown's domination over the other members of the senior management was a further feature of his leadership, although here again some latent resistance was present which surfaced in the later period, for example with respect to the need for customer-based information systems. Nevertheless, Brown was undoubtedly the primary actor in the senior management group, and his dominance was reproduced on a continuing basis by his central role in all important decision-making. In addition, Brown drew on control facilities which he had created, such as direct access to databases on branch performance, which enabled him to monitor branch activities directly, thus curtailing the power of the senior management 'barons' with responsibilities in this area. Similarly, Brown frequently communicated directly with computing staff, using his sound knowledge of IT and its capabilities, and thus further reinforced his domination over decision-making.

By the end of the period of Brown's leadership, a relatively stable climate had been created and reproduced based on linked social structures. The structures of legitimation were centrally based around norms of high profitability and growth, the structures of domination around Brown's autocratic leadership, and the structures of signification around the need for good customer service facilitated by decentralized information systems. It is likely that Brown would have continued to maintain his dominance and pursuit of the profitability and growth norms if he had remained as Chief Executive, although one can speculate that a new business focus may have been been needed to address the changing market conditions of the latter half of the 1980s. Brown's resignation triggered off some rather more dramatic changes, and some key elements of the changes in the subsequent period are now analysed.

Period 2: Taylor's Leadership from 1987 to 1989

The most important initial step taken by Taylor can be seen as an attempt to create new structures of signification based around participation and collectivity of action. The approaches used to communicate these ideas included the development of a corporate plan and the use of brainstorming sessions at the quarterly conferences. These can be viewed as interpretative schemes which, in being drawn on by a wide range of company staff, were designed to produce the participative signification structures referred to above. It is worth noting that the business focus was unclear at this stage, and largely remained unclear throughout the next two years. A number of competing 'structures of signification' were suggested in this area including 'a focus on retail banking', 'integrated customer-based systems', and 'customer loan systems', but none of these were accepted by all major interested parties.

The two years following Taylor's arrival can be seen as a period of struggle to establish new structures of domination. The old structures were suddenly ruptured by Brown's departure, and the competition for dominance was further sanctioned by Taylor's emphasis on participation. Thus interest groups felt able to express their views in a relatively open fashion. For example, branch staff started to question decisions made at the centre, and opposed the interpretative scheme of the corporate plan since it violated their shared structure of signification *vis-à-vis* the centrality of their work to the business, which had been consistently drawn on and reproduced during the time of Brown's leadership.

With respect to information systems, computing staff had been dominated by Brown in terms of the direction of systems enhancement but, when this structure of domination was removed, they were able to appeal to the norm of well-planned systems development to exert their own autonomy in the area of computer systems. The interpretative scheme of 'a formal approach to systems development' was put forward and accepted by management, sanctioned by appeals both to the norms of planned systems and to a participatory approach. However, by the end of the research period, shared structures of signification had not been created in the area of new computer systems, due to the diversity of different views, no clear business focus, and a concern on the part of some members of senior management that such approaches tend to lead to 'systems for today' rather than for the future.

This concern about the slowness and difficulty of achieving an agreed way forward with respect to computer systems is one example of the new senior management thinking which was starting to take shape at the end of the research period in 1989. Senior management, including Taylor, had been reflexively monitoring the results of their actions since 1987, and were not satisfied that the central concept of participation had been successful. It is interesting to note that Taylor's remarks at the end of the period imply a shift towards more central direction, although it still remained unclear as to what senior management intended with respect to the key structure of signification of the business focus for Sky.

CONCLUSIONS

This final section draws together some conclusions from the case study with respect to the IS issues of strategy, evaluation, design and development, and implementation. These issues are interdependent, but the discussion is divided into sections for analytical convenience. It should be noted that computer-based IS were central to Sky's business throughout the 1980s, and thus IS issues were inseparable from those of the business as a whole, and the discussion which follows interweaves the two strands.

Strategy

The context of Sky in 1981 contained many negative features with a history of stagnation, low growth and poor profitability at a time of rapid and profound change within the financial services sector as a whole. Brown, however, saw these problems as representing a strategic opportunity for major change within Sky; he pointed out that periods of crisis provide the right 'climate' for change, and that this needs to be exploited in an opportunistic fashion.

Brown's strategic vision for change involved a clear business focus on better customer service via decentralized information systems in the hands of branch staff. This vision represented Brown's views of the likely evolution of the financial services sector in the UK during the 1980s, and an appropriate and early positioning of Sky with respect to this wider context; this certainly placed Sky among the leaders in the field, despite their relatively small size, and vastly improved financial performance followed in due course. All the evidence suggests that Brown's strategic ideas were his own, formed and developed during his previous experiences in marketing in the 1970s and supported by his sound knowledge of the capabilities of computing systems. Other members of the senior management team were peripheral in the formation of strategy at this stage, and no formal strategy process was gone through. Brown dominated strategic direction throughout his time as Chief Executive of Sky, and as a key input to his thinking he continued to monitor developments in the wider context of the financial services via formal bodies such as the Building Societies Association and, more informally, through involving himself in regular contact with the media.

Brown also had a strategic view on the process of organizational change which was needed to support and implement his strategic vision. He reduced the size of the senior management team and then circumvented them to some extent by adopting a style of direct intervention with various key groups, such as the branch staff and the computing professionals, in order to influence their attitudes and views with respect to their work and its place in the organization. He devoted major financial resources to training programmes designed to aid the process of cultural change. With respect to political change, he ensured that key groups such as the branch staff perceived personal advantage to themselves in the changes which took place. Any opposition from senior management was muted over the period of his leadership by the spectacular achievement of the norms of high profitability and growth, which continuously reproduced Brown's dominance.

Brown's approach to strategy and its implementation was effectively conceived by himself alone, and this created a negative contextual condition of a strategic vacuum when he resigned in 1987. Taylor attempted to fill this vacuum with a changed vision of participation as the cultural goal. He widened the senior management team and adopted approaches such as that of a formal corporate plan, with a view to involving a much larger constituency in the discourse on strategy and thus obtaining widespread support for an agreed strategic view on the way forward. This agreed view had still not been achieved two years later, and a major contributory factor can be considered to be a lack of clear strategic business focus. Alternative targets included retail banking, loan systems, and customer-based systems, but the participatory approach encouraged a process where vested interests pressed their own views, with little resolution into a shared strategic vision.

One could argue that the two-year debate was necessary to help create a new style of strategic policy formulation, that would then be capable of producing a strategy which commanded more genuine commitment and support than was the case under the autocratic leadership of Brown. This author's interpretation, however, is that the strategic vision was still unclear at the end of the research period, and that far too long had been taken in debating the strategy for change at a time of high turbulence in the financial services sector, where Sky, in line with all other companies, faced severe competitive pressure.

Evaluation

Formal evaluations of computer-based IS were non-existent throughout the period of Brown's leadership. He effectively formed his own evaluations of the merits of particular systems, and then ensured that these were implemented, using a variety of strategic approaches and opportunistic tactics. However, as noted in the previous chapter, people formed their own informal evaluations. On the part of the branch staff, with some grumbles about increased workload, evaluations were consistently positive, since the new systems increased the importance of their work to the business and enabled them to deliver improved customer service. However, for the computer staff, more ambiguity can be perceived in their informal evaluations during the Brown period. They took a largely positive view of Brown's interest and involvement in their work and certainly of their improved status in the business. On the other hand, there was a recognition of their loss of autonomy, and there was a widely-held negative view concerning ad hoc systems development. These informal evaluations, held in check by Brown's dominance, surfaced immediately after his departure, and resulted in the adoption of a more formal approach to systems development and more autonomy for computing staff in developing this approach.

A second example of the informal evaluations of the Brown period emerging after his departure is the Deputy Chief Executive's resurrection of the proposal for customer-based systems which reflected his own background and interests in banking. However, the formal development process which was then started to carry this proposal forward offered many opportunities for the evaluations of other interested parties to be expressed, and no clear agreement had been reached two years later. It can be argued that the formal process avoided a rush into the development of new computer systems which may well have not been beneficial to Sky as a whole. Nevertheless, this example illustrates the rather haphazard management of the evaluation and learning process with respect to computer systems under Taylor's leadership. Computer and user staff were sometimes left to their own devices and their evaluations formed the key inputs to the process at these times. At other times, senior management intervened directly themselves. Taylor's relatively hands-off style with respect to computer systems resulted in him and his senior colleagues not being centrally involved in all stages of the evaluation process for new systems, and undoubtedly contributed to the length of time which the process took and the indecisiveness in the results achieved.

Design and Development

Although Brown's approach to strategy was autocratic, it is interesting to note his learning approach to design and development. He talked of his inability to know exactly what was needed at the 'sharp end of the business', and thus the right approach being to develop 'half-baked' systems which were consistently improved with use until they 'fitted the business'. In other words, Brown was a proponent of participation in design and development of the computer systems themselves, rather than participation in the development of strategic vision of how to locate Sky within its broader context and the contribution of computer systems with respect to this vision.

The role of the computer staff in the design and development process under Brown was largely that of technical experts, and sufficient expertise in this domain appears to have been available. Brown drew on facilities such as his sound knowledge of computing capabilities, his wider knowledge of the business in its context, supported by a style of direct intervention, to dominate the computer staff with respect to the more strategic aspects of systems design. This resulted in systems being developed very rapidly which produced clear short-term gains with respect to key norms such as profitability; thus staff were provided with no opportunity to question Brown's approach, despite them having reservations about the long-term problems produced, in their view, by his insistence on an incremental systems development style.

Following the departure of Brown, the structured systems design method which was then introduced involved significant user and analyst participation in the planning process. However, the approach was slow in producing results and, in contrast to the period under Brown, did not involve participation on how to implement a particular strategic vision of the role of computer systems in the business, but rather the opportunity for the expression of different views with respect to both strategy and implementation. A further point worth emphasizing is that many people's long-term vision is heavily influenced by the existing situation, and it is not surprising that a senior management view had emerged at the end of the research period that the structured design method had tended to result in proposals for 'systems for today' rather than systems with a more strategic and forward-looking orientation.

Implementation

Brown was highly aware of implementation issues with respect to new computer systems and the way in which they are interwoven with the processes already discussed. He was directly and actively involved in strategy, evaluation, and design and development, and succeeded in linking these together and orchestrating sufficient common purpose to enable new systems to be developed rapidly and effectively. There is no doubt that the implementation of these systems was the cornerstone of the turnaround in performance of Sky under Brown, and a major reason for the remarkable results for the organization in terms of profitability and growth. Brown also achieved his personal goals, as these were seen by a senior management colleague, in terms of demonstrating a high level of top management capability enabling him to be recruited for a similar job in a larger organization. There were some negative aspects of the implementation successes under Brown, at least in the view of some staff, in terms of the short-termism inherent in Brown's strategy and the excessive work which was required in some cases. Nevertheless, one must conclude that implementation of computer systems under Brown was successful under most criteria.

Taylor was certainly aware of implementation issues with respect to computer systems, and treated them with equal importance to that accorded them by Brown. Indeed, the primary purpose of the participative approach with respect to strategy, evaluation, and design issues was to arrive at shared views and approaches to which everyone was committed, and thus to create the right conditions or prerequisites for successful implementation. However, Taylor's approach may have been unrealistic in some respects. There are as many different visions of the way forward in an organization as there are people in it, and the goal of total consensus is infeasible. Adequate leadership from the top is essential and this appears to have been lacking to some extent in the two years after Brown. There were signs that senior management were coming round to this view themselves by the end of the period, although one can speculate that there may have been a subsequent danger of them swinging too far the other way towards the attempted use of the power of their position to simply 'overcome' resistance.

This case study could be taken to imply that the strategic development and implementation of computer systems requires an autocratic leader such as Brown, and that more participative styles are less successful. This is not an intended conclusion, and each individual case needs to be considered on its own terms and with respect to its own conditions. With respect to this case study, there is no doubt that Brown was successful in many respects, and that the following period involved considerable delay and indecision with respect to new developments. However, we have seen that Brown's style was actually more involved and participative in some respects, and in some stages, than that of Taylor. From the perspective of senior management, there is a need for a delicate and shifting balance between participation and direction at all stages of the strategy formation and development of new computer systems, with the dual goal of achieving an adequate level of support by all interested parties for the implementation of systems, which have high value to the business.

REFERENCES

Waema, T. M. (1990) *Information Systems Strategy Formation in Financial Services Sector Organizations*, unpublished PhD thesis, University of Cambridge.

Waema, T. M., and Walsham, G. (1990) 'Information systems strategy formulation', *Information and Management*, **18**, No. 1, 29–39.

Chapter 6
THE GOVERNMENT CO-ORDINATION AGENCY

The case study described in this chapter concerns the computer-based information systems developed by a central government agency in a Third World country, which were designed for the purpose of monitoring and controlling development projects in the country. Three information systems will be described and their development and use over a period of about 12 years will be discussed. The first two systems were implemented in a technical sense, but there were many problems in such areas as data validity and usefulness and the systems were largely ineffective. The third system was still in the process of being developed at the end of the research period, but there were strong indications that a similar fate to that of the first two systems was likely in terms of ineffectiveness in use. Elements of the case were described in Han and Walsham (1990) and fuller detail is given in Han (1991); the description of the case in this chapter draws extensively from these sources.

The field research for the case study was carried out in two main periods, consisting of three months in mid-1989 and two months in early 1991. The research involved a historical reconstruction of the information systems development and use from 1978 to 1989 and a longitudinal study of the period 1989–91. It should be noted, however, that one of the research workers had studied the first two systems at an earlier period in the 1980s, and therefore additional background was available from that source. The primary method of data collection during the main research periods was through in-depth interviews with government officials at a wide variety of levels in the administration, from very senior civil servants down to middle-level officials in ministries and state offices. The interviews were mainly semi-structured discussions; a preparatory note containing background information on the organizational function of the interviewee, a description of the objectives of the meeting, and specific areas to be covered served as an aide-mémoire to the interviewer with respect to the research objectives of the meeting. The interview sessions were tape-recorded and many were transcribed in full. More than one interview was normally conducted with key actors, with the first interview being largely of a fact-finding nature, concluding with a request for relevant documents. Subsequent interviews were more focused, and questions were asked to elicit the interviewee's perceptions on why events happened as they did, the roles of particular individuals, and the broader context of actions.

Questions concerned the sequence of past events, the present situation, and possible future trajectories. Other sources of data included documentary evidence from both primary and secondary sources. The primary sources included minutes of meetings, policy documents and project reports, although the availability of these was restricted due to confidentiality considerations. Secondary data sources included trade magazines and the daily press.

The description of the case in this chapter uses the broad framework developed in Chapter 3 and summarized in Table 3.1. The next section provides an outline case history as a general introduction, and this is followed by three sections which analyse the case, firstly in terms of social context, then in terms of social process, and finally using a structurational analysis of context/process linkage. The organizational and IS content of the change programme is addressed throughout, rather than being treated separately. The final section of the chapter draws some conclusions with respect to the information systems issues of strategy, evaluation, design and development, and implementation.

OUTLINE CASE HISTORY

The three computer-based information systems which are the focus of this case study were developed within the Government Co-ordination Agency (GCA) in the Third World country which will be called Polonia. The first part of this section addresses the wider context of the focal IS by giving some brief details on Polonia and the role of the GCA. This is followed by an outline case history of the development and use of the three IS over the period 1978 to 1991.

Polonia and the Role of the GCA

Polonia had a population of around 15 million people during the research period in the 1980s, with a variety of racial backgrounds, although there was a dominant majority group who had largely controlled the political system since independence in the early 1960s. In constitutional terms, Polonia was divided into a number of states; the federal government was responsible for activities at the national level such as defence, and the state governments were responsible for matters of local importance such as land and water supply. Other activities such as public health and irrigation were shared responsibilities between the federal and state governments. States were divided into administrative districts, each headed by a district officer. In political terms, the federal government was run by the Prime Minister and his Cabinet of Ministers. Each of the states had its own Chief Minister and its state executive councils. In economic terms, Polonia was basically a free-enterprise economy, based on primary products but with increasing levels of industrialization.

Socio-economic planning in Polonia had been a cyclical process repeated every five years. Eight development plans had been published since political independence, with objectives reflecting the changing requirements of the Polonian political and economic situation. Development goals emphasized modernization of the traditional sectors in the 1950s, infrastructural development and agricultural diversification in the 1960s, and society restructuring and poverty eradication in the 1970s and 80s. In these last three decades, major development initiatives had been mounted by both federal and state governments, in a number of priority areas such as agriculture, education, health, water resources, and transportation. An outline of the formal bodies responsible for the planning and implementation of development projects is shown in Figure 6.1. The planning exercise carried out in the five-year cycle was complex, but involved inputs from district and state levels, from ministries and other central agencies, and from the various interagency planning groups. The ministries and agencies finally submitted their programme and project proposals through the National Planning Council and the Cabinet for approval.

Implementation of projects was the task of the operating agencies, but monitoring of implementation progress and evaluation of impact was a joint responsibility of the operating agencies and central agencies, the latter including the National Action Council at the federal level. At the state level, the State Action Committee supervised and co-ordinated project implementation with the State Development Office (SDO) providing the secretariat. Parallel mechanisms were in place at the district level. The role of the GCA, the focal agency in this case study, included monitoring project implementation in detail, reviewing the physical and financial progress of projects, identifying bottlenecks, suggesting actions on remedial measures, and formulating new strategies to speed up national development. The GCA worked with the SDOs on the monitoring of implementation at the state level, but was a federal agency which formed a part of the influential Prime Minister's Department.

Focal Information Systems 1978–1991

Various manual systems had been in use from the 1960s onwards for the monitoring of development projects, but these had been placed under increasing strain by the upsurge in development activities during the 1970s and were widely perceived to be inadequate. A new system was needed and, in 1977, the decision was made to computerize project monitoring activities at the GCA. An IBM computer was installed in 1978 and a project monitoring database system was set up, which will be called Premis. By 1980, around 20,000 projects were being monitored by Premis.

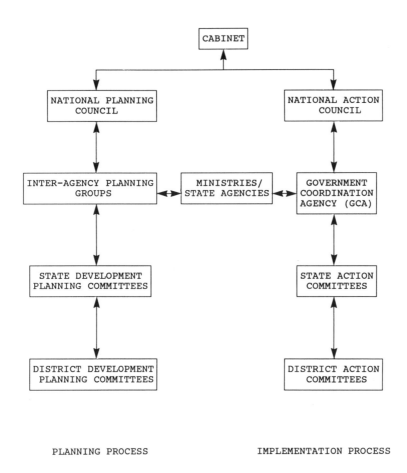

PLANNING PROCESS   IMPLEMENTATION PROCESS

FIGURE 6.1 Development planning and implementation: formal organization

Premis was a centralized system based on quarterly report forms sent by the implementing agencies to the GCA for processing. By the time that the large number of forms had been processed and returned, the information generated was already out of date and consequently of little use to the agencies. In addition, forms were frequently incomplete and only about half the agencies actually reported on their projects; thus the information in the central database gave a very partial picture. The new computer forms allowed for a range of implementation problems to be reported, including delays in the completion of a physical stage of the project, and problems arising from staff shortages, raw material quality, or the provision of utilities. However, the value of the computerized data as a diagnostic tool leading to remedial action was low.

For example, difficulties frequently arose from interdepartmental conflicts and lack of co-ordination, and these aspects were not captured in the computer database.

A new government came into power in Polonia in 1981, and its policies included an emphasis on efficiency and productivity in the public sector. A study was carried out on the implementation of development projects and the findings were critical of the existing information systems for project monitoring and management. In addition to the problems of incomplete, late or non-reporting mentioned above with respect to Premis, the study criticized the lack of co-ordination in the different systems being used by various central agencies including the GCA. As a direct consequence of the study report, the GCA was charged with developing a new computerized system, which will be called Intis. Intis was aimed to co-ordinate and standardize the information systems in use by the central bodies and agencies concerned with development projects, including Premis used by the GCA itself, and various systems in use by the Treasury, the Accountant General's Department, and the Economic Planning Department. An outline of the conceptual structure of Intis is shown in Figure 6.2.

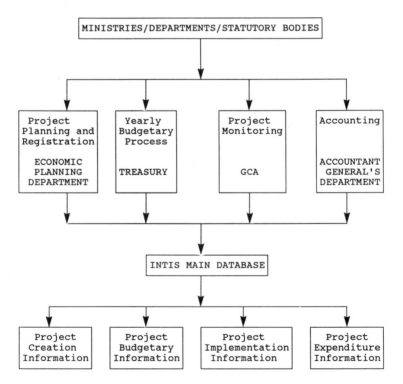

FIGURE 6.2 Conceptual structure of Intis

The twin objectives of Intis were to provide a common database with a common data source, and to provide end-user facilities to government agencies to plan and control development projects. By 1984 Intis was implemented within the GCA and provided information, for thousands of development projects, on project plans, budget allocation, implementation progress, and finance. The Intis Distributed Processing Subsystem was made available in 1987, and various government ministries and state development offices were provided with a computer and printer which were linked directly to the main computer system at the GCA in the capital city. The distributed processing subsystem provided the facility for various simple output formats. Some query programmes were also provided for access to the main database. Intis was a mandatory reporting procedure for operating agencies, and all agencies did report as mandated.

Despite the technical implementation of Intis and the completeness of the data reporting by the agencies, the system can be considered largely ineffective in its central purpose of the monitoring and control of development projects. Qualitative criteria such as continued dependence on government versus self-reliance were important measures of development not captured by Intis. Even the measures of financial and physical progress in terms of 'percent spent' and 'percent completed' were relatively meaningless indicators given the complexity of most development projects which cut across various ministries, as well as the absence of any comparison with performance standards. Thus, the information provided by Intis did not enable senior government officials to judge the impacts or cost effectiveness of projects or programmes towards national or sectoral goals.

In addition to the criticism of the low value of the measures of performance generated for the GCA itself, the Intis system was not considered valuable by many of the participating agencies. It was often seen as involving extra work by the agencies with no reward, since the information generated was of little value for their purposes, being either too detailed in some areas, or not detailed enough in others. Intis did not replace their existing systems but had to be handled in parallel. It was not used by other agencies in the way that had been envisaged in the original concept for a common reporting and monitoring system.

Even in the early 1980s, senior management at the GCA realized that Intis would not be adequate for monitoring purposes at the lower levels of the district and the state. Details at the district level, and even village level, were required to monitor development activities in the field. An earlier manual information system in the 1960s had operated at these levels in support of a district development programme involving the direct leadership from the centre of the then Deputy Prime Minister. In 1986, a new programme was launched by the Deputy Prime Minister at that time, broadly based on the same rationale as the earlier programme, with the centre being seen to be directly involved at the lower levels. The stated purpose of this initiative revolved around co-ordinating and integrating development activities at the district level in order to stimulate economic growth at the grass roots. Information was felt to be a critical ingredient and a computerized IS in support of the programme was envisaged.

Responsibility for this new computerized information system, which will be called Devplan, was given to the GCA. In mid-1988, a prototype IS for a particular district was developed by a subsidiary of one of the main computer vendors. However, the prototype exercise did not address such organizational aspects as whose responsibility it would be to update the data on the stand-alone machine. By the time the prototyping exercise ended, GCA's thoughts were moving from a district-level IS to a more comprehensive system that would link up with its existing project monitoring systems, notably Intis. Further work on the Devplan system continued until the end of the research period, involving amongst other things attempts at developing pilot applications linking health and educational IS at the district level. Some scepticism was expressed by government officials outside the GCA about the likely usefulness of Devplan, mainly centred around the lack of genuine involvement in the IS of those actually working at the lower levels. In addition, the relative failure of Intis as a common IS for central government agencies did not appear to have dimmed the drive in the GCA for large integrated systems, and the research period ended with the GCA actively considering a national development information system involving the whole machinery of government at local, state and federal level.

SOCIAL CONTEXT

We start the analysis of the case by considering the social context of the focal computer-based IS. An aspect of particular importance in this case study, part of the multi-level context of the focal IS, is the context of the culture and politics of Polonia. Although the national context within which events occur is always relevant, the cases described in the previous two chapters took place in the UK, one of the industrialized countries within which computer-based IS were originally developed. A critical issue for a country such as Polonia is whether these experiences transfer to the rather different social context of their country. A second feature of the context of a country such as Polonia is the social infrastructure for computing development. These issues are now briefly considered under the headings of the political context of Polonia, social relations, and infrastructure; some elements of the discussion are summarized in Table 6.1.

TABLE 6.1 GCA: some elements of social context

Political Context

- Dominant racial group wished to see material progress in rural areas
- Development projects were key instruments for rural development, and the related computer-based IS were thus a political issue
- GCA were close to the centre of power, and their IS projects were geared to programmes with political purposes

- -

Social Relations

- Characterized by strong sense of social hierarchy/respect for authority
- IS team in GCA saw themselves as carrying out instructions from senior levels in the GCA
- IS for development project monitoring and control seen as providing information for central control

- -

Infrastructure

- No significant understanding of IT and computer-based IS amongst top politicians or senior managers of the GCA
- Skilled human resources within the IS team very limited

Political Context

Polonia had achieved considerable economic growth since independence, but there had been a number of serious political problems, including racial tension culminating in major race riots in the late 1960s. The dominant racial group who controlled the political system had a particular desire to see material progress in the rural areas, where the villages were largely populated by members of their racial group who were in the poorest economic category. Development projects, which were the focus of each of the three computerized IS in this case study, were key instruments for economic development in general, and rural development in particular. Thus the whole area of development projects and their monitoring, and the computer-based IS to support this, was a highly sensitive political issue.

Within this broad national context, the GCA was close to the centre of political power, including the Prime Minister himself. Initiatives for computer-based IS thus tended to be driven from the political centre and to be geared to programmes with political purposes. For example, Intis was a response to the drive for more efficiency in the public sector brought in by the new government in 1981. Devplan was part of a vigorous political effort from 1986 onwards to demonstrate government commitment to the rural areas, following political concerns about the weakening of grass roots support for the government in these areas. It is not bad in itself for development initiatives and their supporting IS to be politically driven, but we will see later that this feature of the Polonian case, combined with other elements of social context and process, resulted in major problems for the effectiveness of the IS developed.

Social Relations

As is the case in many developing countries, general social relations in Polonia were characterized by features such as a strong sense of social hierarchy, high respect for authority figures, and an unquestioning approach to instructions from superiors. Civil servants always see themselves as the 'servants' of their political masters to some extent, but members of the GCA in Polonia reflected the general social characteristics discussed above, and largely saw their role as carrying out orders issued from above. This was certainly the case for the IS team in the GCA, who were not represented at the highest political levels and saw themselves as a service unit carrying out instructions from senior levels in the GCA.

The social relations discussed above are also related to the view which was taken concerning the purpose of computer-based IS, this being seen as the provision of information upwards and decisions downwards. Thus IS for development project monitoring were primarily viewed as providing information for central control, rather than as aiding the personnel at lower levels to carry out their jobs. One central official said that 'district-level people know nothing about computers', and the implication was that the centre was best placed to determine their needs for them. This hierarchical view of the role of IS can be seen in all three focal IS. Premis and Intis were thought of as providing information for the centre on what was happening in the field. Devplan was aimed at district-level planning and monitoring, but its content and development were controlled by the GCA at the political centre.

Infrastructure

The physical infrastructure for computer-based IS is much better in Polonia than in many developing countries, with generally adequate provision of utilities such as electricity, and the availability of computer equipment and spare parts. However, social infrastructure for computing involves other aspects such as the availability of human resources, and the management understanding and authority to make these available when needed. In these areas, Polonia was less well provided and some features of this are now outlined.

IS initiatives in the GCA were largely driven by political considerations, but none of the politicians or the top management of the GCA had a real understanding of information technology and the opportunities and risks involved in the development of computer-based IS. Polonia had no central IT plan or any coherent view of how information technology could be used within the economy. There was some knowledge concerning the application of computers amongst some of the middle-level officials in the GCA forming the IS team, and in a number of other government agencies outside the Prime Minister's Department. These latter agencies were, however, not consulted with respect to the development of the three focal IS, and the IS team in the GCA itself viewed their role largely as carrying out orders. In addition, skilled human resources within the IS team in the GCA were very limited, necessitating the frequent use of outside consultants. This could have been a benefit in terms of bringing in outside expertise, but the common view expressed by government officials was that these consultants lacked experience on government systems, and they appear to have had little impact on the rationale and design of the focal IS in the GCA.

SOCIAL PROCESS

In this section, the social process surrounding the focal IS will be analysed over the period 1978 to 1991. The analytical framework in Chapter 3 identifies two elements of cultural and political change in social process, but the two elements will be discussed together in this section, focusing on subcultures and their interaction, the management of change, and aspects of autonomy and control; some elements of the discussion are summarized in Table 6.2.

Premis 1978–1981

The decision to computerize development project monitoring activities, producing the Premis system, was made by the head of the GCA, following the recognition of the difficulties of keeping pace with the increased level of development activities. The subculture of the GCA IS staff viewed their role as producing a computer system matching the broad specifications they had been given, and the Premis system was implemented in a technical sense in 1978. However, the data produced by the system were of little value, since the subcultures of the various agencies did not submit data in some cases, submitted incomplete data in others, and the data were in any case not adequate to diagnose the real problems in the field to enable those at the centre to direct appropriate remedial action. Summarized data were returned to the agencies themselves, but these data were out of date by the time they were received by the agencies, in addition to being inadequate as a basis for detailed action.

The management of the process of cultural and political change in connection with the new computerized IS was almost non-existent. The senior management

TABLE 6.2 GCA: some elements of social process

Premis   1978–1981

- Decision to computerize project monitoring activities made by head of GCA, with IS staff seeing their role as technical implementation
- Subcultures of various other agencies resisted supplying data
- Management of process of cultural and political change in connection with the new computerized system almost non-existent
- Enhanced monitoring and control at the centre not achieved

Intis   1981–1991

- Highest level political backing for Intis system, so that all agencies supplied data as required
- Many agencies perceived the system as of no value to them
- Integration between agencies was a key goal, but no one saw themselves as managing the change process
- IS staff in the GCA became aware of deficiencies in the system, for example in terms of data quality and system usefulness

Devplan   1986–1991

- High-level political support for centrally-directed development programme at district level, supported by computerized system
- Little account taken of actual work at district level and below
- Philosophy of increased top-down control still pervasive, reflecting elements of nature of social relations in Polonia

of the GCA could not exert any significant influence on the agencies in order to obtain fuller co-operation. The IS staff saw their role as technical, and did not view the change process, in terms of generating a shared view of co-operation between the GCA and the other agencies, as being their responsibility.

One of the main purposes of the Premis system, as viewed from the GCA and the Prime Minister's Department, was increased monitoring and control of development projects at the centre, and this was certainly not achieved. Indeed, the introduction of the computer system was accompanied by other changes in the monitoring of development projects, including a reduction in the number and intensity of field briefings and inspections by personnel from the centre. Ironically, in view of the goal of Premis, this resulted in more autonomy at local levels, and the state development officers assumed greater responsibility for local development activities. The question as to whether this helped or hindered development progress is not easily answered; it is, however, clear that Premis was ineffective in achieving closer central control.

Intis 1981–1991

The initiative for Intis derived from the very top of the political system, with the new Prime Minister focusing on improving the efficiency of the public sector, and the committee which recommended the development of Intis being at Cabinet level. The head of the GCA was the main champion for the new system, and it was aimed at remedying the data deficiencies of the previous Premis system, in addition to providing an integrated system across different central agencies for the better monitoring and control of development projects. In view of the high level of political support, the subcultures of the individual ministries and agencies did provide the data as required, but this was a response to a political directive, rather than any more basic change in attitudes as to how to do their work in a way which was integrated with other agencies.

This lack of perceived value of the Intis system by many of the participating agencies can be illustrated with some direct interview quotations. A senior official in one of the other central agencies which was intended to be both a supplier and user of data from the system said:

> The work involved in providing information for Intis is additional as we do not want to use the more micro-level information Intis requires . . . For the micro type of data Intis requires, it should be decentralized.

The information needs at the ministry level also differed from what was provided by Intis. According to an official in one Ministry responsible for providing input data to Intis:

> Intis, being designed for all ministries for all types of development project, is too simplified to be of use to this Ministry. What this Ministry keeps track of and what is given to the GCA (for Intis) are two different things. Intis is useless to the Ministry.

At the state level, the difficulty lay in providing data from the relevant agencies working in the field on actual projects. Thus, an officer from one State Development Office said:

> They (local agencies in the field) don't keep records and don't have the required data. We (the State Development Office) have our own format for data collection, and don't use the GCA's prescribed format (for Intis). In addition, we have detailed information on problems in project implementation, which are not required by the GCA but are required by the State Secretariat.

The last sentence in the above quotation illustrates the main reason why the Intis system, in addition to being of little value to the participating agencies, produced data for the GCA itself which was of limited usefulness for central monitoring and control. Detailed information on problems in the field, adequate as a basis for proposing remedial action, was not available through Intis. It was noted earlier in the chapter that the information on physical and financial progress which was available from Intis was not helpful to senior government officials in judging the development impact of programmes and projects.

The intention of Intis in the minds of some politicians and high-level administrators at least was to assist in the process of cultural change, whereby government agencies would work together in a more integrated fashion on the planning and control of development projects. However, as with the previous Premis system, no one individual or group saw their role as managing this cultural and political change process surrounding the focal IS. Directives were issued to agencies on the provision of data for Intis and these were obeyed, but this does not achieve better co-operation in itself, and indeed can produce resentment and the reverse effect as some of the above quotations from officials in the agencies imply.

With respect to changes in the autonomy/control balance mediated by Intis, it is difficult to make a definitive statement since other changes took place over the seven years from the first technical implementation of the system in 1984 to the end of the research period in 1991. However, the general impact of the system was low, and agencies at all levels appeared to have continued to work much as before. One aspect of change worth mentioning is that IS staff in the GCA monitored the progress and achievements of Intis and, despite still taking a largely reactive stance to IS development, were critical of a number of aspects of the system. In interviews in 1989, different officials noted that Intis was 'a top management information system', that the system was 'not well used' by other agencies, and that 'data quality was a problem'.

Devplan 1986–1991

The political initiative for a new district development programme again came from the top of the political hierarchy, being announced by the Deputy Prime Minister in 1986. As mentioned earlier, the approach echoed an earlier centrally-directed development programme in the 1960s supported by a manual information system on district-level activities. It is interesting to note that, no doubt because of the experience of earlier systems such as Intis, officials at the GCA expressed some doubts about how easy it would be to develop the Devplan system to provide valuable data for officers in the field, within the timescale envisaged by politicians. A senior IS official in the GCA said, in 1989, following relatively slow progress in the Devplan project:

> Politicians tend to want something fast in IS which can be a problem . . . Government is a bureaucracy and tends to think in national terms. Development of management information systems is most difficult in this sort of context.

Despite increasing recognition of the difficulties of providing genuinely effective IS for users, the GCA still adopted a relatively centralized approach to the determination of user needs, taking little account of the actual work of the subcultures of district level officials and below, and the needs of the different agencies and ministries operating at that level. Criticisms of the GCA's approach to Devplan were expressed in a forthright manner by a senior official of another central government agency, who was knowledgeable about computing systems and their implementation:

> The GCA are yet to clarify the mechanism of integrated planning, the information requirements to support integrated planning, and how the various databases at the district are to be integrated ... People at the grass roots are not much involved in the whole process ... The GCA don't know what they want and have not gone to the districts. The districts may not be ready to accept Devplan or even to sit behind a computer terminal and input data. The state development officers themselves don't think they can collect the required data as they are too busy with routine duties.

It is worth noting that the main purpose of the new district development initiative started in 1986 can be thought of as involving a process of cultural and political change at the district level. Yet, once again, no one saw themselves as managing this change process in connection with the introduction of Devplan. The pilot scheme in a particular district in 1988, carried out by a consultancy firm employed by the GCA, ignored issues of organizational change. The tender document for further consultancy work issued in 1989 made little mention of organizational issues and, equally worrying, none of the short-listed consultants had any experience of implementing government information systems projects.

Politicians and senior government officials in Polonia still appeared to see computer-based IS as an opportunity for increased control, rather than being aware of the subtle balance between autonomy and control at all levels which is a critical feature of successful management and should guide approaches to IS development. This 'control' view of IS can be suggested as a key reason why the concept of an integrated national development information system was being seriously debated by the central agencies at the end of the research period, despite the relative failures of Premis and Intis to provide improved co-ordination between agencies or good data for central control, and the uncertainties and difficulties surrounding the Devplan system at the district level. The social context of Polonia discussed earlier, and in particular the nature of social relations, is reflected in the model of all-seeing top-down control, and it is perhaps fortunate, from an ethical stance, that computerized IS are unlikely to deliver mechanisms to achieve this.

CONTEXT/PROCESS LINKAGE

This section presents a formal analysis of some elements of the case study using structuration theory as a basis. The description shows how social structure and action are inextricably interlinked via the modalities of interpretative schemes, facilities and norms; structuring processes take place over time in which action, influenced by structure, reinforces or modifies structure. This structurational analysis should be seen as complementary to the preceding analytical sections. The discussion is divided into three consecutive periods, each starting with the initiation of a new computerized IS for monitoring and controlling development projects; some elements of the discussion are summarized in Table 6.3.

Period 1: 1978-1981

The head of the GCA was able to ensure development of the Premis system by drawing on his facility to allocate human and material resources within

TABLE 6.3 GCA: some elements of context/process linkage

Period 1: 1978-1981

- Head of GCA drew on facility to allocate human and material resources in GCA to initiate Premis system
- Reflected structure of signification viewing economic development as best achieved through centrally directed projects
- GCA attempted to exercise power over other agencies to provide data, with limited success
- Intended strategy was closer central monitoring and control, but unintended consequences included increased local power of action

Period 2: 1981-1986

- New strategy for IS, reflected in Intis system, involved better co-ordinated control between key central agencies
- Information provided to agencies by Intis perceived as of little use, so routinization of activities in agencies is not disrupted
- In minds of IS staff, norm of obedience to orders probably stronger than norm of usefulness of computerized systems

Period 3: 1986-1991

- Approach taken to systems development for district-level Devplan system reflected persistent social structures of top-down control
- Reflexive monitoring by IS staff provided seeds for future change
- However, little sign of changed attitudes among dominant coalition

the GCA, sanctioned by the norm of improved central monitoring and control of development projects. The Premis system reflected a long-standing structure of signification which viewed economic development as best achieved through centrally directed projects; this view had been widened by the late 1970s to see a key role for computer-based systems in monitoring and control. This modified structure of signification partly arose from the experiences prior to 1978, when the manual monitoring system had not kept pace with the upsurge in development activities.

GCA staff attempted to draw on structures of domination, arising from their powerful position within the Prime Minister's Department, to compel other agencies to provide data for the Premis system. In some cases, the relational power of the GCA *vis-à-vis* other agencies was not strong enough to make this happen; and other agencies were unlikely to participate voluntarily, since they did not in general share the strategic approach of the central control of development projects being co-ordinated by the GCA. Other agencies who did supply data to the Premis system found that the system did not embody an interpretative scheme on development activities which could be usefully drawn on in communication as to what was happening in the field. The summary data from the system were out of date by the time they were received by the agencies, and they were insufficiently detailed; thus the Premis system was not used by agencies outside the GCA, and was of little use to the GCA itself.

Premis reflected a conscious effort on the part of the GCA leadership to change the power of the centre with respect to people at the local state and district level, by closer central monitoring of development activities in the field. However, other changes such as a reduced number of briefings and inspection visits at the local level, together with the failure of the Premis system to provide good data on local activities, combined to provide local staff with more autonomy. They had increased facilities to allocate local resources to development activities, and thus changed structures of domination involved increased power of action for people at the local level. This is an interesting example of the unintended consequences of intentional action of the centre designed to produce the reverse effect.

Period 2: 1981–1986

The arrival of the new Prime Minister in 1981 resulted in major modifications to existing political structures and attitudes, including an increased emphasis on the norm of efficiency in the public sector. This norm was used by the Cabinet Committee on the implementation of development projects as part of the sanction for their proposal of a new computerized monitoring system. The Cabinet Committee's report embodied an interpretative scheme that was drawn on by the head of the GCA to communicate the desirability of the new

Intis system. The new strategy for information systems, as conceived by senior GCA staff, involved not only IS for central control, as was the objective of the Premis system, but also better co-ordinated control between the key central agencies concerned with development projects.

The power of the Prime Minister's Department with respect to other agencies was enhanced by the arrival of the new Prime Minister, and a circular from this Department on the new procedures for reporting development activities provided a facility which could be used to put pressure on all agencies; the result was that all agencies were compelled to provide data to the Intis system, in contrast to Premis. However, in common with its predecessor, Intis embodied an inadequate interpretative scheme to be drawn on in communication regarding development activities. This applied not only at the district and state levels, where insufficient local-level detail was available from Intis, but also within the ministries and other central agencies where the Intis system provided data which were not perceived to be of value to people in doing their work. Thus the routinization of the activities of agencies outside the GCA was not disrupted by the Intis system; they carried on largely as before with little change to their structures of signification with respect to their role and work on development activities, and the need for this to be co-ordinated between agencies.

It is worthwhile here to expand the boundaries of our discussion beyond the social actions and structures at the level of the focal information systems, and the government agencies developing and using them, to the broader social context at the national level. The GCA IS staff sanctioned their actions on Intis, and the previous system Premis, by the norm of carrying out orders of their superiors. This norm reflects the social structure of legitimation within Polonian society concerning the acceptability of hierarchical top-down control, and in drawing on the norm to sanction action, the structure of legitimation is reproduced. The fact that the norm of usefulness of the computerized system was not achieved by either of the two systems, Premis or Intis, was probably not perceived by the GCA staff as being as important as following the societal norm of obedience to authority.

The above discussion should not be taken to imply a criticism of the approach taken by the IS staff in the GCA, since in the case of resistance by their juniors, senior GCA staff could have drawn on their facility to punish and even dismiss staff who resisted, with little comeback in the asymmetric structures of domination of Polonian society. However, despite little evidence in terms of action, the GCA IS staff did reflexively monitor their own activities and the consequences. They were prepared to follow orders, but views expressed in interviews in 1989, that the Intis system was not well used and that there were problems of data quality, indicate clear evidence that they had formed their own opinions regarding the value of the computerized monitoring systems. Indeed, the seeds of change to social structures are here, since the members of the IS staff were starting to form and communicate a new structure of signification regarding the problems inherent in top-down approaches to computerized IS driven by political imperatives.

Period 3: 1986–1991

The political leadership of the dominant racial group were concerned in the mid-1980s about the gap between the political centre and activities at the local level. This resulted in a programme for improved rural development via integrated development planning at the district level, with IS being seen as supportive of this, leading to the Devplan initiative in 1986. Although the system could be perceived as an attempt to focus on local-level activities, the approach taken to systems development reflected the persistent social structures within Polonian society concerning the acceptability of control from the top-down. We have seen that some of the IS staff in the GCA were beginning to question these structures with respect to computerized IS, but the attitudes of the dominant coalition of politicians and administrators over the whole research period seem to have shifted little, and they continued to utilize their power to ensure a similar top-down approach to the development of Devplan to that used for the Premis and Intis systems.

Indeed, not only was there little change in the top-down approach amongst senior politicians, but discussion was starting to take place over this later period of a new role for computer-based IS as an opportunity for integrated control at all levels. A proposal was made for an integrated national development information system, incorporating existing systems such as Devplan and Intis, which would embody an interpretative scheme for development activities at all levels, encapsulate the norm of central control, and provide a facility to enable this to happen. However, there is no evidence from the history of the earlier systems that such an approach would lead to an effective system, either in terms of capturing the variety of development activities at the local level in an adequate way, or in facilitating a shared interpretative scheme regarding development activities and their particular role amongst the multiple agencies operating in the field.

As noted above with respect to Intis, the views regarding IS and their role amongst some of the IS staff were changing over the research period, and staff expressed specific doubts concerning Devplan. These reservations included aspects such as the feasibility of providing systems as rapidly as the politicians wanted, and whether the systems provided would be of any use to those managing and monitoring development projects at the local level. The views of some government officials in other agencies, with experience of computerized IS, tended to support these reservations. We thus see some evidence of changing structures of signification amongst knowledgeable government officials, away from IS for central control and towards IS for local management.

However, the norms of obedience within the social hierarchy were deep-rooted within Polonian society, and it would require at least a significant shift in the social structures in the minds of senior politicians regarding the role and purpose of computerized IS before any real change at the level of action would be likely with respect to government systems in Polonia.

CONCLUSIONS

This final section draws together some conclusions from the case study with respect to the interdependent issues of IS strategy, evaluation, design and development, and implementation. The history of the focal information systems for the monitoring and control of development projects is inextricably interlinked with cultural, political and development issues in Polonia, and the discussion which follows interweaves these various strands.

Strategy

The strategic discourse which lay behind the development of the information systems by the GCA was political in nature and largely conducted by senior politicians and those appointed by them, including the head of the GCA itself, who had no real understanding of computer-based systems or of experiences with them in other environments. However, each of the information systems had a clear strategic focus. For the Premis system, the goal was improved central control of development projects by the GCA, whilst for Intis this goal was enlarged to include co-ordinated control by the central agencies. The Devplan system was aimed at integrating district-level monitoring and control, and the proposed national development IS envisaged linked control at all hierarchical levels.

The critical question with respect to the strategic focus of each of the computerized systems is whether the goal was desirable and feasible, and the interpretations presented in the case study suggest a largely negative answer. The systems developed with a view to top-down control did not support the work of the people and agencies supplying data, and thus were seen by them as irrelevant at best, or as a significant burden in some cases. This negative perception on the part of the agencies could perhaps have been offset if the data produced for the GCA at the centre had been valuable, but in general this was not the case. The data supplied by the Intis system were incomplete and out of date by the time they were available; in addition, the data supplied by both Intis and Premis did not capture what was happening at the local level in a way which was useful to central government in judging the impact or cost effectiveness of development programmes and projects. It was too early to say conclusively whether Devplan would repeat the history of Premis and Intis and produce data of little value, but the evidence by the end of the research period, including the lack of contact with those working in the field and the top-down strategic focus, suggested that a similar fate was quite likely. The proposal for the national integrated IS appeared to be extremely overambitious, bearing in mind the relative failure of the rather more modest earlier attempts.

In trying to understand human actions which appear to ignore earlier evidence, such as the later proposal for the national integrated IS, we can perhaps look to deep-seated attitudes and values which are slow to change, and in this case the top-down approach to IS strategy and the philosophy of central control were endemic to the culture and social relations of Polonia. The actions of the IS staff in the GCA, in following the norm of obedience to orders and largely discounting the norm of the usefulness of the IS produced, reproduced the social structures within the GCA and Polonian society at large. It would be simplistic to assume that cultural attitudes and social relations within a whole society can be easily changed, or that it is always desirable for this to occur. Nevertheless, it should be recognized that a top-down and central control approach to IS strategy, whilst it may be in tune with local culture, may well produce computerized information systems of little value in practical terms, other than as a symbolic reaffirmation of the culture of following orders from the political centre. It can be suggested that this represents a waste of economic and human resources, which are in relatively short supply in countries such as Polonia.

Evaluation

No formal evaluation on economic or management efficiency grounds was carried out for any of the information systems described in this case study, although the political debate at the centre was a form of evaluation discourse which provided the impetus for system approval. Other interested parties outside the political centre made no direct input to this political evaluation process, but they made their own informal evaluations of the systems and used these as the basis for action. For example, informal evaluations led some agencies to not even supply data for the Premis system; in the case of the Intis system, all agencies were compelled to supply data, but made no significant use of the system, having evaluated it as useless for their needs. A similar situation could occur with the Devplan system when completed, since it would be informally evaluated by lower level officers in the districts, and not utilized by them if classed as unhelpful. Some supportive evidence for this latter hypothesis is provided by the Crisp system in India. This is a computerized information system for district-level planning which was imposed on all districts in India by a central government agency in New Delhi; research evidence (Madon 1992) demonstrates that the system was not used at all in the districts investigated, since the system was not thought to be of value by local officers at the district level.

The informal evaluations carried out by some of the IS staff in the GCA itself are interesting. Their evaluations of the Premis and Intis systems over a number of years made them start to question, at least in their own minds, the concept of top-down control as the underlying rationale for the IS developed by them. They were starting to show concern by the end of the research period that IS should be of benefit to local-level management in the districts, a move towards a philosophy of end-user computing. The informal evaluations of the IS staff at the centre thus provided some evidence of seeds for future change, although there was no evidence that this had affected the views of the politicians themselves to any appreciable extent.

The informal evaluations of the computerized IS amongst the relevant politicians and senior administrators no doubt placed more emphasis on obedience to their directives than on the usefulness of the IS produced. It could be argued that this obedience reproduced their political domination and thus that it served their needs. However, if we consider the Devplan system, it is not at all obvious that the approach taken would serve their needs. The system was envisaged as part of a signal of commitment by central government to development at the lower levels, following concern that dissatisfaction was being expressed at these levels. However, if the Devplan system were to be evaluated by local officers as being of little use, then this would tend to reinforce feelings of dissatisfaction with the political centre and thus produce the reverse effect of that intended. A simple contributory factor to the behaviour of politicians in Polonia with respect to computerized information systems was their relative ignorance of such systems, and hence they had a deficient basis for evaluation. In other words, their actions partially reflected a lack of knowledge of other ways to approach the strategy and development of IS, one based on end-user computing, for example. However, such a changed philosophy would have been at odds with general cultural attitudes in Polonia, and central government officials no doubt feared the loss of power and privilege which could result from societal change away from the philosophy of central control.

Design and Development

The history of the design and development of the computerized IS in this case study can be succinctly summarized as one of technical implementation, with no significant concern for organizational usefulness, particularly with respect to agencies outside the GCA itself. The specification for the design of the Premis and Intis systems, derived from political imperatives, was elaborated at the centre by GCA staff with little consultation, and the task was then seen as one of producing software and systems which worked in a technical sense.

Participation of other agencies was minimal in the case of Premis, and for Intis was restricted to ensuring that technical integration of the different central agency systems was achieved, with no effort being directed to trying to generate systems which would be valuable to other agencies in their work. Training was largely concerned with data collection and input, rather than with actual use of the system in practice for real work. With respect to Devplan, there was no evidence of serious efforts towards participation of staff in the field in the design of the eventual system. Some pilot projects had been initiated, but the focus of interest was not towards helping local-level staff in their work activities, although as we have seen, there were some signs of a recognition by central IS staff in the GCA that there perhaps should be movement in this strategic direction.

There was little evidence of serious technical deficiency in the systems produced. Much of the effort in software design and development is towards tools and methodologies to aid technical implementation, which would have been of little value in addressing the problems in this case study, which were largely organizational and contextual in nature. It is true that inadequate resources in the IS staff of the GCA meant that outside consultants were used at various stages of the design and development of the focal information systems. This could have been a blessing in disguise if the outside consultants had had a good grasp of organizational issues and a drive towards IS effectiveness in use, since they may have compensated for deficiencies in this respect in the GCA IS staff. However, the consultants replicated the technical implementation focus of the GCA approach, and appear not to have questioned the overall strategy or system goals; this may, again, have reflected national cultural attitudes of not questioning higher authorities, although an ignoring of issues of IS usefulness is not solely a characteristic of IT consultants in developing countries such as Polonia, but is also common in industrialized societies.

Implementation

The Premis and Intis systems could be perceived as having achieved a measure of success with respect to some implementation goals, in terms of technical implementation, and in terms of meeting important political stakeholders' objectives of visible systems designed for central control purposes, reproducing the legitimacy of the norm of central control. However, the implementation goal of effectiveness in use was largely not achieved. Both Devplan and the proposed national integrated IS could be seen similarly as symbolic systems, demonstrating central concern for local development activities linked to an overall system of top-down control. There was no real evidence to suggest that they would be effective in helping people to carry out their work, except perhaps for some signs of changing attitudes towards end-user systems on the part of the IS staff in the GCA itself.

Two qualifications should be made to the rather bleak conclusion on implementation in the above paragraph. Firstly, it would be wrong to suggest that no data from the Premis or Intis systems were ever of any value; for example, both systems were used internally within the GCA itself, and whilst the data were inadequate in many ways, no doubt some useful information was generated by debates stimulated by data from the systems. In addition, it is impossible to measure any benefit which may have accrued in terms of improved understanding from those people and agencies inputting data to the system. Such individuals were normally negative about the benefits of this process, but we cannot conclude that they gained no benefit, although questions of the opportunity cost of their time if used for other purposes are clearly relevant. A second qualification to the negative implementation picture is the argument that learning was taking place, in a slow way, and that the IS staff in the GCA, for example, were better informed about IS and their potentialities by the end of the research period when compared to a decade earlier.

Despite the above qualifications, there is a certain irony in the largely unsuccessful implementation of the computerized IS developed by the GCA, in that its central *raison d'être* was the monitoring of the implementation of development projects in the country. The location of the GCA in the Prime Minister's Department meant that it was very close to the centre of political power and therefore could draw on powerful facilities to ensure compliance with respect to data input, for example. However, this location also made it more difficult for IS staff in the GCA to take an openly critical stance of the IS strategy and development approach, since this would no doubt have been perceived as political dissent. Nevertheless, this group could perhaps play a catalytic role in the future of government IS in Polonia, by starting to articulate some of their growing doubts concerning the effectiveness of systems produced.

REFERENCES

Han, C. K. (1991) *Information Technology Policies and Government Information Systems: A Multiple Level Perspective*, unpublished PhD thesis, University of Cambridge.

Han, C. K., and Walsham, G. (1990) 'Public policy and information systems in government: a mixed level analysis of computerization', Management Studies Research Paper No. 3/89, University of Cambridge.

Madon, S. (1992) 'Computer-based information systems for decentralized rural development administration: a case study in India', *Journal of Information Technology*, **7**, No. 1, 20–29.

Part III
MAJOR ISSUES

Chapter 7
STRATEGY

This chapter addresses the issue of information systems strategy, and is divided into four sections. The first section discusses *relevant literature on strategy*, and relates ideas from this literature to aspects of the earlier case studies. The second section focuses on the analysis of the case studies in Part II, and discusses *themes on IS strategy* arising directly from this material. The third section draws on the discussion in the first two sections to generate a *synthesized perspective* on IS strategy and the role of the IS strategist. The final section of the chapter then develops this perspective by discussing the *practice of IS strategy* based around the set of themes from the case material; the discussion aims to provide some vocabulary and issues for debate in any particular practical context, rather than a set of prescriptions.

RELEVANT LITERATURE ON STRATEGY

The purpose of this section is not to survey the literature on strategy in its entirety, but rather to identify and discuss work which is relevant to the interpretive approach taken in this book, and also to use this work to interpret aspects of the earlier case material. Much of the strategy literature is concerned with strategy formulation, taking a formal-rational view of organizations as systems with coherent purposes and shared goals, and seeing the strategy formulation process as a series of logical steps. The material in this book is concerned with interpretations of the way in which strategy forms in practice, viewing the whole concept of organization as problematic, and strategy formation as a dynamic socio-political process within multi-level contexts.

The majority of this section is devoted to discussing the general business strategy literature rather than the literature on information systems strategy itself, and there are two reasons for this. Firstly, information systems are a central issue in business strategy in an increasing number of organizations, including the focal organizations in all three case studies in Part II; thus IS strategy is an important subset of business strategy for such organizations. Secondly, there is more reported work on general business strategy than there is on IS strategy that is of relevance to the interpretive approach. The review is divided into three parts. The first part concerns a major body of work on strategy formation carried out by Mintzberg, and the second part then considers other literature on business and corporate strategy; in the final part, some relevant work on IS strategy itself is reviewed.

Mintzberg on Strategy

A prolific and much-cited writer on strategy in the management literature is Henry Mintzberg. In an early article (Mintzberg 1978), he coined the term 'strategy formation' to reflect the emergent nature of the strategy process:

> ... the usual definition of 'strategy' encourages the notion that strategies, as we recognize them ex post facto, are deliberate plans conceived in advance of the making of specific decisions. By defining a strategy as 'a pattern in a stream of decisions', we are able to research strategy formation in a broad descriptive context. Specifically, we can study both strategies that were intended and those that were realized despite intentions. (p. 934)

Mintzberg and McHugh (1985) later gave a modified definition of strategy as 'a pattern in a stream of decisions and actions', the additional two words reflecting the point that decisions themselves represent intentions whereas actions represent realized activity. This later article describes strategy formation in some detail in an organization which resembled an ideal type known as an adhocracy (Mintzberg 1979), characterized by such features as complex and unpredictable work, a dynamic environment, highly trained staff in multi-disciplinary teams, and relatively informal and non-hierarchical management style. This case study is an example of Mintzberg's work on how strategy forms in a wide variety of different organizations.

In summarizing the range of work referred to above, Mintzberg and Waters (1985) note a distinction between unrealized strategies, namely intentions not successfully realized, and realized strategy that is unsuccessful in its consequences. They present a synthesized view of strategy formation as follows:

> Our conclusion is that strategy formation walks on two feet, one deliberate, the other emergent. . . . managing requires a light deft touch—to direct in order to realize intentions while at the same time responding to an unfolding pattern of action. (p. 271)

A further set of ideas in Mintzberg and Waters is an attempt to classify different approaches to strategy observed in the extensive case material into eight categories. Five of these are outlined here, being of relevance to the subsequent discussion. These are 'the planned strategy', involving detailed planning, normally from an initial vision; 'the entrepreneurial strategy' based on the personal control of a single individual; 'the umbrella strategy', setting general strategy guidelines without detailed plans; 'the process strategy', involving control of the process of strategy making rather than its content; and 'the imposed strategy', determined largely by pressures outside the control of management.

Some of the ideas from the above literature provide useful ways of interpreting the formation of IS strategy in the case studies in Part II. In the Processing Company, the intended strategy can be thought of as an MRP system for automation and control. The realized strategy involved one element of that intended, namely the existence of the sales order processing system, but the goal of automation of procedures and tight control by management can be thought of as an element of unrealized strategy. An emergent aspect of strategy was to view MRP systems as 'a whole new way of working', which then contributed to the intended strategy for the later phases. The approach to strategy making can perhaps be classed as one of 'planned strategy' from the initial vision of MRP systems.

In Sky under Brown, we can view a key element of deliberate strategy as decentralized IS for improved customer support. This aspect of strategy was realized, although it also led to closer central control of the branches; this latter aspect could be considered to be a part of Brown's intended strategy at the outset, but the way in which it developed can be thought of as a part of emergent strategy. Under Taylor, we see no clear IS strategy being agreed upon, although Taylor's intentions were that the strategy would emerge from the formal corporate planning procedures. Sky seems to relate well to two of Mintzberg's categories of strategic approach, moving from the 'entrepreneurial strategy' under Brown to the 'process strategy' under Taylor.

The intended IS strategy for the Government Co-ordination Agency can be interpreted as central systems for improved monitoring and control of development projects. The implemented systems, Premis and Intis, represented an element of realized strategy, but the improved monitoring and control of development projects can be regarded as largely unrealized strategy. The approach can be viewed as an 'umbrella strategy' on the part of central government during the whole research period, shifting the coverage of its umbrella from central monitoring by the GCA, to the integration of monitoring by central agencies, with the inclusion of district-level monitoring in the latter part of the period. From the perspective of the GCA itself, and certainly from that of the IS team, the approach can perhaps be seen as an 'imposed strategy', since the strategy was essentially being driven by political forces outside the GCA itself.

The above analysis of the case material suggests that Mintzberg's ideas provide a useful way of thinking about the IS strategy formation process, at least at a broad conceptual level. Similarly, the categorization of different approaches to strategy can be related to the case studies, although individual cases are more complex and confused than these simple categories would suggest. Finally, Mintzberg's work is a reminder of the diversity of organizations which are encountered in practice, and that our case studies analysed in Part II represent only a small element of that diversity.

Other Literature on Business Strategy

A number of other writers, in addition to Mintzberg, have been concerned with the process of strategy formation. A major body of work is that by Pettigrew and others at the University of Warwick in the UK. This work will not be elaborated on here, since it was described in some detail in Chapter 3, and has contributed significantly to the theoretical and methodological basis of the work described in this book, including the content/context/process analysis of organizational change.

Another author who has written extensively on the strategy formation process is Quinn, who has argued that successful strategic managers practise 'logical incrementalism' (Quinn 1980). This is described as a jointly analytical and behavioural process in which managers proceed flexibly and experimentally from broad concepts to specific commitments, making the latter concrete as late as possible. The idea of logical incrementalism is similar to Mintzberg's 'walking on two feet', making deliberate policy but also monitoring emergent effects. The 'most successful' strategic manager in our case studies, at least measured by criteria such as organizational profitability, was undoubtedly Brown at Sky. He certainly exhibited some elements of logical incrementalism, in terms both of having clear concepts concerning strategy, and of being prepared to learn from the unfolding nature of events. An example of the latter is provided by Brown's strategic approach to design and development of IS, where he talked of his inability to know exactly what was needed and hence the need to proceed incrementally.

In the remainder of this subsection, we turn away from the broad school of management writers on strategy formation such as Mintzberg and Quinn, towards two more questioning and critical views of the whole concept of strategy in organizations. The first of these (Smircich and Stubbart 1985) draws on the interpretive approach which underpins this book, and views organizations as socially constructed systems of shared meaning. Organizational members are considered to form or enact their environments (Weick 1969) through their social interaction. This implies a way of viewing strategy as part of the enactment process:

> The task of strategic management in this view is organization making—to create and maintain systems of shared meaning that facilitate organized action. (Smircich and Stubbart 1985, p. 724)

The authors argue that this enactment model implies that an environment of which strategists can make sense has been put there by strategists' patterns of action; not by the process of perceiving the environment, but by the process of making the environment. They further argue that this implies a research question as to how patterns of organization are achieved, sustained and changed; and their own answer is that this is largely through the sharing of norms and values, communicated through such devices as metaphors and stories.

This enactment model of strategy is similar in analytical approach to that already taken in Part II, and so no further direct analysis of the case studies from this perspective will be given here. A summary of the approach can be given using the terminology of structuration theory. Discourse about IS strategy is based on interpretative schemes, reflects norms and provides a facility for co-ordinating and controlling action; the discourse when drawn on in communication reproduces or modifies existing social structures, viewed as shared attitudes and perceptions in human minds.

Smircich and Stubbart draw some conclusions for those involved in strategic management. They argue that such managers should see themselves as enactors of their own world, and should be consciously self-reflective about their own actions. They should intensify the debate concerning the values and norms on which their strategies are based. Multiple views of reality should be encouraged, since novel interpretations may be positive creative forces in strategy making. Finally, they argue that strategists should be concerned with testing and experimenting with what they think they know, being prepared to change their ways of viewing their environments.

It is interesting to note that the work discussed above is focused on two of the analytical dimensions in structurational analysis, namely structures of signification concerned with meaning and structures of legitimation concerned with norms and values. The third dimension is structures of domination and concerns power, and this is the main focus of the paper by Knights and Morgan (1991), which is the final piece of work reviewed in this subsection. It provides a more radical analysis than the work on strategy reviewed so far, in that it views the discourse on strategy as a mechanism of power that transforms individuals into subjects who are self-disciplined or socialized by it. They draw on the work of Foucault (1980) in emphasizing the inseparability of power and knowledge, and the way in which knowledge is always intricately bound up with technologies of power which reproduce particular discursive practices.

The theoretical summary above can be made more concrete by noting some of the power effects which Knights and Morgan consider to arise from the discourse on corporate strategy. It can provide a rationalization of management's successes and failures; it can sustain and enhance the prerogatives of management and negate alternative perspectives on organizations; it can generate a sense of personal and organizational security for managers; it can demonstrate managerial rationality; and it can facilitate and legitimize the exercise of power by management. Knights and Morgan compare their views with that of the 'processual theorists' such as Mintzberg and Pettigrew:

> Although processual theorists see strategy as an outcome of negotiated and political relations and as often emergent rather than deliberate, they do not seem to question the rationalist view that it (strategy) exists to solve problems *vis-à-vis* the organization and its environment . . . our analysis suggests that strategy does not simply respond to pre-existing problems. In the process of its formulation, strategy is actively involved in the constitution, or redefinition, of problems in advance of offering solutions for them . . . The concern of our own research is . . . to examine the various sites of power relations where strategic discourse becomes articulated and embodied through constituting or redefining the problems for which it claims to offer a solution. (Knights and Morgan 1991, pp. 267, 270)

The essence of these ideas can be expressed in the terminology of structuration theory by the view that the discourse on strategy is based on interpretative schemes and reflects norms, as noted earlier, but also that it provides a co-ordination and control facility that can be drawn on in power relations; thus the strategy discourse is intimately involved in the constitution of what is meaningful and, simultaneously, in the production and reproduction of particular structures of domination.

Elements of the above analysis can be used to interpret aspects of our case studies. In the Processing Company, IS strategy was discussed centrally by senior management with no reference to the rest of the workforce, reproducing the prerogative of management to determine organizational direction. This is 'normal' in Western business organizations, but it can be seen as an example of the application of power legitimized by the discourse on strategy, and a radical analysis would question whether it was 'desirable' as well as 'normal'.

In Sky, Brown can be viewed as using a complex discourse on IS strategy to facilitate his power of action in relation to the rest of senior management and various subcultures in the workforce such as the branch staff and the IS group. The discourse centred on norms such as profitability and growth, and the success in achieving these contributed and reinforced a sense of personal and organizational security for management. Taylor initiated a debate on IS strategy which could be viewed as attempting to demonstrate managerial rationality, and thus facilitate the later exercise of power by management to implement the resultant intended strategy. However, the discourse reflected many vested interests and it proved difficult to generate a shared view of reality as a common basis for management action.

The discourse on IS strategy with respect to the systems in the GCA was seen to be the prerogative of senior politicians, thus reproducing that view of the world, and perhaps contributing to a feeling of security on the part of those involved, since the approach was in line with cultural values, despite the relative 'failure' of the later systems. There was similarly no grass roots involvement in the discourse on IS strategy at the district level; again, this can be seen as 'normal' in many developing countries, but this prerogative of the centre and the emphasis on hierarchy in the strategic discourse is a social construction which a radical analysis would challenge.

IS Strategy Literature

There is a large literature on IS strategy in organizations, but almost all of it is concerned with prescriptive methods and frameworks aimed at aiding management in the formulation of strategy. Much of this literature takes an implicit formal-rational view of organizations, and views strategy formulation as a series of logical steps. There is very little published work to date which attempts to describe interpretations of the way in which IS strategy forms in practice, or which discusses the discourse of IS strategy as a topic of importance in itself. Since these latter issues are the main focus of this book, no substantial review of the conventional IS strategy literature will be presented here; however, a brief mention is made of this literature in the paragraph below, and then some work of relevance to the book's theme is outlined.

Earl (1989) provides a summary of much of the conventional literature on strategy with respect to computer-based information systems. He distinguishes between development or formulation of IS strategy, and management approaches to its implementation which he calls information management strategy. Earl gives a wide-ranging description of frameworks and contingency approaches in each of these areas. Many of the techniques are based on a formal-rational view of organizations as coherent entities with shared goals and management as a rational process of decision-making, although Earl does touch on more diverse views, for example by emphasizing the existence of different stakeholder perspectives. The book aims to provide support for an approach to the management of IS strategy which could broadly be considered to be in the spirit of Quinn's logical incrementalism.

Published work in the literature on interpretations of the process by which IS strategy forms in practice is difficult to find. An exception is an article by Waema and Walsham (1990) which uses a methodological approach similar to that described for the case studies in Part II to trace the process of IS strategy formation in a developing country bank in an Anglo-African country. The process was characterized by political conflict at all stages with no commitment to any particular strategic direction by the end of the research period; the strategy formation process is related to aspects of the organizational and wider multi-level contexts.

With respect to the perception of strategic management as an enactment process, there are few references in the IS literature, but Winograd and Flores

(1986) is worth mentioning. They do not refer directly to IS strategy but they see management action as an enactment process without using that exact phrase:

> We may say that managers engage in conversations in which they create, take care of, and initiate new commitments within an organization. (p. 151)

Zuboff (1988) similarly takes a view of management activity as linked to the communication of meaning and the enactment of reality, and regards this as a critical activity for the future of work:

> ... when work involves a collective effort to create and communicate meaning, the dynamics of human feeling cannot be relegated to the periphery of an organization's concerns. How people feel about themselves, each other, and the organization's purposes is closely linked to their capacity to sustain the high levels of internal commitment and motivation that are demanded by the abstraction of work ... (p. 401)

Zuboff explicitly mentions strategy formulation as a major domain of future managerial activity, and argues that all such areas should be much more open to inputs from all levels in the organization. She argues for a new vocabulary— one of colleagues and co-learners, of exploration, of experimentation and innovation. This idea of a new vocabulary in organizational discourse is discussed further in the later sections of the chapter.

THEMES FROM THE CASE STUDIES

The discussion in this section brings together interpretations on IS strategy arising directly from the analysis of the case studies in Part II. Some brief conclusions on IS strategy were given at the end of each of these earlier chapters, but this section provides a fuller and more integrated discussion based around a set of themes derived from the earlier analyses, and summarized in Table 7.1. The discussion is grouped under the headings of content, social context and social process.

Content

A major element of the content of an IS strategy can be thought to involve the *vision for change* which is embodied in it, either by deliberate design or as an emergent phenomenon. For the Processing Company, the vision was that a material requirements planning system could provide a major improvement in the way that the company collected, used and communicated information on all aspects of its business from order processing to sales despatch. The company's market conditions had changed significantly, and management saw

TABLE 7.1 Themes on IS strategy from the case studies

Content

- Vision for change
- Autonomy/control balance

- -

Social Context

- Historical context
- Multi-level context

- -

Social Process

- Process of cultural change
- Process of political change

the MRP system as a key initiative to help the company to succeed in their changed environment. The general content of this broad vision appears to have been sensible, and the major disaster which occurred in the first phase of implementation relates to other aspects of the Processing Company's management attitude to the project, including the underlying norm of automation and control and the lack of thought with respect to the process of organizational change, both of which will be discussed later in this section.

For Sky Building Society, the vision for change embodied in the IS strategy emanated from Brown and was aimed at providing improved customer services through decentralized IS in the branches, ahead of most of Sky's competitors. This vision was largely realized during Brown's leadership, and most people in Sky were either prepared to support his approach to realization during his period of office, or were unable to mount any significant opposition to it. The vision for change under Taylor was not clear, either in general business terms, or with respect to IS strategy. Taylor had views on the appropriate processes which were to be followed to generate a strategy, including participation and more formalized planning approaches. However, no consensus vision for change had resulted from this process by the end of the research period, and senior management were starting to consider other ways of generating a vision for future action.

With respect to the Government Co-ordination Agency in Polonia, the vision for change with respect to computerized IS was driven directly from the political centre, by politicians with no intimate knowledge of computerization, and was aimed at gaining improved control of development projects. This vision for change was imposed from the top down, and debate at other levels was not encouraged, in keeping with the cultural attitudes of Polonia, with a strong emphasis on hierarchy and the norm of obedience to superiors. Some members of the GCA IS staff were starting to modify their personal vision for change by the end of the research period, towards a philosophy of end-user computing, but this vision had not yet had any major impact on the thinking of their seniors.

A key issue in the vision for future change embodied in any IS strategy can be thought of as the view which is taken on the desirable *autonomy/control balance* at various organizational levels. For the Processing Company, the focus from the perspective of senior management was on automation to achieve better management control. This is a narrow strategic view, and underestimates the importance of allowing scope for autonomous action at all levels. This was well illustrated by the reduced efficiency which resulted from curtailing the autonomy of the warehousemen in deciding how best to utilize the warehouse space. Apart from issues of the morality of deskilling work, the point is that the strategy of total control is naïve; it cannot be achieved and attempts to move in that direction can often result in reduced organizational effectiveness.

A good contrast to the Processing Company's strategy with respect to the autonomy/control balance was provided by Brown's approach at Sky. He adopted a much subtler strategy, involving considerably increased autonomy for action on the part of staff in the branches in areas such as the provision of mortgage loans. However, the computerized IS which enabled this relatively autonomous action also provided data which could be captured to provide better information for central monitoring of branch performance. This is an example of the 'informating' capability of information technology, and illustrates the idea of delegation and decentralization without loss of control. Child (1988) notes that whether this amounts to a real increase in discretion for lower level staff is debatable, since a strong element of central control is built in to the local software via such devices as pre-planned menus. Under Taylor's leadership, the strategy of 'participation' and the use of formal procedures was aimed at generating a greater shared sense of purpose; no explicit or coherent strategy was pursued with respect to the autonomy/control balance, which was symptomatic of the lack of clarity of purpose in general under Taylor's leadership.

For the Government Co-ordination Agency, the IS strategy was aimed at shifting the autonomy/control balance towards closer central control. The Premis and Intis systems were directly geared to control from the political centre and, whilst the Devplan system was concerned with the district level, the focus was still the co-ordination of district control, monitored by the central agency. We have seen that these efforts at increased central control largely failed, and indeed that a combination of the actions of the central government, including those with respect to computerized IS, contributed to an increase in the scope for autonomous action of the district level officers in the first half of the 1980s. The differences here from the systems developed under Brown at Sky were that the latter systems genuinely supported the work activities of those at the lower hierarchical level and, rather ironically, this enabled improved central monitoring of their activities. On the other hand, the Premis and Intis systems were not used at the lower hierarchical levels, and did not capture what was actually happening at those levels; this ensured that the data which were generated for the centre were of little use for monitoring and control purposes.

Social Context

The discourse on IS strategy on any point in time takes place from a background provided by the *historical context* of any previous systems, together with wider aspects such as the organization's history and past performance and its location within broader sectoral and national boundaries. This historical context is multi-faceted and highly complex, but we will focus here on the way in which this context may be viewed as both a threat and an opportunity. For the Processing Company, there were many negative aspects of the historical context at the time that the strategy for the new MRP system was being discussed. These included the poor financial performance of the company in the changing market conditions, the relatively low morale of the declining labour force, and inadequate internal resources with experience of the development and use of computerized IS. These factors in the historical context could perhaps be taken as reasons why the introduction of the MRP system was such a notable failure, or at least as contributing factors.

However, an interesting contrast to the case of the Processing Company is provided by Sky under Brown. He inherited an historical context which shared a number of similar features with that of the Processing Company, including poor financial performance and a workforce who could see that the society was in a declining situation in a changing market. A major difference between the two cases is that Brown explicitly viewed the historical context as being supportive of change; he expressed this, in his own words, as the 'right climate for change'. He saw that this climate could be exploited, provided that a sufficiently shared basis for action could be developed and managed. In contrast, senior management in the Processing Company were 'demotivated' and had 'no incentive to make any significant change'. The difference in result between the two cases appears to be related more to attitude to the historical context, seeing and communicating it either as a threat or opportunity, rather than to measurable features such as actual past performance. Taylor took over Sky following the exceptional financial and growth performance under Brown and, interestingly, this appears to have contributed to a perception that there was plenty of time to discuss policies such as IS strategy. This attitude can be seen as dangerously complacent in the rapidly changing financial services environment of the late 1980s in the UK. One decidedly negative feature of the historical context for Taylor was the domination which Brown had exercised over senior management and the IS staff during the period of his leadership; this created conditions suited to the break-out of strategic vested interests which occurred in the period after Brown's departure, although it should be noted that this was encouraged and legitimized by Taylor's explicit strategy regarding the importance of participation.

For the Government Co-ordination Agency, the most important components of the evolving historical context which impacted the IS strategy can be considered to be political issues in the national context of Polonia. Development projects were seen throughout the period as of high significance to the government and its perception by the people. The government's lack of control of these projects at the grass roots level was seen as a political threat, and computerized IS were viewed as a strategic opportunity to do something about this lack of control, at least in symbolic terms. The context of the failure of Premis to achieve adequate data quality for monitoring and control purposes, coupled with a change of government, were aspects of the historical context which led to Intis being seen as an opportunity to do better. Devplan was a later response to the threat of loss of grass roots support for the government, although the action taken with respect to the development of the Devplan system by the end of the research period had been largely symbolic in addressing genuine local issues.

In attempting to analyse the social context within which IS strategy is developed or emerges, we have traced above some aspects of the historical context of previous IS, the organization within which the IS were developed, and elements of the broader context within which this organization functioned. However, the concept of *multi-level contexts* is wider even than this, incorporating not just sectoral, national or international contexts within which the focal organization is located, but more nebulous yet crucial social contexts represented by both constant and changing social practices and cultural attitudes. For the Processing Company, multi-level contexts included its location within a holding company, who intervened in later stages with dramatic effect by removing the whole senior management layer, and its location within a changing industry. The political context of Thatcherism in the 1980s has not been explicitly addressed in the analysis of the case to date, but is a contextual feature which was supportive of profitability being regarded as the critical goal of an organization, helping to legitimize actions such as the sacking of members of the workforce in conditions of declining growth.

For Sky Building Society, we can see the impact of the Thatcher years more directly and clearly as a major contributory element of the multi-level context within which the IS strategies developed. Brown led the society during an unprecedentedly turbulent and changing period for the financial services sector as a whole in the UK, largely brought about by government legislation on deregulation and liberalization of the sector. Brown's perceived success on financial and growth criteria occurred at a time when such criteria were being presented as central to the country's well-being by the government in power. This was a supportive context for the strength of Brown's position throughout his period as leader. A similar turbulent and changing context confronted Sky during Taylor's leadership, and if the relative inaction and slow response during the research period were to be continued and contribute to a later decline in profitability and growth, Taylor's position would no doubt have been under threat, since these remain central norms in contemporary UK society.

For the development of IS strategy in the Government Co-ordination Agency, we have seen the importance of the multi-level contexts at the district and national levels in influencing the approaches taken. A rather less tangible but critical context is created by the cultural attitudes within the Polonian society at large, which include an acceptance of orders from those perceived to be in authority, or at least the following of these in a mechanistic fashion even if they are questioned internally by the individual involved. This aspect of the multi-level context of the IS strategy is very deep-seated, and may be a force against the effectiveness of computerized IS in developing countries where similar cultural attitudes prevail, or at least imply that rather different approaches are needed in comparison to countries such as the UK. For example, Tricker (1988) described some of the major differences in cultural attitudes of the Chinese business community compared to the West, and noted that this should have a major influence on the design of computerized information systems; this observation extends naturally to the area of IS strategy.

Social Process

A vision for the strategic content of change and an appreciation of the complexity of the social context within which change takes place leads on to a consideration of social process and, in particular, the strategy with respect to the *process of cultural change*. In the case of the Processing Company, the view taken by senior management during the first phase of the sales order processing system focused on automation of work and there was no appreciation of the need for fundamental attitudinal change; only after the disastrous implementation was MRP seen as 'a whole new way of working' involving major cultural change on the part of all employees, in terms of their work roles and their understanding of the nature and purpose of their work. No one saw themselves responsible for the management of this change process, neither the senior management of the company, nor the IS team. Thus no significant action was taken during the critical design and development phase of the sales order processing system to attempt to influence the perceptions and working practices of subcultures such as the sales order processing staff and the warehousemen.

The case of Sky provides a marked contrast, in that Brown appears to have had a clear strategic view of the need for cultural change and management of the process throughout his time as leader. His focus was on changed approaches and attitudes of the branch staff leading to better service to customers, supported by decentralized IS; he pressurized other staff such as senior management and those in the IS department to at least acquiesce in the delivery of such systems. He saw himself as the key actor in managing this change process by direct action, such as the early and drastic rearrangement of the senior management group, and by symbolic action on his part in terms of involvement with detailed systems design and the support of costly and extensive training programmes for branch staff. Taylor also had a strategic view of cultural change, but saw his role as facilitating the development of a new culture based around participation, at least within the middle and senior levels of management, based around formal methods of corporate planning and, in the IS domain, structured methodologies for system design. He was starting to have serious doubts by the end of the research period about this approach to cultural change, in view of the lack of tangible results and the fact that consensus in key areas had not been achieved.

With respect to the Government Co-ordination Agency, senior politicians directing the formal IS strategy saw the need for cultural change within government agencies towards more integrated working, involving central agencies in the case of the Intis system and district-level agencies for Devplan. Computerized IS were seen as a major instrument in achieving this improved co-ordination and control. However, no one individual or group saw their role as including the management of the cultural change process surrounding the focal IS. The IS staff had a perception of their role as technical, and senior staff in the GCA were not involved in the detailed management of process. Nevertheless, some cultural change is detectable by the end of the research period, not in terms of better integrated systems, but in terms of doubts in the minds of some IS staff about the wisdom of the whole strategic approach to IS.

The *process of political change* is inextricably interlinked to that of cultural change, but some additional aspects can be identified from this perspective. In the case of the Processing Company, the lack of common goals on the part of various subcultures did not result in open political conflict in the first phase, but the avoidance of such political issues by senior management can be seen to have contributed to the disaster after switch-over. For example, the lack of involvement of the sales order processing staff in systems design was not tackled during the design phase and major problems then occurred in later use of the system. One of the few areas where senior management directly intervened politically was to insist on an early switch-over date; this contributed significantly to the negative outcome. Management's later attempt to exert rigid control over the warehousemen using the rules and procedures of the new computer system was a further example of inept intervention in the political process.

In contrast, Brown's political actions at Sky involved a conscious and continuous intervention in the political change process, linked to a strategy of personal domination over the organization's direction. He took actions such as severely reducing the senior management group and restricting the use of committees to exert dominance over this group. He enhanced the role of the computing staff, although the price which they paid for this increased status was a reduction in their autonomy. The suppression of overt political opposition under Brown was followed by a period of political liberation under Taylor, where many vested interests were openly expressed in the new political climate. Taylor's hands-off style to the management of this political process resulted in a long and inconclusive debate on future direction, with respect to both business and IS strategy.

In the Government Co-ordination Agency, the approach taken to political process was largely one of the issuance of directives and orders by those at the political centre. This often had the effect of compliance, as in the case of data supply for the Intis system on the part of the agencies involved, but the core strategy of integrated control was subverted by the lack of use of the system by these agencies. With respect to the Devplan system, it was not clear who was supposed to manage the political process at the district level to gain political support for the system from the multiple agencies operating at that level. It seemed likely that no one would see their role as including this, least of all the IS staff in the GCA, and that political support would not be forthcoming.

A SYNTHESIZED PERSPECTIVE ON IS STRATEGY

The purpose of this section is to synthesize and summarize a view of IS strategy arising from the preceding discussion in the chapter. The section is divided into two subsections. The first of these presents a view on the nature of IS strategy, and the second describes the role of the IS strategist related to this view. The key features of this perspective are summarized in Table 7.2, and the abstract ideas will be illustrated more fully in the final section of the chapter.

The Nature of IS Strategy

The *formation of IS strategy* can be viewed as a process of continuous discourse. This *discourse on IS strategy* is a way of communicating meaning, centred on norms and values, and linked to power in relation to others. The communication

TABLE 7.2 A synthesized perspective on IS strategy

The Nature of IS Strategy

- The formation of IS strategy can be viewed as a process of continuous discourse
- The discourse on IS strategy is a way of communicating meaning, centred on norms and values, and linked to power relations to others
- The language of the discourse uses vocabularies which influence its content
- The core content of the discourse concerns computer-based IS. These can be viewed strategically as embodying interpretative schemes, providing co-ordination and control facilities and reflecting norms

The Role of an IS Strategist

- An IS strategist is anyone who takes part in the discourse on IS strategy
- Leadership is important in the strategic enactment process
- The IS strategist can be viewed as an enactor of meaning, through the discourse on IS strategy
- A second dimension of the role of an IS strategist is as a moral agent, involved in the production and reproduction of normative values, and in the maintenance and change of power relations

of meaning can be thought of as an enactment process in which individuals select and communicate ideas, concepts and plans; these embody particular normative views of the way the world is or should be; their communication through language is inextricably interlinked to the maintenance and change of power relations between the parties involved in the acts of communication.

The *language of the discourse* on IS strategy uses vocabularies which influence the content of the discourse. The use of Mintzberg's vocabulary of intended, emergent and realized strategies contributes to a shift in emphasis away from the view of IS strategy formulation as a discrete rational process carried out in a series of stages prior to implementation. The use of Zuboff's suggested vocabulary, of colleagues and co-learners, exploration, experimentation and innovation, would influence a further shift towards a more egalitarian approach to strategy formulation, involving a wider constituency of interests and less asymmetric power relations.

The core *content of the discourse* on IS strategy concerns computer-based information systems. These can be viewed strategically as embodying interpretative schemes, providing co-ordination and control facilities, and reflecting norms; the IS being drawn on in action reproduce or modify social structures. The consequences of action and interaction around the focal IS, which may be intended or unintended, are reflexively monitored by all human agents involved, and provide a basis for future communication and action, including future discourse on IS strategy.

The Role of an IS Strategist

An *IS strategist* can be thought of as anyone who takes part in the discourse on IS strategy at any level. Of course, existing power relations will condition the influence of any particular individual's ideas. Nevertheless, the reflexive monitoring of action and its consequences on the part of all individuals provides them with a basis on which to contribute to the strategic discourse. Existing attitudes that the legitimate contributors to the discourse consist solely of a small top-management group are not immutable in the future.

The enlargement of the constituency of IS strategists in the previous paragraph is not intended to suggest a diminished importance for *leadership*, which is an important aspect of any organization of human beings. For example, Noël (1989) discusses the role of Chief Executive Officers (CEOs) in the business strategy formation process, illustrates this with three case studies, and concludes that the wishes, desires, and visions of these visible leaders are central to the organizational processes which produce strategies. This high level of influence of the views of the CEOs reflects existing power relations in the particular organizations studied, but is likely to be common in most contemporary organizational forms.

The IS strategist can be viewed as an *enactor of meaning* through the discourse on IS strategy. Following Smircich and Stubbart (1985), the task of the strategist is to contribute to 'organization making', the creation and maintenance of systems of shared meaning that facilitate organized action. The IS strategist is an agent of organizational change through the medium of language. Choice of vocabulary implying particular enactments of the organization and its environment is a key element of the role of the strategist.

A second dimension of the role of an IS strategist is as a *moral agent*, involved in the production and reproduction of normative values, and in the maintenance and change of power relations. Computer-based information systems and the related discourse on IS strategy reflect norms and values concerning the individual, the organization, and the broader society at large; at the same time, they provide facilities for co-ordination and control, linked to particular forms of power relations. The process of organizational change associated with the information system will contribute to the reinforcement or change of social structures of legitimation and domination based on these values and facilities. IS strategists are thus implicated in moral choices regarding norms and power relations, even if this does not reflect any conscious intention on their part.

THE PRACTICE OF IS STRATEGY

The material in the previous section, summarized in Table 7.2, provides a general but abstract perspective on the nature of IS strategy and the role of an IS strategist. In this final section, the perspective will be applied at a less abstract level to the strategic themes which were developed from the case studies in Part II and summarized in Table 7.1. These themes were discussed in some detail in the second section with reference to the case studies; the discussion below addresses the themes more generally.

The flavour of the discussion which follows is oriented to the practice of the 'IS strategist', and is divided into three broad task areas, namely forming of strategic content, understanding strategic context, and facilitating strategic change. The discussion does not aim to provide a set of prescriptions for strategic practice, but is intended as interesting food for thought and debate in any particular context. Key elements of the discussion in this section are summarized in Tables 7.3 to 7.5.

Forming Strategic Content

A major theme arising from the case studies concerned the *vision for change* which is embodied in a particular IS strategy, either by deliberate design or as an emergent phenomenon. The need for such a vision appears to be linked to a sense of purpose and security in organizational members, and no articulated vision can be seen as an absence of effective leadership. Visions tend to be rather general in nature, and their very ambiguity is their strength, since it enables them to be incorporated into a variety of personal enactments. Many techniques have been offered in the IS literature to aid the generation of the content of a strategic vision (see, for example, Earl 1989, Chapter 3). Such techniques may prove of some use in a particular context, but vision

---

TABLE 7.3 Some issues for debate on forming strategic content

Vision for Change

- Linked to security and sense of purpose/concept of leadership
- Ambiguity enables vision to be incorporated into personal enactments
- Generation of vision may be aided by techniques but remains largely tacit
- Conscious reflexive monitoring needed to refresh and adapt vision
- Moral agenda include norms and values which underpin the vision, impact on power relations, and organizational involvement in vision generation

Autonomy/Control Balance

- Strategy of total control is infeasible
- One approach is delegation of tasks with enhanced central monitoring; this approach to control is uniquely enabled by computer-based IS
- Enactment of meaning can be aimed at manipulation
- Discourse needed on ethical limits on issues such as surveillance

appears to derive largely from tacit knowledge and cannot be reduced to a series of logical inferences and steps.

An important point about a vision for change is its fluid nature; even if a particular vision is incorporated by organizational members at a given point in time, conscious reflexive monitoring of action and its consequences is necessary to detect changing attitudes and circumstances, and thus to refresh and adapt the vision over time. The choice of vocabulary used to communicate a particular vision for change can also be a matter for careful deliberation and choice, in order to maximize the chances of its incorporation in the enactments of different organizational subcultures.

Other issues in connection with a vision for change concern the norms and values which underpin the vision, the possible impact on power relations, and the question of organizational involvement in the generation of vision. These issues concern the role of the IS strategist as moral agent; no simple prescription can be made here, but it is worth noting that discussion of such issues is rarely part of the explicit agenda of contemporary organizations. The suggestion being made here is that this dehumanizes the process of strategy formation and the role of the IS strategist, since human beings cannot divorce themselves from a concern with such issues.

A key element in the vision for future change embodied in any IS strategy is the view which is taken, implicitly or explicitly, of the desirable *autonomy/control balance* at various organizational levels. A naïve strategy of total control is infeasible, since human agents can subvert attempts to impose this. One strategic approach is to use IS to support the delegation and decentralization of tasks, whilst retaining central monitoring and control. Indeed, IS can facilitate this form of task-related decentralization coupled with increased central surveillance in a way which has not been possible with previous technologies of control. The enactment of meaning by the IS strategist in this context of autonomy/control could emphasize the delegation aspects and play down the surveillance issues; this could be viewed as manipulation, reflecting a simplistic or cynical stance on issues of empowerment. The role of the IS strategist as moral agent should include consideration of desirable ethical limits in these areas.

Understanding Strategic Context

The discourse on IS strategy at any point in time takes place from a background provided by the *historical context*. This includes the history of the previous computer-based information systems in the focal organization, the history of the focal organization itself, and the broader contexts within which the organization is located. Human beings enact past events and actions in order to give meaning to the present and to speculate and make plans concerning the future. The role of the IS strategist as enactor of meaning is

TABLE 7.4 *Some issues for debate on understanding strategic context*

Historical Context

- Need for knowledge of history of previous IS, focal organization, broader contexts
- People enact past events and actions in order to give meaning to the present, and to speculate and make plans concerning the future
- IS strategists can facilitate shared views of historical context, which encourage positive future action

Multi-Level Contexts

- Broader contexts can be used as a legitimizing device for action
- The IS strategist at the organizational level is an agent for broader social change

to facilitate shared views of the historical context in order to help generate commitment for future action.

Past events or circumstances can be consciously selected and presented in ways which facilitate present action; for example, by viewing poor organizational performance as an ideal opportunity to improve. A related point is that positive aspects of the historical context can be viewed in such a way as to encourage complacency. The role of the IS strategist as enactor of meaning cannot be separated from the role of the IS strategist as moral agent, and ways of presenting the historical context can be manipulative devices for personal ends, as well as methods to aid beneficial social change in a more general sense.

The *multi-level contexts* within which an IS is developed include sectoral or national contexts, but also more nebulous social contexts represented by social practices and deep-seated cultural attitudes. National level political contexts, such as Thatcherism in the UK in the 1980s, can be used as legitimizing devices for action within the focal context; this has the effect of reinforcing the central political philosophy and has implications for the IS strategist as moral agent. Deep-seated cultural attitudes, such as deference to authority, do not change rapidly within a society, and indeed are a key component in retaining stability and social order. However, the IS strategist operating at the organizational level is implicated in changes in cultural and political attitudes at that level, and is thus an agent for broader social change.

Facilitating Strategic Change

The *process of cultural change* surrounding a focal IS involves new ways of thinking and working, and strategy in this area is concerned with the creation

TABLE 7.5 *Some issues for debate on facilitating strategic change*

Process of Cultural Change

- Many different subcultures enacting their own worlds
- IS strategist can help create new meanings and understandings, compatible with vision for change, and with enactments of other subcultures
- Responsibility can fall between IS developers and strategic management
- Methods to facilitate change include symbolic commitment, through devices such as training schemes

Process of Political Change

- IS strategist as moral agent on issues such as imposition of change
- Hands-off approach or issuance of orders can both be ineffective
- IS strategist can monitor and facilitate change, rather than control it

and communication of new meaning within and between subcultures. Different subcultures enact their own worlds, and the role of the IS strategist is to help create new meanings and understandings, which are not homogeneous between subcultures, but are broadly compatible with the overall vision for change and with the enactments of other subcultures.

The responsibility for the strategy with respect to the process of cultural change in connection with computer-based IS can easily fall into a gap between IS developers and strategic managers, since both groups can assume a role for themselves which assigns responsibility to the other party. The methods which can be used to facilitate cultural change include such obvious approaches as training schemes, but it is worth noting that the power of such approaches often rests in the symbolism of commitment on the part of all parties involved, rather than solely in the content of the programmes.

The *process of political change* involves shifting interests and coalitions, and strategy in this area is concerned with the creation and communication of meaning to generate political commitment. The role of the IS strategist as moral agent is clearly relevant here, and includes issues such as the desirability of the imposition of change in cases of resistance. A hands-off approach to the imposition of strategic direction by senior management does not necessarily lead to enhanced consensus and reduced political activity, and indeed the reverse can be the case. An approach based on the issuance of orders can produce compliance in areas such as data delivery, but the effective use of the resultant systems may not be achieved. A final point on the process of cultural and political change is that it will occur naturally as a consequence of the reflexive monitoring of all interested parties in the change process; the role of the IS strategist is in monitoring and facilitating change, rather than in controlling it in any total sense.

REFERENCES

Child, J. (1988) 'Information technology and organization', in *Innovation and Management: International Comparisons* (eds K. Urabe, J. Child and T. Kagono), Walter de Gruyter, Berlin.

Earl, M. J. (1989) *Management Strategies for Information Technology*, Prentice-Hall, New York.

Foucault, M. (1980) *Power/Knowledge: Selected Interviews and Other Writings 1972–77* (ed. C. Gordon), Harvester Press, Brighton.

Knights, D., and Morgan, G. (1991) 'Corporate strategy, organizations, and subjectivity: a critique', *Organization Studies*, **12**, No. 2, 251–273.

Mintzberg, H. (1978) 'Patterns in strategy formation', *Management Science*, **24**, No. 9, 934–948.

Mintzberg, H. (1979) *The Structuring of Organizations: A Synthesis of Research*, Prentice-Hall, Englewood Cliffs.

Mintzberg, H., and McHugh, A. (1985) 'Strategy formation in an adhocracy', *Administrative Science Quarterly*, **30**, No. 2, 160–197.

Mintzberg, H., and Waters, J. A. (1985) 'Of strategies, deliberate and emergent', *Strategic Management Journal*, **6**, No. 3, 257–272.

Noël, A. (1989) 'Strategic cores and magnificent obsessions: discovering strategy formation through daily activities of CEOs', *Strategic Management Journal*, **10**(S), 33–49.

Smircich, L., and Stubbart, C. (1985) 'Strategic management in an enacted world', *Academy of Management Review*, **10**, No. 4, 724–736.

Tricker, R. I. (1988) 'Information resource management—a cross-cultural perspective', *Information and Management*, **15**, No. 1, 37–46.

Quinn, J. B. (1980) *Strategies for Change: Logical Incrementalism*, Irwin, Homewood.

Waema, T. M., and Walsham, G. (1990) 'Information systems strategy formation in a developing country bank', *Technological Forecasting and Social Change*, **38**, No. 4, 393–407.

Weick, K. E. (1969) *The Social Psychology of Organizing*, Addison-Wesley, Reading, Massachusetts.

Winograd, T., and Flores, F. (1986) *Understanding Computers and Cognition*, Ablex Publishing, Norwood.

Zuboff, S. (1988) *In the Age of the Smart Machine*, Basic Books, New York.

Chapter 8
EVALUATION

This chapter addresses the issue of information systems evaluation, and is divided into four sections. The first section examines *elements of the evaluation literature*, with a focus on work which supports and complements the interpretive approach of the book. The second section then compares and contrasts the findings from the case studies in Part II, based around *selected themes on IS evaluation* arising from the earlier analyses. The third section *synthesizes a perspective* on IS evaluation drawing from material in the preceding sections. The final section then applies this new perspective to a discussion of the *practice of IS evaluation* based around the set of themes from the case material; this discussion aims to provide some issues for debate in any particular context, oriented to the practice of an IS evaluator.

RELEVANT LITERATURE ON EVALUATION

The purpose of this section is to identify and discuss literature of relevance to an interpretive approach to IS evaluation, and to relate this work to the previous case material where appropriate. Much of the literature on evaluation in general, and IS evaluation in particular, takes a formal-rational view of organizations, and sees evaluation as a largely quantitative process of calculating the preferred choice and evaluating the likely cost/benefit on the basis of clearly defined criteria. In contrast, the approach taken in this book is concerned with interpretations of the way evaluation takes place in practice, viewing it as a dynamic socio-political process within multi-level social contexts. The literature discussed in this section is divided into three parts. The first two parts describe some interesting work on evaluation in the field of education, and the evaluation of organizational change programmes. The final part of the section examines some relevant literature on IS evaluation itself.

Evaluation in the Field of Education

A major amount of research activity has taken place on evaluation in the education field, particularly on the evaluation of educational programmes, and some valuable ideas from this literature are summarized here. A useful distinction was drawn by Stake (1975,1983) between a preordinate approach to evaluation and a responsive approach. The former emphasizes the statement of goals, the use of objective tests, and the production of research-type reports; the latter emphasizes the usefulness of the findings of the evaluation research to the people concerned with the programme.

Guba and Lincoln (1981) develop the theme of responsive evaluation as being organized around the concerns and issues stemming from the several audiences that the evaluation will serve, based on their underlying sets of values. A concern is defined as any matter of interest or importance to one or more of the involved parties. An issue is a statement, proposition, or focus that allows for the presentation of different points of view. A value is any principle or standard that leads to judgements of either relative or absolute utility, goodness, or importance, or that guides choices amongst alternatives. Values range from the very tangible to the very intangible.

A later development of this work (Guba and Lincoln, 1989) proposes an approach entitled fourth generation evaluation, distinguished from previous evaluation generations characterized as measurement-oriented, description-oriented, and judgement-oriented. The key dynamic of the new approach is negotiation. This later work is explicitly linked to an interpretive approach, although called a constructivist perspective by Guba and Lincoln. They take the position that evaluation outcomes are not descriptions of the way things really are or really work, but instead represent meaningful constructions that aid individual actors or groups of actors to make sense of the situations in which they find themselves. The approach considers that the constructions through which people make sense of their situations are shaped by the values of the constructors. Power relations are also recognized as important by the view that evaluations can be shaped to enfranchise or disenfranchise stakeholding groups in a variety of ways.

The above descriptions are theoretical in emphasis, but the proposed evaluation approach has an action orientation towards defining a course to be followed, stimulating involved stakeholders to follow it, and generating and preserving their commitment to do so. Twelve steps of a defined methodology are given (Guba and Lincoln 1989, p. 185) aimed at setting up the evaluation study, developing and enlarging constructions, resolving concerns and issues, negotiating unresolved concerns and issues, and recycling if necessary. The authors state that fourth generation evaluation is a means to empowerment of stakeholders (p. 227), but they do not say how conflicts should be resolved in cases of fundamental disagreement between actors or interest groups. They view the evaluator not as a controller, investigator, and discoverer as in the preordinate approach to evaluation; but as a collaborator, learner and teacher, reality shaper, and change agent.

Although the above ideas were generated from evaluation research in the very different domain of education, they can be used directly to illuminate some aspects of IS evaluation in the earlier case studies. In the Processing Company, the two formal evaluations resulting in the selection of the Prosys system can be thought of as a preordinate approach based largely around technical and economic criteria such as hardware, software and costing data. The concerns and issues of stakeholder groups were not surfaced at all in the formal evaluation process, and only started to be considered by management after the initial failure of the sales order processing module. The values held by stakeholders other than senior management were neither sought nor considered by the evaluators who saw their role as investigator and report generator, very much as described by Guba and Lincoln for preordinate evaluation.

In Sky Building Society under Brown, no preordinate approach to evaluation was conducted. No formal responsive approach was carried out either, but it is interesting to note that Brown as the key evaluator in this case took account of the concerns and issues of a wide variety of stakeholder groups, and formed his own interpretations of the underlying values they placed on various changes associated with IS developments. His approach as an evaluator had strong elements of learner and teacher, reality shaper and change agent, as described by Guba and Lincoln for the responsive approach. Only in the dimension of collaborator do we see a clear difference, where the alternative description of controller fits Brown's actions rather better. Latent conflict regarding evaluation of IS was suppressed by his tight control of the direction of the organization and the IS to be developed. For example, the IS developers' reservations on ad hoc systems development were basically ignored by Brown.

The approach to IS evaluation at Sky under Taylor was not preordinate, and is better characterized as a form of responsive approach towards the concerns and issues of various stakeholder groups, in a rather more formal and less personal manner than was the case under Brown. Taylor himself could be seen as a collaborator, learner and change agent, in line with the responsive approach. However, he cannot be classed as a teacher or reality shaper with respect to the evaluation of computer-based IS at Sky, and the sense of a leadership vacuum and unclear vision for change enabled stakeholder conflict to flourish, and no agreed agenda for action was developed.

In the Government Co-ordination Agency, we see the evaluation of the proposed computer-based IS being conducted on the basis of political and technical criteria. There was no consideration of the concerns and issues of importance to a variety of stakeholder groups, such as the other central agencies in the case of Intis, or those actually working at the grass roots village and district level in the case of Devplan. The evaluation approach can be thought of as preordinate, with the evaluators seeing themselves as investigators and controllers, and certainly not as collaborators, learners and teachers, or reality shapers.

Evaluating Organizational Change

A second area of evaluation research is rather broader in concept than that in the field of education, and embraces a wide variety of work undertaken by 'professional' evaluators in the field of organizational change. According to Legge (1984), these include people engaged in evaluating federally funded US social change programmes, evaluators in industry drawn from external or internal consultancy groups, and applied social scientists in universities and research institutions concerned with such issues as the effectiveness of different project payment systems in enhancing motivation, the relationship between job design and productivity, or the effectiveness of different leadership styles.

Legge notes that the whole process of planned organizational change reflects an evaluatory act, since planning models involve the notion of an assessment, however unsystematic, of some gap between the present and a desired future state. Resistance to change often reflects individuals' or groups' negative evaluations of the likely consequences for them. Legge argues for a form of contingency approach to evaluation research by undertaking a matching process to achieve compatibility between evaluation functions sought and the research design employed. For example, a distinction can be made between formative evaluation which aims to provide systematic feedback to programme designers and implementers, and summative evaluation concerned with identifying and assessing the worth of programme outcomes in the light of initially specified success criteria after the implementation of the change programme is completed (this distinction is due to Scriven 1967). Legge argues that interpretive evaluation designs are best suited to the purpose of formative evaluation.

Legge describes in detail some of the characteristics of interpretive evaluation designs. These include explanation through developing understanding, an emphasis on actions and taken-for-granted meanings, an iterative and emergent process, an emphasis on the richness and meaningfulness of data, and the use of mainly qualitative rather than quantitative methods. In discussing strategies and techniques for interpretive evaluation designs, Legge refers to the earlier work of Guba and Lincoln, and indeed their later work on fourth generation evaluation can be thought of as a particular development of the general concept of an interpretive evaluation design.

Legge goes beyond the work of Guba and Lincoln in her discussion of the politics and ethics of approaches to evaluation. She notes that the choice of an evaluation design is likely to be constrained by the information the most powerful participants require and why they require it. She distinguishes between overt functions of evaluation concerned with the provision of information for decision-making, and covert functions which are understood as those functions of evaluation which one or more stakeholders in the evaluation consider it inappropriate to admit publicly, because they perceive it as against their interests to do so, to the possible detriment of others. These covert functions include rallying support or opposition to a change programme, postponing a decision, evading responsibility, and fulfilling grant requirements. Legge also argues that the meta-function of all evaluations is to either sustain or question the status quo, and asks whether all evaluation research tends to be conservatively biased towards existing power structures and a gradualist approach to change. Further, she hypothesizes that interpretive evaluation methods may be more open to manipulation by powerful interest groups than traditional positivistic designs, since an admission of multiple realities and values may actually help the powerful to impose their own interpretations. Thus interpretive design may act as a rhetoric for an evaluation ritual, whereby the appearance of democracy and non-elitism serves to disguise the greater room for manoeuvre accorded to the powerful.

In discussing the purpose of evaluation in organizational contexts, Legge refers to an interesting paper by Brunsson (1982) on organizational action. Brunsson argues that the main problem for organizations is not the problem of choice but that of organizing action. Thus what may appear to be irrational behaviour in decision-making can be explained as action rationality. For example, it may be better from an action perspective to consider only one or two alternatives; considering multiple alternatives may appear to be a better support to rational decision-making, but multiple alternatives evoke uncertainty and this reduces motivation and commitment. An implication of Brunsson's perspective for evaluation is that whereas a rational model might prescribe that alternatives should be formally evaluated against predetermined criteria or objectives, this is a dangerous approach from an action perspective, since there is a high risk that decision-makers will formulate inconsistent objectives and will have difficulty assessing alternatives. Brunsson quotes Lindblom (1959) in arguing that a better strategy is to start from consequences and to invent the objectives afterwards. Brunsson ends the paper by noting the important challenge in organizations of combining influence by diverse groups with the ability to act.

A number of ideas were introduced in the discussion above concerning the style and purpose of evaluation, and possible political and ethical impacts. Our IS case studies can be used to make some brief comments on these ideas. With respect to the distinction between covert and overt functions, a good example is provided by the second formal evaluation study in the Processing Company. The covert function from the point of view of the management of the Processing Company was to get agreement from the holding company for the Prosys system. This could not be stated openly in those terms, and the overt function of the evaluation was to compare the Prosys system against an IBM-based proposal.

Legge argued that evaluation methods in general may be conservatively biased, or in other words geared to existing powerful interests, and we certainly see no evidence of radical change in this respect arising from any of the formal approaches to evaluation in the case studies. Legge also hypothesized that interpretive methods of evaluation may be more open to manipulation by powerful groups than more positivistic approaches. Whilst the case studies in Part II provide no direct evidence on this assertion, it is difficult to believe that an interpretive approach to evaluation in the Processing Company, including the views and interests of a wider set of stakeholders such as the sales order processing staff and the warehousemen, would have resulted in a more conservative solution being adopted. The evaluation approach which was used, largely preordinate as we have seen, merely reproduced the attitudes and values of the existing senior management elite. A similar conclusion can be reached with respect to the political evaluations of the computer-based information systems in Polonia, where the evaluations reflected and reproduced senior politicians' attitudes and values concerning central control of development projects. We do not know what the impact of interpretive evaluation designs would have been in these cases, but the evidence from the case studies suggests that Legge's hypothesis is of doubtful validity, at least in these contexts of existing tight central control. The more positive empowerment hypothesis of Guba and Lincoln with respect to interpretive evaluation designs may have more validity in such contexts.

With respect to Brunsson's views on action rationality, Sky Building Society provides an interesting example. Brown tended to think through alternatives with respect to computer-based IS in his own mind, and narrow down to a single choice. He then worked hard to gain motivation and commitment from all stakeholder groups to implement this choice. Taylor, on the other hand, allowed multiple alternatives to be considered and evaluated at all stages, but as Brunsson suggested can happen, this resulted in no commitment to action. Taylor and his management team can be seen to have failed to manage the combination of the influence by diverse groups with the ability to act.

IS Evaluation Literature

Computer-based information systems can be evaluated at various stages, including feasibility studies at an early stage, ongoing evaluations to provide feedback during the design and development process, and post-implementation evaluations. There is a large and growing literature in this area (see, for example, Bjorn-Andersen and Davis 1988) and many different theoretical and methodological approaches have been suggested. One common theme in the literature is that IS evaluation is difficult. Symons and Walsham (1988) note that information systems are frequently used to enhance organizational performance without necessarily any reduction in costs, and produce benefits which are often intangible, uncertain, and extremely difficult to quantify in a meaningful way. Some costs are fairly clear but others are less obvious, and there may be insidious effects such as a deskilling of work or a decline in job satisfaction. Stone (1991) notes that the different approaches suggested in the literature to address the difficult issues of IS evaluation are not interchangeable, but rather represent fundamentally different ways of understanding. The focus of the discussion here will be on interpretive approaches to evaluation, rather than a comprehensive review of alternative ways of thinking.

A number of authors have proposed interpretive approaches to evaluation and have suggested some of the merits of this perspective. Hirschheim and Smithson (1988) argue that most IS evaluation concentrates on the technical rather than the human or social aspects of computerized systems, and that this can have major negative consequences in terms of the system developed, with respect to individual aspects such as user satisfaction, but also broader organizational consequences in terms of system value. They propose an interpretive approach to evaluation research as a way of gaining a deeper understanding of the nature and process of evaluation itself, including recognition of the informal evaluations carried out by all individuals and social groups who are affected by the computer-based IS. Symons (1991) makes a similar point that effective evaluation means understanding and taking seriously the perspectives of individual stakeholders and interest groups. She adds the observation that the evaluation process should be regarded as a means to encourage the involvement and commitment of stakeholders.

Although Hirschheim and Smithson are critical of many of the current approaches to evaluation based on quantification and largely technical criteria, they note that the results of formal evaluation studies of this type often have a considerable legitimacy. This seeming paradox between a rather circumscribed approach to evaluation and the organizational credibility of its results has been explained by some authors in terms of organizational ritual. Symons and Walsham (1988) suggest that when a formal analysis is carried out, it is more likely to be a symbolic expression of a belief in rational management than a trusted aid to decision-making. Floder and Weiner (1983) note a similar point, in the context of the evaluation of major social programmes, that evaluation may be seen as a ritual whose function is to calm the anxieties of the citizenry and to perpetuate an image of governmental rationality, efficacy, and accountability. A recent paper by Kumar (1990) described a survey of the actual practice of post-implementation evaluation of computer-based IS in over 90 US companies. He concluded that, where it was conducted, the primary use of post-implementation evaluation was as a disengagement device for the systems development department. Kumar does not use the term ritual, but the post-implementation evaluation process he describes is ritualistic rather than substantive.

The importance of symbolism and ritual in human affairs generally is very much a part of the philosophy underpinning this book, and ritualistic evaluation exercises are not necessarily to be condemned. The interpretive approach to evaluation may give a deeper understanding, but the purposes of ritual are different, aimed at issues such as reassurance and a sense of security. However, two reservations can be made. Firstly, ritualistic evaluation may be a way of supporting powerful interests and a device to suppress the less powerful in organizational terms; no general judgement can be made here, since each case needs to be considered on its own merits, but ritual cannot be divorced from its moral implications.

A second reservation about ritualistic evaluation in the context of IS is that it can be a major hindrance to innovative organizational change. This is well illustrated by the research of Currie (1989) on the justification of computer-aided design (CAD) technology in 20 UK companies. She notes the frustration of engineering managers proposing the introduction of CAD systems, who were forced to 'play the game' and engage in 'Return on Investment (ROI) and Discounted Cash Flow (DCF) rituals' based on simple cost-accounting techniques, in order to justify the technology to top management. One way of 'getting round the system' was noted as putting additional costs on other budgets. This game playing continued in summative evaluation exercises after the technology was installed, where Currie notes that engineering management continued to manipulate the information to demonstrate to top managers that CAD was achieving the benefits outlined in the proposal documents. The reason for all this deception was that engineering managers perceived the benefits of the CAD technology as rather intangible aspects such as better quality design linked to long-term organizational goals of quality products and thus an enhanced and competitive position in their markets. Short-term cost savings were not the goal, but these had to be manipulated to produce the right picture for justification purposes. A crucial observation in Currie's paper for our purposes here is that 'a more qualitative and holistic approach (to investment appraisal for new technology) . . . was unacceptable'.

The above discussion has not attempted to present a case for the elimination of ritualistic evaluation in the context of IS, or to suggest that accounting techniques such as DCF have no place in the evaluation of new technology. The argument is, rather, that there are circumstances where such approaches are highly deficient in generating real understanding of the costs and benefits of a computer-based system and its human and organizational consequences. In such circumstances, it is suggested that interpretive approaches to evaluation have something extra to offer in terms of understanding. Specific interpretive IS evaluation methodologies have been suggested in the literature (see, for example, Iivari 1988, on the Pioco methodology). The later sections of this chapter will not attempt to provide a rival to such approaches, but rather to present a broader discussion of an interpretive perspective on IS evaluation and its implications for practice.

THEMES FROM THE CASE STUDIES

The discussion in this section compares and contrasts the findings on IS evaluation from the case studies in Part II, organized around a set of selected themes arising from the earlier analyses in those chapters. The themes are grouped under the headings of the content, social context and social process of evaluation, and are summarized in Table 8.1.

Content

A key element of the evaluation of an actual or proposed computer-based information system is the *purpose* for which the evaluation is being carried out; this purpose may be explicitly stated or may be implicit, and the evaluation may be a formal exercise or part of a largely tacit process. In the Processing Company, two formal evaluations were carried out prior to the development of the Prosys system. The purpose of the first of these evaluations was to choose between four different MRP system proposals, based on a set of largely technical criteria. The second evaluation was carried out at the insistence of the holding company, and the purpose of this from the perspective of the senior management of the Processing Company was to legitimize their previous choice of system.

In Sky Building Society during Brown's leadership, central evaluation of proposed and on-going systems was a largely personal activity carried out by Brown himself. The purpose from his point of view was to determine which systems to develop linked to his personal vision for change, and to monitor the performance of existing systems, seen from his own perspective. Taylor's view of the purpose of evaluation was very different, in that he encouraged management at various levels to input their own evaluations of existing

TABLE 8.1 *Themes on IS evaluation from the case studies*

Content
- Purpose
- Factors

Social Context
- Stakeholder assessments
- Stakeholder conflict

Social Process
- Multi-stage process
- Evaluation as learning

systems and proposals for new systems into a formal planning process. The purpose of this from his perspective was to generate consensus approval on proposals for change, although this was not actually achieved in practice.

The evaluation of the Premis and Intis systems prior to their development was part of a high-level political process in Polonia, carried out by senior politicians and civil servants. The purpose of these deliberations from their perspective was to determine political priorities and to consider how IS could be used to support these political goals. Post-implementation evaluation of the Premis system noted such aspects as poor data supply by the agencies, and this formed part of the input into the formal Cabinet Committee proposal for the Intis system. The purpose of the proposal and evaluation of the proposed Devplan system was similarly linked to central government perceptions on political priorities.

A related issue to that of the purpose of an IS evaluation is to consider what *factors* are included in the evaluation. In the Processing Company, the factors that were included in the formal evaluations were captured in the Invitation to Tender, and consisted of equipment, applications programmes, costs, and the supplier's experience and support available. It is noticeable that there were no evaluation factors related to organizational issues such as implied changes in work practices, and to possible difficulties of achieving organizational change to accommodate the proposed new systems.

Since the evaluations carried out by Brown in Sky were largely a personal affair, he could include a broad range of factors. It is clear that he considered many factors in addition to purely technical and economic criteria; for example, a major factor of concern to Brown was the acceptability of proposed systems to branch staff, and the potential value to them in carrying out their work. The formal planning procedures instigated by Taylor certainly involved a large number and variety of factors to be considered in evaluations of proposals for new systems; the lack of resolution which followed can be thought of as partly due to the lack of any clear vision for change in a strategic sense, and thus no central vision against which to prioritize the evaluation criteria.

In the Government Co-ordination Agency in Polonia, the factors included in the evaluations of the Premis and Intis systems combined political and technical criteria, but with no serious account taken of organizational issues. The political desirability of central control, and the technical feasibility of combining existing systems, were included as evaluation criteria in the Cabinet Committee report recommending the development of the Intis system. No consideration appears to have been given to organizational issues such as the potential value of data from the system to central agencies other than the GCA itself. A similar approach was pursued in the central evaluation of the proposal for the Devplan system based on political and technical factors alone. However, the personal views of some members of the GCA IS staff were starting to change by the end of the research period towards consideration of an end-user computing philosophy, which would imply the incorporation of evaluation factors such as user acceptability and perceived value.

Social Context

The above discussion of the content of an IS evaluation exercise has focused on a formal or tacit activity backed by the organizational authority to carry out the recommendations of the evaluation. A key element of the social context within which such an exercise is carried out is provided by the *stakeholder assessments* of the various individuals and interest groups involved in or affected by the computer-based information system. These assessments or personal evaluations always exist, and are sometimes taken account of and even incorporated within the formal evaluation activity; in other cases, they remain outside the formal activity as an informal context.

The Processing Company provides a good illustration of this latter condition. For example, the sales order processing clerks assessed the proposed new computer system as an enforced change, for no particularly clear reason, from a previous system they were reasonably happy with. This informal assessment formed no part at all of the formal evaluation exercises. Similarly, the warehousemen formed their own informal assessments of the demerits of the new system with respect to the efficient utilization of warehouse space. In this second case, following the disastrous implementation of the sales order processing module, elements of the warehousemen's assessment were incorporated into a re-evaluation of procedures with respect to the new system, and some changes were made to accommodate their views.

In Sky under Brown, the branch staff's informal assessments with respect to proposed, prototype, and implemented systems were listened to by Brown as an input to his personal evaluation activities. The IS staff formed their own personal assessments of the problems associated with ad hoc and incremental systems development, but although Brown was aware of these, and they were therefore an input to his evaluations, he did not respond to their views by modifying the systems development approach in any significant way. However, after the departure of Brown, these assessments formed an important part of the social context for the evaluation exercises conducted as part of the formal planning procedures instigated by Taylor.

In the Government Co-ordination Agency, the assessments of the other agencies with respect to the value of the Premis system resulted in a number of them not even supplying data to the system. This did not occur for the Intis system, but agency assessments in this case resulted in them complying with central directives on data supply, but largely ignoring the system as a support for their own work. The informal assessments of some of the GCA IS staff with respect to existing systems led them towards a more user-oriented way of thinking with respect to Devplan, but these assessments had not been incorporated in the thinking of senior politicians and administrators by the end of the research period, and were thus not an input to formal evaluation activity.

Stakeholder assessments are sometimes sufficiently diverse, and are recognized as a legitimate input to the formal evaluation activity, that this can be seen to be taking place in the social context of *stakeholder conflict*, where the result of the evaluation activity can be viewed as a way of resolving this conflict, at least in the short term. In the Processing Company, the second evaluation exercise was carried out in the context of conflict between senior management of the Processing Company and the holding company over the recommendation of a non-IBM system. The formal evaluation exercise enabled this conflict to be resolved in favour of the Processing Company management.

In Sky, explicit stakeholder conflict with respect to the evaluation of the computer-based IS was kept in check during Brown's period of leadership, since he dominated the formal evaluation activity and resolved differences of opinion by personal decision. Following his departure, the social context in the period under Taylor can actually be characterized as one of stakeholder conflict, and this context impacted evaluation activity; differences in stakeholder assessments, seen as legitimate inputs to the evaluation process with the new emphasis on formal planning and participation, had not been resolved by the end of the research period.

In the Government Co-ordination Agency, we see no overt stakeholder conflict with respect to the political priorities incorporated in the evaluation of the computer-based IS, although it is possible that this occurred within the inner deliberations of high-level government. The resistance of other central agencies to the concept of the GCA being the focal agency for development projects can be seen in their reluctance to supply data for the Premis system. The evaluation of the weaknesses of previous systems, incorporated in the Cabinet Committee report, removed this resistance, but only in the sense that it cleared the way for the technical implementation of the Intis system; this latter system was not subsequently used to any extent by the other agencies.

Social Process

A way of conceptualizing the evaluation process during the planning, design, implementation, and subsequent use of a computer-based IS is as a *multi-stage process*, where the use of the term stage implies various discrete periods punctuated by major events or actions. Of course, shifts in the evaluation content and context take place in the periods between major events, but a division into stages can be a useful analytical construct to describe elements of an essentially continuous social process. In the Processing Company, major events included the results of the first two evaluation exercises, which was followed by the stage of the development of the sales order processing system.

The subsequent major problems associated with system implementation were an event which triggered a major re-evaluation by all interested parties.

In Sky, the period of Brown's leadership could be broken into different evaluation stages, punctuated for example by the introduction of the various systems which were developed during the period of his leadership. However, the broad evaluation process based on personal decisions taken by Brown himself remained constant throughout his time in office. The leadership change from Brown to Taylor resulted in a dramatic change in the evaluation process, and informal assessments, which formed part of the latent social context of evaluation during Brown's time, became incorporated as part of the formal evaluation process under Taylor.

In the GCA, we can see some distinct evaluation stages over the period of the decade of the 1980s, largely triggered by events and actions in the wider political context. For example, the change of government in Polonia in 1981 resulted in the establishment of the Cabinet Committee whose brief included the evaluation of computer-based IS to support the monitoring and control of development activities, and their report led to the development of the Intis system. The proposal and evaluation of the Devplan system followed a 1986 government initiative directed towards regional development, arising from political fears concerning the distance between the political centre and the grass roots.

An evaluation exercise supported by organizational authority for action, whether formal or tacit in nature, can be regarded as a stage in its own right, and provides an opportunity for personal appraisal, the sharing of ideas between individuals and interest groups, with the aim of generating consensus agreement and thus commitment to the resulting proposals for action. This can be summarized in the phrase *evaluation as learning*. We have already noted that the social context of an evaluation activity can sometimes be characterized as one of stakeholder conflict. Learning still takes place in an evaluation activity conducted under these conditions since, for example, the views of others are better understood even if they conflict with one's own. However, unless the conflict arises from misunderstanding which can be resolved by the evaluation activity, a result may only be reached by non-consensual approaches such as majority vote, or dictate.

In the Processing Company, the philosophy of evaluation as learning was not adopted in any serious sense in the first two evaluation exercises. Although senior management no doubt learnt more about each others' views with respect to computer-based IS, there was no significant involvement of other interest groups, and thus no chance of a consensus commitment to the proposed system on the part of company staff in general. Some change in attitude on the part of senior management took place following the initial failure, recognizing for example the view of MRP systems as a new way of working for everybody in the company. Senior management were replaced soon after this realization, so there is no evidence as to what approach they would have pursued in later evaluation exercises.

In Sky, Brown's personal approach to evaluation had a strong self-learning flavour, reflected in his willingness to be involved directly with all interested parties. However, his central control over the evaluation process meant that it was not a major vehicle for learning on the part of other members of the management team. On the other hand, Taylor's approach to evaluation could be argued to fall neatly into the definition of evaluation as learning given above, with its emphasis on widespread sharing of ideas between all interest groups. However, consensus and commitment were not generated by the process, at least by the end of the research period; conflict of views between stakeholders was present and, in the absence of a clear vision for change and in the presence of rather hands-off leadership, it was unlikely that an agreed way forward would emerge.

In the GCA, evaluation exercises such as those contained in the Cabinet Committee report in 1981 can be considered to be a vehicle for political learning and the generation of political commitment amongst the group of senior staff involved. There was little learning about the realities of how to implement computer-based IS in a non-technical sense, since constituencies who could perhaps have articulated ideas in this area were not represented. Some similarities can be observed here with the top management evaluations in the Processing Company designed to share ideas amongst themselves, but without the right level of thought and understanding concerning the perceptions and interests of other affected groups.

A SYNTHESIZED PERSPECTIVE ON IS EVALUATION

The purpose of this section is to synthesize a perspective on IS evaluation drawing from the preceding discussion in the chapter. The section is divided into two subsections; the first of these presents a view on the nature of IS evaluation, and the second describes the role of an IS evaluator related to this view. The key features of this perspective are summarized in Table 8.2, and the ideas will be illustrated more fully in the final section of the chapter.

The Nature of IS Evaluation

The *process of IS evaluation* involves a discourse, that is often mediated by formal techniques and procedures, but where the social context always includes the informal assessments of individuals and stakeholder groups, which are rational in their own terms. Symons (1990, p. 189) argues that the discourse of evaluation thus comprises a public rationale undershot by a multiplicity of private rationalities, the formal procedures of evaluation interwoven with informal process.

TABLE 8.2 A synthesized perspective on IS evaluation

The Nature of IS Evaluation

- The process of IS evaluation involves a discourse, often mediated by formal procedures, but in the context of informal stakeholder assessments
- The outcome of a formal evaluation exercise forms an interpretative scheme, which embodies norms and provides a control and co-ordination facility
- A formal evaluation can have both overt and covert functions, and can be seen in some cases as a ritual
- Interpretive evaluation designs focus on learning and understanding, but consensus cannot always be achieved

- -

The Role of an IS Evaluator

- IS evaluators include those with formal authority, but also other stakeholders
- A ritual element is a part of the evaluator's role in both preordinate and responsive evaluation designs, but the symbolism is different
- An IS evaluator is both an enactor of meaning involved with organization making, and also a moral agent concerned with norms, values and power relations

The *outcome of a formal evaluation exercise* forms an interpretative scheme which embodies norms and values and provides a facility to be drawn on for the control and co-ordination of material and human resources. The degree to which the interpretative scheme represents a shared viewpoint by the various stakeholder groups depends in part on the social process during the conduct of the formal evaluation activity. Individuals reflexively monitor actions and consequences following an evaluation outcome, and these informal assessments form part of the context for future actions and evaluations.

A formal evaluation can have both *overt and covert functions*, and in some cases can be seen as a *ritual*. This ritual may express, for example, symbolic belief in management competence, or it may provide an underpinning for an action rationality where choice has been restricted in order to reduce uncertainty. Rituals are an important aspect of human life, but a formal IS evaluation viewed as a ritual can be a device to reinforce structures of domination, and can also be a *major hindrance to innovative organizational change*.

Interpretive evaluation designs aim to involve a wide variety of stakeholder groups, and their focus is on a discourse for learning and understanding, in order to generate involvement and commitment. This responsive approach is organized around the concerns, issues and values of stakeholders. However, it is important to note that consensus is not always achievable by such approaches, and ways of resolving conflict involve power relations and necessitate moral choices.

The Role of an IS Evaluator

An *IS evaluator* can be taken to include any person charged with carrying out a formal evaluation exercise, or a manager conducting a more personal evaluation study that has a formal legitimacy due to the individual's organizational function. However, in addition to those in formal positions, an IS evaluator can be considered to include anyone concerned with the proposed or actual computer-based IS, who is monitoring actions and consequences and forming their own assessments, often involving a discourse with members of their own stakeholder group at least.

In the case of a *preordinate evaluation exercise* based largely on technical and economic criteria, the role of a formal IS evaluator can be taken to include not only quantitative and other assessments, but also a ritual element of demonstrating management competence. In the case of a *responsive evaluation design*, the role of a formal IS evaluator is as a facilitator of the evaluation discourse amongst a wide variety of stakeholder groups. The evaluator in this context can be seen as a collaborator, learner and teacher, reality shaper, and change agent. Ritual may also be present under these circumstances, where involving people represents a symbolic expression of a form of democracy.

The roles of an IS evaluator as an *enactor of meaning* and a *moral agent* are present in any evaluation exercise. The IS evaluator is contributing to organization making, namely the creation and maintenance of systems of shared meaning that facilitate organized action. The IS evaluator is also involved in the production and reproduction of normative values, and in the maintenance and change of power relations.

THE PRACTICE OF IS EVALUATION

The perspective on the nature of IS evaluation and the role of an IS evaluator, outlined in the previous section, will now be applied to a general discussion of the evaluation themes derived from the case study findings. The discussion is oriented to the practice of an IS evaluator, and in particular focuses on evaluation in the context of an interpretive or responsive evaluation design rather than a preordinate design based largely on technical and economic criteria. The latter approach may be useful in certain contexts and indeed may be 'required', but it is not compatible with the focus of this book, and in addition there is a large normative literature on how to carry out such exercises. The discussion is divided into three broad task areas, namely those of considering evaluation purpose, understanding evaluation context, and facilitating evaluation process. The section aims to provide some ideas and issues that it would be worthwhile to discuss in any particular practical context; key issues are summarized in Tables 8.3 to 8.5.

TABLE 8.3 Some issues for debate on considering evaluation purpose

Purpose

- For interpretive evaluation, broad purpose is to deepen understanding, and generate motivation and commitment

- Purpose of evaluation at various stages of IS development life cycle can be feasibility study, design feedback, or post-implementation review

- An interpretive evaluation can be carried out at any stage of IS cycle

- Interpretive evaluation emphasizes overt rather than covert functions, but covert motives cannot and should not be eliminated

Factors

- Use of word 'criteria' in preordinate designs prioritizes technical/quantitative data

- For interpretive designs, vocabulary is concerns, issues and values; and these include human, organizational, and political factors

- Important issue is agreed strategic focus, which reduces choice/aids action

Considering Evaluation Purpose

A key element of any IS evaluation can be considered to be the *purpose* for which it is being carried out. For interpretive evaluation exercises, the broad purpose is to deepen understanding and to generate motivation and commitment. This goal would normally be stated explicitly, although the form of the exercise will implicitly carry this symbolism of participation in any case. The involvement of a wide range of stakeholder groups is essential to this style of design, and may be one of the practical deterrents for the approach where time or resources for the evaluation are deemed to be in short supply.

The purpose of the evaluation may also be viewed in relation to the different stages in the cycle of the development of a computer-based IS. At an early stage, an evaluation can be considered as a form of feasibility study. During the process of technical implementation, evaluation may be concerned with providing feedback for design modifications. After technical implementation is complete, the purpose of the evaluation may be to decide how well the system achieves various goals with a possible view to further modification, or design of a follow-on system. The latter case has summative and formative elements, whereas the other two are formative from an interpretive design perspective. The crucial distinction with respect to the purpose of an IS evaluation exercise seems not to be the distinction between formative and summative evaluation, but between preordinate designs based largely on technical and economic criteria, and responsive evaluation concerned with social and organizational issues. A responsive evaluation can be carried out at any stage of the development life cycle of a computer-based IS with the goal of learning and understanding at that stage.

Another distinction mentioned earlier with respect to evaluation purpose is the inclusion of both overt and covert functions. The general philosophy of interpretive evaluation designs would imply being more open concerning motives and possible actions, and thus emphasizing overt rather than covert evaluation functions. Nevertheless, it would be naïve to assume that the covert could or should be eliminated; people will retain covert motives in the most open of interpretive designs, sometimes for reasons of self-interest, but also with rather higher motives in some cases. The latter can occur, for example, because it is often unwise to 'tell the truth' if this can be hurtful to others; another instance is that radically new ideas may need to be introduced gradually in order not to shock or threaten people.

A related issue to that of the purpose of an IS evaluation is to decide what *factors* should be included in the exercise. It is interesting to note that the word criteria is often used in relation to preordinate designs, and the use of this term has a 'hard' scientific feel which supports a tendency to prioritize technical and quantitative data. In the case of an interpretive evaluation design, factors to consider could be centred around the vocabulary of concerns, issues, and values of stakeholder groups. These factors will certainly include technical and economic issues, which it would be foolish in any context to underemphasize, but the language also supports a much wider social perspective.

Thus the factors considered in an interpretive evaluation design will include human, organizational and political concerns, issues and values in addition to technical and economic criteria. It is worth noting one specific concern or issue related back to the previous chapter on IS strategy. It was argued there that a broad vision for change is a key strategic element which, if it is not present or broadly shared, can create major problems. An interpretive evaluation design without any agreed strategic focus for change may degenerate into factionalism or arguments for the status quo. This view is also linked to the earlier discussion on the need for a rationality which stimulates action; a broad strategic focus in this context can be seen as a means of choice reduction, providing a valuable starting point and variety reducer for an interpretive evaluation exercise.

TABLE 8.4 *Some issues for debate on understanding evaluation context*

Stakeholder Assessments

- Interpretive evaluation designs incorporate more stakeholder assessments in formal process; one rationale is to avoid later implementation problems
- Informal assessments will always be there, even in interpretive designs
- All assessments are worth listening to, but are not equally valid

Stakeholder Conflict

- Where differences are irreconcilable, decisions are imposed, and this may be necessary as a way of taking action
- Morality of imposed decisions depends on specific case, but involves IS evaluator as moral agent which needs more emphasis in literature and practice
- Overriding of stakeholder conflict by dictate can result in later problems, since effective implementation may require shared norms and values
- More time spent in interpretive evaluation may repay itself in longer term

Understanding Evaluation Context

The importance of *stakeholder assessments* in evaluation activity has been emphasized throughout the chapter, and interpretive designs aim to incorporate more of such assessments within the formal process. A key rationale for this is that they are present in any case, and if ignored may create a context which enables the sabotage of later activity on system development and implementation. Two qualifications are worth making to a view of interpretive evaluation design as incorporating stakeholder assessments. Firstly, it is not possible to do so in any complete way, and informal stakeholder assessments, which change subtly over time, will always shadow and be outside any formal evaluation activity, even if based on an interpretive design. Secondly, the view is not being put forward here that all assessments are equally valid. The philosophy of interpretive evaluation design from this author's perspective would see all assessments as worth listening to, but that the evaluation process should be an opportunity for learning, and this will and should involve more attitudinal change on the part of some stakeholders than others.

This brings us to the important and difficult question of *stakeholder conflict*. No matter how an interpretive evaluation is carried out, circumstances will arise where differences are irreconcilable, and in these cases decisions are normally reached by the exercise of power to impose. Indeed, it is essential that there is a tie-breaking mechanism in any human society, or total inaction would result, which would be unlikely to be in anybody's interests. There are no simple prescriptions on the morality of imposed decisions, and each situation must be decided on its own merits. The only point worth making here is that this involves the role of the IS evaluator as moral agent, and the author's view is that this role needs more emphasis and discussion than it is accorded at the present time, both in the literature and in practice.

On a more pragmatic level, the overriding of stakeholder conflict by dictate or as the 'results of the evaluation exercise' can be a hollow victory. The evaluation outcome may provide a facility to enable the co-ordination and control of resources in the short term, but in the longer term effective implementation in an organizational sense may not be achieved if norms and values are not shared, and indeed if the imposition of a decision regarding a computer-based IS actually strengthens the opposition of a particular stakeholder group. It seems clear that in most cases consensus is a more desirable state of affairs if it can be achieved, but it may be felt that there is a trade-off between the time taken to achieve this and the cost of delay. However, more time spent in an interpretive evaluation activity may well repay itself in the longer term.

Facilitating Evaluation Process

The assessment of computer-based IS on the part of all stakeholders is a continuous process taking place in a changing set of contexts. It is unlikely to be desirable to conduct formal evaluation exercises as a continuous process, and thus the evaluation process can be conceptualized as a *multi-stage process*, punctuated by major events or actions, in which a formal evaluation exercise

TABLE 8.5 Some issues for debate on facilitating evaluation process

Multi-Stage Process

- Assessment of computer-based IS is continuous process in changing contexts
- Can be conceptualized as a multi-stage process, punctuated by major events or actions, in which a formal evaluation exercise is a specific stage
- Regular review desirable for all stakeholders on need for formal evaluation exercise
- Individuals and groups monitor the actions and consequences from previous evaluation stages, which form part of the social context of future evaluations
- An IS evaluator should gain understanding and facilitate the sharing of experiences on previous evaluation stages

Evaluation as Learning

- An IS evaluator can consciously attempt to create and support an evaluation climate within which learning should flourish
- Ritual of participation needs to be linked to other actions and enactments
- Values to promote include the legitimacy of all assessments in the evaluation discourse, that everybody is a learner, and that moral issues can be debated

is thought of as a specific stage. However, a regular review of the need for a more formal interpretive evaluation exercise would seem to be desirable on the part of all stakeholders, bearing in mind the process of continuous change in both assessments and contexts.

A further point worth noting with respect to the multi-stage nature of the evaluation process is that individuals and groups monitor the actions and intended and unintended consequences from previous evaluation stages. These help form the informal stakeholder assessments that are elements of the social context for future evaluations. In some cases, these assessments remain suppressed in formal organizational activity due for example to the domination of a particular individual; they can, however, surface again after such a constraint is removed. One implication for the IS evaluator in an interpretive evaluation design is the need to gain an understanding and to facilitate the sharing of experiences from previous evaluation exercises and stages.

A key phrase from an interpretive perspective to describe the social process during a formal evaluation stage is that of *evaluation as learning*. An IS evaluator can consciously attempt to create and support a climate within which learning activity should flourish. The ritual of participation embodied in the interpretive design itself is one aspect of symbolic action, but this may be viewed as a sham if it is not linked to other actions and enactments. Specific action for a given context cannot be prescribed, but certain values can be proposed as likely to provide a supportive environment if explicitly promoted by participants in the social process. These include the view that questioning is acceptable, that all assessments are legitimate in the evaluation discourse, that everybody is a learner during the evaluation process, and that moral issues can be debated.

REFERENCES

Bjorn-Andersen, N., and Davis, G. B. (1988) (eds) *IS Assessment: Issues and Challenges*, North-Holland, Amsterdam.
Brunsson, N. (1982) 'The irrationality of action and action rationality: decisions, ideologies and organizational actions', *Journal of Management Studies*, **19**, No. 1, 29–44.
Currie, W. L. (1989) 'The art of justifying new technology to top management', *Omega*, **17**, No. 5, 409–418.
Floder, R. E., and Weiner, S. S. (1983) 'Rationality to ritual: the multiple roles of evaluation in governmental processes', in *Evaluation Models: Viewpoints on Educational and Human Services Evaluation* (eds G. F. Madaus, M. Scriven, D. L. Stufflebeam), Kluwer-Nijhoff, Boston.
Guba, E. G., and Lincoln, Y. S. (1981) *Effective Evaluation*, Jossey-Bass, San Francisco.
Guba, E. G., and Lincoln, Y. S. (1989) *Fourth Generation Evaluation*, Sage, Newbury Park.
Hirschheim, R., and Smithson, S. (1988) 'A critical analysis of information systems evaluation', in *IS Assessment: Issues and Challenges* (eds N. Bjorn-Andersen and G. B. Davis), North-Holland, Amsterdam.
Iivari, J. (1988) 'Assessing IS design methodologies as methods of IS assessment', in

IS Assessment: Issues and Challenges (eds N. Bjorn-Andersen and G. B. Davis), North-Holland, Amsterdam.

Kumar, K. (1990) 'Post implementation evaluation of computer-based IS: current practices', *Communications of the ACM*, **33**, No. 2, 203–212.

Legge, K. (1984) *Evaluating Planned Organizational Change*, Academic Press, London.

Lindblom, C. E. (1959) 'The science of "muddling through"', *Public Administration Review*, **19**, 79–88.

Scriven, M. (1967) *The Methodology of Evaluation*, Rand McNally, Chicago.

Stake, R. E. (1975) (ed.) *Evaluating the Arts in Education: A Responsive Approach*, Merrill, Columbus.

Stake, R. E. (1983) 'Program evaluation, particularly responsive evaluation', in *Evaluation Models: Viewpoints on Educational and Human Services Evaluation* (eds G. F. Madaus, M. Scriven, D. L. Stufflebeam), Kluwer-Nijhoff, Boston.

Stone, D. N. (1991) 'Language, training and experience in IS assessment', *Accounting, Management and Information Technologies*, **1**, No. 1, 91–108.

Symons, V. J. (1990) *Evaluation of Information Systems: Multiple Perspectives*, unpublished PhD thesis, University of Cambridge.

Symons, V. J. (1991) 'A review of information systems evaluation: content, context and process', *European Journal of Information Systems*, **1**, No. 3, 205–212.

Symons, V., and Walsham, G. (1988) 'The evaluation of information systems: a critique', *Journal of Applied Systems Analysis*, **15**, 119–132.

Chapter 9
DESIGN AND DEVELOPMENT

This chapter is concerned with the issue of information systems design and development, and is divided into four sections. The first section reviews some of the extensive *design and development literature*, focused on work which is related to the broadly interpretive approach of this book. The second section compares and contrasts the findings from the case studies in Part II, based around a set of selected *themes on IS design and development* arising from the earlier analyses. The third section of the chapter then *synthesizes a perspective* on IS design and development drawing from the material in the previous sections. In the final section, this perspective is applied to a discussion of the *practice of IS design and development*, based around the set of themes from the case material, and aimed to provide some issues for debate in any particular context.

RELEVANT LITERATURE ON DESIGN AND DEVELOPMENT

There is a large literature on IS design and development and, in contrast to the issues of IS strategy and evaluation discussed in the previous two chapters, there is a considerable body of work which derives from a broadly interpretive approach to research and understanding. The purpose of this section is to discuss some ideas and approaches from this work, and to relate these ideas to the earlier case studies where appropriate. The review does not aim to be comprehensive, but to provide discussion of some interesting streams of work on IS design and development under the headings of structured methodologies, ethical issues, and the analyst's perspective.

Structured Methodologies

There are a very large number of structured methodologies available, which are intended to aid the IS analyst during the design and development process. Some of these methodologies take no account of human and organizational issues, and others treat such issues from a managerialist stance that takes little account of multiple realities and the sense-making aspect of the process (Boland 1979). Such methodologies will not be reviewed in this subsection, although it is recognized that some of them are in fairly common use, and brief comments on this will be made in the final subsection of this literature review.

The first interpretive methodology we will consider here is the participative design approach known as the Ethics method (Mumford and Weir 1979), which derives from the research of the socio-technical school on the design of work in organizations. The socio-technical approach to work organization places emphasis on the need to match social and technical systems in an appropriate way, and not to emphasize the technical system at the expense of the human system; the approach also recognizes the importance of job satisfaction, autonomy, and self-determination for social groups. The Ethics method has been applied in a range of real settings (see, for example, Mumford 1981), and aims to involve users directly in the design of their work activities and the supporting computer-based systems. A recent overview of the method is provided by Maclaren, Hornby, Robson, O'Brien, Cleg and Richardson (1991):

> Ethics is intended to provide users with the means to take control of systems' analysis and design. It does this by involving them in the process of analysis and providing them with the means to analyse requirements and design the system from an organizational perspective. It also provides the design team with a means of trading off social and technical features of the design to ensure an 'optimised' socio-technical outcome. It is largely process orientated (i.e., it is concerned with 'getting right' the process of analysis and design through participation) but it does, also, recommend some useful tools and techniques for collecting and analysing information. These are all paper based. (p. 83)

Mumford (1981) states that critics of the Ethics method see it as too complex, too time-consuming and too expensive. She argues that in reality this is not the case, and her view is somewhat supported by Maclaren *et al.*, who see Ethics as cheap in direct cost terms, and say that the increased amount of time spent by user department staff may be compensated for in a reduction in maintenance time and later hidden costs such as user dissatisfaction, stress, and absenteeism.

A rather different critique of participative system design in general, and the Ethics method in particular, is summarized by Floyd, Mehl, Reisin, Schmidt and Wolf (1989). Although the method recognizes that different groups in an organization normally have different goals and perceptions, an implicit assumption is that these different goals may be pursued and attained jointly if the values underlying them are made as explicit as possible from the start. This assumption has been labelled the 'harmony perspective' (Nygaard and Sorgaard 1987), and takes little account of circumstances where conflict is endemic and cannot be resolved by democratic means or open debate.

A second stream of work on IS design and development from an interpretive perspective is based on soft systems methodology (SSM) (Checkland 1981; Checkland and Scholes 1990), which was introduced in Chapter 1 as a general approach to organizational intervention. In the domain of the design and development of computer-based IS, the ideas of SSM have been used as the basis for a number of approaches and methodologies. An example is the work of Wilson (1984, 1989), where aspects of SSM are used to create a staged methodology starting with the formation of a consensus primary task model as the basis for information requirements analysis. Other methodologies for IS design and development that make use of SSM include FAOR (Functional Analysis of Office Requirements) (Schäfer 1988) and Multiview (Avison and Wood-Harper 1990).

It was noted in Chapter 1 that SSM has been criticized as conservative in nature and likely to be geared to the vested interests of those in authority. It is interesting to note, with respect to our focus here on IS design and development, that Iivari (1989) draws on SSM for some of his ideas on systems design and, as observed by Alvarez and Klein (1989), Iivari emphasizes the conflictual perspective on organizations in contrast to the consensus-based approach to design of Wilson referred to above. This lends some support to Checkland's own view that SSM can be applied in a variety of ways, not all of them being consensual in their approach.

The final broad approach to IS design and development that will be outlined here arises from work in the Scandinavian countries. As noted by Floyd *et al.* (1989), there are a number of schools of thought rather than one well-defined 'Scandinavian approach', but the different schools tend to share some common features in their underlying philosophy. This philosophy emphasizes efforts towards humanization and democratization as overriding design goals, in keeping with the broad aim of building a relatively egalitarian society.

The participative design method is one approach that has been pursued and used in Scandinavia. The criticism of its underlying 'harmony perspective' discussed earlier led to the suggestion (Ehn and Kyng 1987) of an alternative approach to design known as the collective resource approach. This approach explicitly allies itself with trade union interests, and adopts a conflict perspective on organizations. It is a deliberate attempt to provide empowerment for workers at the lower hierarchical levels, and it has led to specific initiatives and projects (see, for example, Bødker, Ehn, Kammersgaard, Kyng and Sundblad 1987, on the Utopia project). These initiatives are innovative and challenging although, as observed in Alvarez and Gaffney (1989), Scandinavian society provides a supportive cultural and legal environment for such activity, in contrast to most other countries in the world. In addition, the initiatives represent only a small part of IS design and development activity in Scandinavia, the majority of which is not conducted as a joint project between management and labour.

The above discussion of structured methodologies for IS design and development can be briefly related to our earlier case studies. In the Processing Company and the Government Co-ordination Agency, human and organizational issues and multiple stakeholder perspectives were largely ignored. It is not possible to be certain, but it seems likely that the use of a structured methodology based on participative design or soft systems methodology would have ensured that such issues were at least addressed, if not necessarily resolved by consensus. Sky Building Society under Brown provides a more complex example. The vision for change driving the IS design and development activities was created by Brown, but the activities themselves involved a form of participative design, although no explicit structured methodology was used. On the one hand, the design and development approach was very successful in producing systems that were user-friendly and adapted to the work activities of the branch staff. On the other hand, a view arising from the radical end of the Scandinavian spectrum would see the approach as manipulation of the workers in the interests of management in general, and Brown in particular. The lower level employees were not consulted at all with respect to strategy, and the key goals of the strategy, such as increased short-term profitability, were not necessarily in the best interests of the workforce.

Ethical Issues

The above discussion of structured methodologies has touched on a number of issues with an ethical dimension, and a summary of some of the key points in this area can be given by considering the role of the IS analyst. Hirschheim and Klein (1989) discuss four roles of the IS analyst as systems expert, facilitator, labour partisan, and emancipator or social therapist. The first of these relates to the purely technical role of the IS analyst in developing systems to agreed specifications. The second role of the analyst as facilitator is an approach which would be natural when using methodologies such as Ethics and the consensual versions of SSM-based methodologies. Hirschheim and Klein say that, from this perspective, any system that then meets with the approval of the affected parties is legitimate. They argue that:

> Because of its relativist stance, it is *completely uncritical* of the potential dysfunctional side effects of using particular tools and techniques for ISD (information systems development). Different products of systems development are simply viewed as the result of different socially constructed realities. (p. 1206)

Since IS analysts are human beings, who reflexively monitor actions and consequences, such a completely uncritical position does not occur. However, the view of the analyst as a total relativist is useful as an ideal type for analytic purposes, and can be seen as a strong element of the analyst's role in consensual-type interpretive approaches to design and development.

The third role of the analyst as labour partisan suggests that the developer becomes an advocate of labour to redress the balance of power between management and labour as the only morally acceptable course of action. This view of the analyst's role can be seen to underpin the radical Scandinavian school as represented in projects such as Utopia. The need for such a role is also implied by some literature from outside Scandinavia. For example, Robey and Markus (1984) argue that elements of the systems design process can be interpreted as rituals which enable actors to remain overtly rational while negotiating to achieve private interests. They consider that most information requirements analysis methods have an inherent bias to preserve the status quo, which is a beneficial outcome for those who already possess power. Newman and Noble (1990) argue that once conflict has arisen in the IS development process, it may not be possible to resolve it by the exchange of ideas. They describe a case study in which the impasse was resolved by an exercise of power, after several attempts to 'persuade, threaten and coerce the users had failed'. They suggest that this progression from attempted persuasion to the use of force is not an isolated example.

The final role identified for the IS analyst is that of emancipator. This role is developed from critical theory and, in particular, the work of Habermas (Habermas 1972; McCarthy 1978), which was briefly introduced in Chapter 1. The concept is to try to create conditions for free and open discussion that lead to shared understanding, but in contrast to the facilitator role this discussion must include a critical examination of existing barriers to emancipation such as authority and illegitimate power, peer opinion pressure, social differentiation, and the bias and limitation of language use. All of this can read as rather naïve idealism and Hirschheim and Klein say that 'this story is hypothetical to a large degree in that it has been constructed from theory'. However, the action research approach of Jönsson (1991) has strong elements of the analyst as emancipator role, and has been used in a number of cases, not surprisingly in Scandinavia. The idea is to engage with participants in a collaborative process of critical enquiry into problems of social practice in a learning context. The distinction to the facilitator role is the incorporation of the critical dimension. A key difference from the role of labour partisan is that the simple view of the workers as oppressed and management as the oppressors is not accepted uncritically, but is one of the dimensions for critical analysis.

If we consider the relevance of the above subsection on ethical issues to the case studies in Part II, the role of the IS analysts in all three cases can be largely viewed as that of systems expert, with some element of the facilitator role in Sky under Brown. The labour partisan or emancipator roles were not present in any direct way. However, it is worth noting that analysts monitored and assessed what was occurring in the cases, but without any strong focus on the ethical dimension.

The discussion of ethical issues so far has largely been focused on relatively traditional contexts for the development of computer-based IS. A brief discussion now follows with respect to such issues in the new area of computer-supported co-operative work (CSCW). The definition of CSCW is ambiguous with respect to the types of work which are included and excluded. However, the term has been coined at a time when changes in technological capability in areas such as electronic mail systems, electronic conferencing facilities, shared group software, and multi-media systems have spawned new possibilities for computer-mediated group work, leading to a vigorous debate on the social issues connected to the development and use of such systems.

Howard (1987) argues that we may be moving towards more collective work, where the individual's actions and views are more transparent to others and reliant on others. This will shift us into new interpretations of work, involving new meanings and changed social relationships. Much of this 'co-operative' work will be highly dependent on computer-based technology, and the design of this technology is thus intimately involved with the design of new social structures in organizational life. Howard argues that this brings with it a responsibility for the IS designer to become involved in and contribute to an organizational and social debate about how IS are and should be used; he describes this as 'a social ethics of systems design'.

Kyng (1991) considers that crucial aspects of work are often poorly understood in traditional system development, leading to severe difficulties when the system is introduced. He argues that the several such difficulties are magnified when the system being developed falls in the CSCW category and is concerned with supporting group work and interaction. Thus, on both practical and ethical grounds, Kyng argues that new approaches to computer systems design are needed involving mutual learning between designers and users, so that designers learn about the application area, and users learn about new technological possibilities. Kyng notes that there are limits to mutual learning, and that developers do not become skilled practitioners in the application area and users do not become technical experts; thus he argues that one of the challenges of co-operative design is to support creative collaboration despite the fundamental differences among the participants.

Kling (1991) shows a strong awareness of the ethical issues involved in CSCW-type applications, firstly by noting that the CSCW literature 'resonates with relentless positive social imagery' through such slogans as 'shared minds' and 'intellectual teamwork'. He points out that in practice fundamental processes in the particular work situation strongly influence the ways in which CSCW applications are adopted, used, and influence subsequent work; working relationships are multivalent, involving a mix of elements such as co-operation, conflict, competition, coercion, and co-ordination. It follows from Kling's arguments that an understanding of the ethical issues involved in design of CSCW systems should not take a simplistic view of an ideal world of total co-operation, but should be grounded in the 'rich multivalent social relationships of work places'.

The Analyst's Perspective

The literature discussed above has concerned methodologies to aid the IS analyst in the systems design and development process, and ethical issues of relevance to the analyst's work. However, a highly relevant consideration with respect to any proposed methodology or ethical issue is how the analysts view themselves and their role, seen through their own eyes. One research approach to this question is to carry out detailed ethnographic studies of the design and development activity in its context, with the views and interpretations of the analysts as a key data source. Work of this type includes the in-depth case studies of Zuboff (1988) discussed in Chapter 1, although these tended to focus on the users rather than the analysts; other examples referred to earlier were the case study of a systems analyst's work on a loan application system (Boland and Day 1989), and the paper by Orlikowski (1992) on analysts' use of CASE tools in a software consulting firm. It is interesting to note that in both these latter cases, matters of central concern to the analysts included ethical issues and related considerations of power, autonomy and control.

A further example of an ethnographic study of the systems design and development process is provided by Jones and Walsham (1992). They use a single in-depth case study of software development over a five-year period in a small technical consultancy company to illustrate 'limits of the knowable' on what can and should be known in carrying out systems design and development. Areas where there are theoretical and practical limits on what can be known include organizational knowledge about clients and client companies, domain knowledge concerning the focal technology, and design knowledge shared between members of the development team. Areas where there are ethical and social limits on what should be known include the monitoring of analyst's activity by management related to their need for autonomy, and the amount of visibility between different members of the design and development team.

A related style of research to that of ethnographic studies has been described as 'ecological studies' (Schneiderman and Carroll 1988). These are concerned with empirical work which 'confronts design problems on their own terms', involving the collection of detailed qualitative information, particularly through interviews with analysts. This style of research is interpretive and inductive, rather than seeking to confirm or disconfirm hypotheses. Ecological studies place less emphasis on an in-depth longitudinal case analysis than ethnographic studies, but are able to cover a larger number of cases for the same research effort, and can thus draw wider comparisons.

An interesting ecological study of the software design process is that by Curtis, Krasner and Iscoe (1988), based on interviewing personnel from 17 large software projects. They clustered problems as viewed by the interviewees into three key areas, namely the thin spread of application domain knowledge, fluctuating and conflicting requirements, and communication and co-ordination breakdowns. The first of these areas relates to the unevenness with which application-specific knowledge was spread across personnel, which was a major contributor to the phenomena of 'project gurus'. The authors note that conventional wisdom on software development argues that no project should rely on the performance of a few individuals, but their results suggest that this may be more troublesome in theory than in practice, although loss of crucial gatekeeper personnel would clearly cause problems. Their second and third key problem areas led the authors to view software development, at least in part, as a learning, communication, and negotiation process. They observe that software development tools and practices have had disappointingly small effects in improving practice, and consider that this was probably because they did not improve the most troublesome knowledge, requirements, and communication processes in software development.

The above study used data from the USA, whereas a recent study by Maclaren *et al.* (1991) concerned experiences in the UK, and focused on the 'human dimension' of system design methods. The study examined 15 such methods, and was based on interviews with 'experts' in all but two of these, together with 32 analysts covering seven of the methods. The authors summarized some findings from their work as follows:

> From an analyst's point of view, organizations get the systems they deserve. They feel that management appear to have no comprehensive IT strategy and often ask for systems to support solutions to business problems that are imperfectly understood, in a timescale that is impossible and with inadequate resources.
>
> From a management point of view, IT professionals appear to want to remain as technologists, more concerned with their speciality than the demands of the business. It is clear that a significant number of analysts have no knowledge of human and organizational issues, believing they are 'not my problem'. (p. 7)

It was mentioned at the start of this literature review that some rather functionalist methodologies, which take little account of human and organizational issues and multiple realities, are in fairly common use. The summarized views above give strong pointers to the reasons for this, and for the relatively limited use of more interpretive methodologies. Maclaren *et al.* note that there is a lack of agreement as to who owns human and organizational issues in the design process, that there is a lack of knowledge amongst analysts of these issues and of available interpretive methods, and that these latter methods are based on an alien non-engineering philosophy from a technologist's standpoint. In addition, the authors observed that skilled analysts tended to use methods in a highly pragmatic way, selecting only those sections of the methods that were applicable, in their view, to the problem situation. Thus the 'use' of a functionalist methodology is at most a partial use, with the analyst choosing particular tools such as data flow diagrams to assist with specific tasks, rather than using the methodology in any total fashion.

The above review of some literature on the analyst's perspective on design and development carries a number of ideas with strong echoes in our earlier case studies. In the Processing Company, the analysts felt that the timescale was 'impossible' and that management provided them with inadequate resources. They had limited organizational knowledge of the work activities and perceptions of other stakeholder groups, but regarded the human issues involved and the existence of these multiple realities as not their problem. The whole design and development process was conducted in the context of a breakdown of communication and co-ordination between the different groups, but the standard life cycle approach to systems development, concentrating on technical issues, largely ignored the serious future implications of this lack of mutual understanding.

In Sky Building Society under Brown, the analysts perceived themselves as operating under severe pressure, but the timescales were not impossible, resources were adequate, and leadership on communication and co-ordination issues during design and development was provided directly by Brown. A major practical issue with ethical implications from the point of view of the analysts was the degree to which Brown interfered with their activities, resulting in much reduced autonomy of action on their part. They clearly disliked this closer surveillance and control, but they received other 'benefits' in compensation such as increased status in the organization; however, they quickly reasserted their desire for more autonomy after the departure of Brown.

The IS analysts in the Government Co-ordination Agency had very limited organizational knowledge of the other agencies, and little effort was directed to developing communication and co-ordination between these agencies and the GCA. Such human and organizational issues were not regarded by the analysts as being 'their problem'. They had no knowledge of more interpretive design and development methodologies, and these would in any case have been alien to their view of design and development as a technical process. Ethical issues such as the empowerment of lower level personnel were subsumed under the cultural approach of following orders from above without questioning. Some seeds of doubt concerning the merits of this approach to the development of computer-based IS were present in at least some of the IS analysts' minds by the end of the research period.

THEMES FROM THE CASE STUDIES

The discussion in this section compares and contrasts material on IS design and development from the case studies in Part II, organized around a set of themes derived directly from the analyses in those chapters. The themes are grouped under the headings of the content, social context, and social process of IS design and development, and are summarized in Table 9.1.

Content

A key element of the content of any design and development process for a computer-based information system is the production of a *requirements specification*. This is used by the IS developers as the basis on which to carry out the development process, including organizing the databases and writing the appropriate computer code. However, the origins, purpose, and status of the specification can vary widely in different cases.

In the Processing Company, the origin of the requirements specification can be seen as senior management's desire to implement an MRP system aimed at tighter central control, and the choice of the Prosys system as the underlying basis was legitimized by the evaluation exercises. The purpose of the specification was seen by senior management and IS staff as creating a correct description of the user needs of the system to be developed, but its status was as an embodiment of values emanating from the higher levels of the organizational hierarchy; these values were not widely shared by other stakeholder groups.

The origin of the various requirements specifications for the computer-based IS developed in Sky Building Society during Brown's leadership can be thought of as his strategic vision for change based on decentralized systems

TABLE 9.1 Themes on IS design and development from the case studies

Content
• Requirements specification
• Development focus
Social Context
• Senior management attitude
• Project team composition
Social Process
• Participation
• Training

at the branch level. The purpose of a requirements specification was viewed rather differently than in the Processing Company, in that Brown regarded specifications not as a correct set of requirements, but as intermediate steps to produce 'half-baked' systems, which could be consistently improved until they 'fitted the business'. The status of a specification was thus as a particular embodiment of certain broad norms and values emanating originally from Brown, but specific features of the specification were regarded by everybody concerned as likely to change during the development process.

The structured system design method which was used in Sky under Taylor could be seen to originate from his key strategic vision of participation. One of the purposes of the structured method was to produce requirements specifications that would embody shared norms and values of the stakeholder groups. The process took a long time, was not based on any clear vision for organizational change, and resulted in proposals for 'systems for today', as viewed with hindsight by one of the senior management team under Taylor.

The origins of the requirements specifications of the systems developed by the Government Co-ordination Agency in Polonia can be traced to political imperatives from the highest level of government. Although this was a rather different source to that in the Processing Company, the purpose and status of the resulting specifications can be viewed as similar. The design concept was to embody the political norms and values in a correct set of data and system requirements needed for central co-ordination and control. As in the Processing Company case, there was no real agreement amongst the stakeholder groups on the strategic goal of tighter central control.

A related issue to the requirements specification for a computer-based IS is the *focus* of the *development* activity, which can incorporate both technical and social elements. In the Processing Company, the focus can be thought of as the technical implementation of the design specification. The project team regarded their job as largely concerned with writing the necessary software to customize the Prosys system, and then getting the computer system to 'work' in a technical sense. There was no significant focus on how the systems would be used in practice, or how the requirements specification might need to be modified to accommodate stakeholder perceptions and work practices.

The overall focus of the development activity under Brown at Sky can be viewed as a combination of an emphasis on speed of implementation with the need for 'organizational fit' of the systems developed. The former aspect has not been stressed in the analysis to date, but IS staff commented how they were consistently pressured during Brown's leadership into working long hours to produce systems in relatively short timescales. However, this drive for speed was not at the expense of accommodating stakeholder views on the current system design, and leadership on development activity oriented to this second focus was provided directly by Brown himself. The focus of the design effort under Taylor can be seen as attempting to obtain organizational agreement on a requirements specification, but since this was not achieved, no new systems were actually developed.

The focus of the development activity for the Premis and Intis systems at the GCA can be seen as simply the technical implementation of the requirements specification. The focus for the Devplan system was different in the sense that some efforts were made to develop prototype systems with a view to more user involvement and feedback. The degree to which this user-oriented focus would be taken seriously in the development of the eventual system was not clear by the end of the research period; although some members of the GCA IS staff were interested in moving the development focus in this direction, there was little indication of high-level backing for such a change.

Social Context

A major element of the social context for the design and development activity for any computer-based IS of organizational significance can be thought of as *senior management attitude*. The importance of senior management reflects their facility to authorize and allocate human and material resources, arising from the perceived legitimacy of their organizational position. Their attitude during the design and development process includes their perceived need for personal involvement in the process, their view on the role of the IS project team, and their previous experience and understanding of the nature of the design and development activity.

In the Processing Company, senior management distanced themselves from the design and development process, except in such instances as the imposition on the IS project team of a firm deadline on system switch-over. They did not see the need for continuous involvement with the IS staff, and regarded the development focus of technical implementation as being the IS team's responsibility. They had little individual or collective experience of computer-based IS, and only started to show some evidence of learning after the disaster of the sales order processing system.

In contrast to the Processing Company, Brown at Sky was personally involved in all design and development activities, even down to taking an active interest in the design of the computer screen displays. He had wide experience and understanding of computer-based IS from his previous career, and maintained close contact with the IS staff. This latter aspect was a mixed blessing from the IS staff's perspective, since although they gained status by being close to the centre of organizational activity, they lost autonomy of action due to the design and development activity being tightly controlled by Brown. Taylor was less experienced than Brown with respect to computer-based IS, and took a more hands-off approach to the structured design activity, implying that he might also have adopted a similar stance in any subsequent development phase.

The senior politicians and administrators driving the strategy for the GCA systems did not get themselves involved to any significant extent with the design and development process, or with the IS project team. They had little experience of computer-based systems at the time of development of the Premis system, and showed little evidence of learning from this experience to inform actions on the later systems, except in such matters as insisting on data input from all agencies involved in the Intis system. The cultural context of Polonia would not have been conducive to a style of direct involvement of senior management with activities at a lower hierarchical level.

The *composition* of the *project team* itself can be thought of as a second important feature of the social context of any design and development process. In the Processing Company, the project team was understaffed and relatively inexperienced, particularly with respect to organizational issues related to computer-based IS. This resource shortage reflected senior management's own lack of understanding and relative neglect of the critical systems development process. The IS project team could perhaps have been helped by the outside consultants who were employed, but these consultants were kept at arm's length and did not get actively involved in the development process. Despite the relative weakness of the IS project team, the computer systems did get written and tested in a technical sense in time for the switch-over, but at the expense of other aspects such as user involvement.

In Sky Building Society, there were no obvious inadequacies in the composition of the IS project teams, although left to their own devices they might have had a stronger technical systems focus. Some IS staff members complained about ad hoc systems development, and they would no doubt have preferred 'better-designed' systems with a rather longer time period to implementation. This option was suppressed by Brown, although we saw that it resurfaced again under Taylor, and became an important context for the subsequent design activity. There is invariably a trade-off between speed and quality of computer systems produced, and this is a critical area to balance in any design and development activity.

In the Government Co-ordination Agency, the IS project teams appeared to be technically competent in general, but they had a lack of experience with respect to being involved in the social and organizational aspects of computer-based IS, coupled with a cultural propensity to see their role as carrying out the orders of their seniors in the hierarchy. As in the Processing Company, outside consultants were used at various stages of the design and development of the focal IS. However, the consultants replicated the technical implementation focus of the GCA IS staff, and appear not to have questioned the overall strategy or the broad top-down approach to the design and development activity.

Social Process

It is widely believed that the *participation* of users and other stakeholder groups in the design and development process is an important factor to consider with respect to any computer-based information system. In the Processing Company, there was some recognition on the part of the IS project team of the need for user participation, at least in such aspects as systems testing. However, a combination of other factors such as the short timescale imposed by senior management, and the relatively short-staffed and inexperienced IS project team, resulted in little actual participation occurring before the sales order processing switch-over.

In Sky, Brown provided direct leadership in the social process of participation of stakeholder groups in the design and development activity for the computer systems. He viewed participation as not merely symbolic in generating support for the systems, but substantively necessary to understanding what was needed at 'the sharp end'; however, it is worth noting that participation did not extend to the broad vision for change which was driving the process, which derived largely from his own ideas. Taylor's whole approach to social process was centred on participation, reflected with respect to computer-based IS in the involvement of both potential users and analysts in the structured systems design approach. It is clear from this case study that, whilst participation may be a desirable feature of the approach to a design and development process, it is not a guarantee of consensus generation.

Participation of central agencies other than the GCA itself was minimal in the case of the Premis system in Polonia, and for the Intis system participation was restricted to ensuring that technical integration of the central agency systems was achieved. Although some efforts with respect to the Devplan system were directed towards pilot projects, there was no evidence of serious efforts towards participation of field staff in the design of the eventual system. This reflected the strategic focus of all the GCA systems as being concerned with central control, rather than in helping lower level staff in their work activities.

A related processual activity to that of participation in design and development concerns *training*. This word has a whole variety of meanings from the transmission of narrow technical expertise through to attempts to change fundamental attitudes to work and work activities. In the Processing Company, such distinctions can be seen as largely irrelevant, since there was no significant training activity at all prior to switch-over. If more time for training had been available, it seems likely that it would have had a narrow technical focus, reflecting the prevailing approach to computerized systems of both senior management and the IS project team.

We see a major difference in the approach to training under Brown at Sky Building Society. He was the driving force for a major and costly training programme for branch staff, which in addition to enabling them to use the new systems in their actual work activities, provided an opportunity for them to generate a new conception of their work role, and symbolized senior management's commitment to the importance of their activities. Brown linked training to processual aspects such as communication and monitoring, and indicated that he needed to be 'fairly tough' in sticking with the training programme in the face of high costs, particularly at times when old systems were being run down and new ones introduced simultaneously.

Training with respect to the Premis and Intis systems in the GCA in Polonia was undertaken in order to show staff how to input data to the systems. No significant effort was made towards the other aspects of training, such as enabling people to use the systems for their own work, or stimulating new attitudes and approaches to their work role and relationships to others. A serious effort in these latter directions would have been linked to participation in the design and development process, since training oriented to a person's work and work-role permits trainees to question aspects of the way the system is currently designed, perhaps implying the need for a revision to the requirements specification and development activity.

A SYNTHESIZED PERSPECTIVE ON IS DESIGN AND DEVELOPMENT

The purpose of this section is to synthesize a perspective on the design and development of computer-based IS, drawing from the preceding discussion in the chapter. The first subsection presents a view on the nature of IS design and development, and the second subsection discusses the role of an IS analyst related to this view. Key features of this perspective are summarized in Table 9.2, and the ideas will be illustrated further in the final section of the chapter.

The Nature of IS Design and Development

The design and development of computer-based IS involves a *social process of communication, learning, and negotiation*, both within and between stakeholder groups including IS analysts, users, and other interested parties such as senior management. The nature of this social process varies widely between different settings, depending on such aspects as the degree of commitment and participation of stakeholder groups, the norms and values enacted by the IS analysts and management, and the type of methodologies used to support the process.

Structured methodologies provide an *interpretative scheme* that is drawn on during design and development. Methodologies with a strong technical focus can provide valuable aids to specific analyst tasks, but can help to reproduce a narrow view of social process if used in isolation. Interpretive methodologies, based for example on participative design or soft systems methodology, offer

TABLE 9.2 *A synthesized perspective on IS design and development*

The Nature of IS Design and Development

- IS design and development involves a social process of communication, learning, and negotiation, both within and between stakeholder groups
- Structured methodologies provide an interpretative scheme drawn on during design and development. Such methodologies can be technically-oriented, or interpretive with conservative or radical overtones
- The design and development of computerized systems involves the shaping of new forms of identity at work, social structures, and interests and values
- Current technological developments are providing capabilities for computer-based support of group work, involving a range of new practical and ethical issues

- -

The Role of an IS Analyst

- The role of IS analyst as systems expert largely avoids human and organizational issues, and the existence of multiple realities
- The IS analyst as management change agent involves facilitation of the discourse between stakeholder groups, with conflict resolved by 'legitimate' authority
- The role of the IS analyst as moral agent can involve alignment with labour, or critical reflection aimed at emancipation of all parties to the discourse

ways of addressing human and organizational issues and the multiple realities of different stakeholder groups. Such methodologies do not always enable conflict to be resolved and can reproduce existing inequities; more radical approaches emphasize the need to consciously empower less advantaged groups, or to subject taken-for-granted assumptions of the harmony perspective to critical analysis.

The design and development of computerized systems involves the shaping of *new forms of identity* at work, *new social structures* in organizational life, and new *interests and value systems*. Current technological developments are providing capabilities for computer-based support of group work, and this brings with it a whole series of new practical and ethical issues. These include the need for better mutual learning between analysts and user groups, and the desirability of new forms of computer-supported group work, bearing in mind individual needs in such areas as personal autonomy and privacy.

The Role of an IS Analyst

An IS analyst can adopt a range of very different roles during the design and development process. The relatively common enactment of the *IS analyst as systems expert* largely avoids human and organizational issues and the existence of multiple realities. It assumes that these aspects of the context and process of design and development are not within the scope of the analyst's job. A major problem in this respect is that the need to consider such issues can then sometimes be seen as not being the responsibility of any group, either the IS analysts or management.

A second role for an IS analyst is that of *management change agent*, concerned with monitoring and facilitating the discourse between stakeholder groups on the design and development of the computer-based system. This role is similar to the ideal type of IS analyst as facilitator described by Hirschheim and Klein and discussed earlier in the chapter, where it was argued that the analyst's stance is to see any outcome from the discourse as legitimate. However, one qualification is needed to this ideal type from the perspective of this book. The analyst is a consciously reflective agent, and the role of the IS analyst as management change agent implies their acceptance of the 'legitimate' authority of management to resolve conflict by the exercise of power where necessary.

A third role for the IS analyst is that of *moral agent* in the design and development process. This role can involve, for example, the deliberate aligning of the analyst on the side of labour rather than management. Alternatively, the approach can involve a type of critical action research, that again centres itself on moral values, but does not necessarily align itself with any particular group in advance. This latter role is addressed to the learning and emancipation of all parties to the discourse, and includes critical reflection in such areas as power and political action, social differentiation, and the bias and limitations of particular language use.

THE PRACTICE OF IS DESIGN AND DEVELOPMENT

The discussion which follows is oriented to the practice of an IS analyst adopting a broadly interpretive approach, with the roles of management change agent or moral agent. The purpose of analyst activity in these roles is to seriously address the human and organizational issues in connection with the design and development of a computer-based system. Of course, a major and important part of the analyst's task will also be to carry out rapid and effective development of the technical systems. This latter role should not be seen to be downgraded in importance by our discussion here. The argument is that it is a necessary but not sufficient element in successful systems development; the provision of ideas and methods to support the analyst's technical role is essential, but is not the purpose of this book.

The material below is focused around the themes developed in the second section of the chapter, which derived from the three case studies in Part II. The section aims to provide some ideas and issues that it would be worthwhile to discuss in any particular practical context; the discussion is divided into three broad task areas, namely focusing system design, understanding development context, and facilitating development process. Key issues for debate arising from the discussion are summarized in Tables 9.3 to 9.5.

Focusing System Design

A key element of the content of any design and development activity is the production of a *requirements specification*, but the origins, purpose, and status of such a specification can vary widely between different cases. From the perspective in this book, the origins of the specification should be related back to a shared strategic vision for change. The use of participative methods in the production of a requirements specification, in the absence of any shared vision for change, runs the risk of not generating a consensus for action, in addition to being very time-consuming and perhaps producing 'systems for today'. The 'shared' vision for change may have been largely developed by a single individual or senior group, or in a more participative fashion. A radical view of the former of these scenarios would see the resultant specification as likely to reproduce the authority and reflect the vested interests of the powerful.

The purpose of the requirements specification, from an interpretive perspective, should be seen not as a current description of the organization's needs in the area of interest, but as an identification of desirable capabilities of the planned system as an intermediate step in a continuing process. Even when the 'final' specification is produced, the actual use of the resultant system will differ from that as conceived, and evaluations of this knowledge-

TABLE 9.3 *Some issues for debate on focusing system design*

Requirements Specification

- Origins of the specification should be related to vision for change
- The use of participative design methods, in the absence of a shared vision for change, may not generate a consensus for action
- Purpose of the requirements specification should be the identification of desirable capabilities, seen as an intermediate step in a continuing process
- If the status of the requirements specification merely reflects imposed authority, then the resultant computer system may not be successful in use

Development Focus

- Technical focus is essential, together with focus on organizational fit
- The non-technical development focus can be summarized as one of communication, learning, and negotiation
- To empower less advantaged groups, one approach is positive discrimination
- An alternative approach is to emphasize critical debate on ethical issues

in-use will lead to later modification of the system and eventually to replacement.

The status of a requirements specification should be as an embodiment of the norms and values of the vision for change, based on shared or at least non-contested values. If the status of the requirements specification merely reflects the imposed authority of a central organizational or political group, and does not encapsulate norms which are sufficiently shared by relevant stakeholder groups, then the resultant computer system may not be successful in use. These groups may not incorporate the system into changed work activities or new conceptualizations of their work roles.

A related issue to the requirements specification for a computer-based IS is the *development focus*. From an interpretive perspective, this should not solely be concerned with successful technical implementation, although this is of course essential, but should also be centred on the organizational fit of the developed systems. Consideration should be given to how the new system is likely to modify and facilitate new individual work activities and social interactions. The non-technical development focus can be summarized as one of communication, learning, and negotiation.

From a more radical standpoint, the development focus as stated above may not empower less advantaged groups to exercise adequate autonomy in their work lives, or to have some control of their working environment. One approach to address this issue is to practise positive discrimination in favour of labour in the labour/management divide, for example by giving workers a large element of direct control of the development process. An alternative approach would be to place emphasis on the need to ensure serious critical debate on ethical issues between all interested parties.

Understanding Development Context

A major element of the social context for any design and development activity can be thought of as *senior management attitude*. If we conceptualize the development focus as one of learning, communication, and negotiation, then it is evident that senior management should not be distanced from the process, but must be intimately involved with it. Their lack of involvement is likely to be taken as a symbolic signal of low levels of commitment to the proposed systems. They will also be unable to learn and negotiate during the process, both vital roles for them to play in view of the legitimacy conferred by their organizational position.

Senior management should view the role of the IS project team not as just involving technical matters, but they should also see analysts as facilitators of the change process. A more enlightened view might also suggest that senior management should view IS analysts as moral agents in the discourse concerning design and development, with a legitimate role in questioning

TABLE 9.4 *Some issues for debate on understanding development context*

Senior Management Attitude

- Senior management need to be intimately involved with development activity, in order to signal commitment, learn, and negotiate
- Senior management should view the IS analysts as facilitators of change
- An enlightened view would see IS analysts as legitimately involved in questioning ethical values, including those of senior management
- Previous experience and understanding of computer-based IS is needed; dimensions of understanding include both technical and organizational issues

Project Team Composition

- The project team needs a blend of technical, application domain, and organizational knowledge
- Not all members of the team can possess similar levels of knowledge; gatekeeper role to the team in specific area is one approach
- Consultants can enhance project team capability, but complementary role of the consultants is a critical issue

ethical values, including for example those of senior management themselves. Such a view is rare in contemporary business and governmental organizations, but its incorporation would represent an emancipatory shift for all organizational members.

The need for senior management to have previous experience and understanding of computer-based IS was noted in the findings from the case studies. Experience cannot be easily obtained if not already present, although at least one member of a senior management team could be promoted or recruited to contribute to this dimension. Understanding is a more complex issue, since experience does not always generate enhanced understanding. A relevant component of understanding is knowledge concerning the human and organizational issues addressed in this book, but good technical knowledge is also essential.

The *project team composition* is a second important feature of the social context of any design and development activity. There is a need in this team for a blend of technical, application domain, and organizational knowledge, the last of these being the primary focus of this book. It is not necessary, or feasible, for all members of the project team to possess similar levels of knowledge in all these areas; individuals acting as gatekeepers to the team in a particular area is one way of addressing the practicalities of the thin spread of knowledge. It is worth noting that all IS analysts in the project team have an equal human responsibility as moral agents.

The constructive use of consultants can be one way to enhance an existing project team composition, and to stimulate a learning process on all sides. This requires careful thought on the role of the consultants; such a role could be on technical or social aspects of computer-based systems, or could involve the use of consultants in the role of facilitators of a critical debate in the case of an emancipatory approach to organizational action. However, the choice of consultants with a technical focus, in the case where the IS analysts have a similar view, is likely to be counterproductive by reproducing a narrow technical bias to the exclusion of wider social and organizational issues.

Facilitating Development Process

The *participation* of users and other stakeholder groups in the design and development process can be considered as essential, not just in relatively narrow areas such as systems testing, but also in the refining and modifying of the appropriateness of particular systems to support their work activities and their contact with other work groups. The use of formal interpretive methodologies, such as those based on participative design or soft systems methodology, can be helpful here. If conflict is simply resolved by the exercise of formal authority, or participation takes place after the basic strategy has been decided by others, then such methodologies may support the reproduction of existing power structures, and can even be viewed as an exercise in manipulation.

There are some interesting new issues involving participation with respect to the computer support of group work, where technological developments are

TABLE 9.5 Some issues for debate on facilitating development process

Participation

- The participation of stakeholder groups is essential, in systems testing, but also the refining of systems to support their work and work contacts
- The use of formal interpretive methodologies can be helpful, although may be viewed as manipulation in some circumstances
- New participation issues in computer support of group work, implying need for deeper contact between analysts and users in process of mutual learning

Training

- Training should involve transmission of technical expertise, but also be concerned with attitudinal change towards work, social structures, and values
- The provision of adequate resources is a signal of commitment by management to the computer systems and to attitudinal change
- A radical view of IS training would see it as involving all organizational members in critical analyses of such issues as empowerment

providing the potential for innovative systems. In view of the subtleties of the human interaction in group work, and its considerable reliance on tacit knowledge which cannot be articulated (Ehn 1988), there is a need for new forms of learning between the designers and users of computer systems in the group work area. Designers need to learn about the group's activities in a relatively deep way, perhaps by being actively involved themselves; users need to learn about new technological possibilities. Participation in this context can be viewed as a two-way process of mutual learning.

A related processual activity to that of participation in design and development is that of *training*. This should involve not just the transmission of narrow technical expertise in system use, although this is certainly needed and is often badly handled in practice. Training should also be viewed as centrally concerned with attitudinal change towards new identities at work, new social structures, and new value systems. The provision of adequate resources for training activities represents a symbolic commitment by management to the computer systems and to the need for attitudinal change. The process of mutual learning, referred to above in the context of computer support for group work, can be seen as a form of immersion training for both analysts and users. A radical view of IS training would see it as involving all organizational members, with critical analyses of such issues as empowerment being part of the training agenda for everybody, including senior management.

REFERENCES

Alvarez, R., and Gaffney, M. E. (1989) 'Scandinavian approaches: promises and barriers', in *Systems Development for Human Progress* (eds H. K. Klein and K. Kumar), North-Holland, Amsterdam.
Alvarez, R., and Klein, H. K. (1989) 'Information systems development for human progress?', in *Systems Development for Human Progress* (eds H. K. Klein and K. Kumar), North-Holland, Amsterdam.
Avison, D. E., and Wood-Harper, A. T. (1990) *Multiview: An Exploration in Information Systems Development*, Blackwell Scientific, Oxford.
Bødker, S., Ehn, P., Kammersgaard, J., Kyng, M., and Sundblad, Y. (1987) 'A UTOPIAN experience: on design of powerful computer-based tools for skilled graphic workers', in *Computers and Democracy* (eds G. Bjerknes, P. Ehn and M. Kyng), Avebury, Aldershot.
Boland, R. J. (1979) 'Control, causality and information system requirements', *Accounting, Organizations and Society*, **4**, No. 4, 259–272.
Boland, R. J., and Day, W. F. (1989) 'The experience of system design: a hermeneutic of organizational action', *Scandinavian Journal of Management*, **5**, No. 2, 87–104.
Checkland, P. (1981) *Systems Thinking, Systems Practice*, Wiley, Chichester.
Checkland, P., and Scholes, J. (1990) *Soft Systems Methodology in Action*, Wiley, Chichester.
Curtis, B., Krasner, H., and Iscoe, N. (1988) 'A field study of the software design process for large systems', *Communications of the ACM*, **31**, No. 11, 1268–1287.
Ehn, P. (1988) *Work Oriented Design of Computer Artefacts*, Arbetslivscentrum, Stockholm.
Ehn, P., and Kyng, M. (1987) 'The collective resource approach to systems design',

in *Computers and Democracy* (eds G. Bjerknes, P. Ehn and M. Kyng), Avebury, Aldershot.

Floyd, C., Mehl, W.-M., Reisin, F.-M., Schmidt, G., and Wolf, G. (1989) 'Out of Scandinavia: alternative approaches to software development and design', *Human Computer Interaction*, **4**, 17–57.

Habermas, J. (1972) *Knowledge and Human Interests*, Heinemann, London.

Hirschheim, R., and Klein, H. K. (1989) 'Four paradigms of information systems development', *Communications of the ACM*, **32**, No. 10, 1199–1216.

Howard, R. (1987) 'Systems design and social responsibility: the political implications of "computer-supported cooperative work"', *Office, Technology and People*, **3**, No. 2, 175–187.

Iivari, J. (1989) 'A methodology for IS development as organizational change: a pragmatic contingency approach', in *Systems Development for Human Progress* (eds H. K. Klein and K. Kumar), North-Holland, Amsterdam.

Jones, M., and Walsham, G. (1992) 'The limits of the knowable: organisational and design knowledge in systems development', in *The Impact of Computer Supported Technologies on Information Systems Development* (eds K. E. Kendall, K. Lyytinen and J. I. DeGross), North-Holland, Amsterdam.

Jönsson, S. (1991) 'Action research', in *Information Systems Research: Contemporary Approaches and Emergent Traditions* (eds H.-E. Nissen, H. K. Klein and R. A. Hirschheim), North-Holland, Amsterdam.

Kling, R. (1991) 'Cooperation, coordination and control in computer-supported work', *Communications of the ACM*, **34**, No. 12, 83–88.

Kyng, M. (1991) 'Designing for cooperation: cooperating in design', *Communications of the ACM*, **34**, No. 12, 65–73.

Maclaren, R., Hornby, P., Robson, J., O'Brien, P., Cleg, C., and Richardson, S. (1991) *Systems Design Methods—The Human Dimension*, D.T.I. Project IED/4/1249, London.

McCarthy, T. (1978) *The Critical Theory of Jürgen Habermas*, MIT Press, Boston.

Mumford, E. (1981) 'Participative systems design: structure and method', *Systems, Objectives, Solutions*, **1**, 5–19.

Mumford, E., and Weir, M. (1979) *Computer Systems in Work Design: The ETHICS Method*, Wiley, New York.

Newman, M., and Noble, F. (1990) 'User involvement as an interaction process: a case study', *Information Systems Research*, **1**, No. 1, 89–113.

Nygaard, K., and Sorgaard, P. (1987) 'The perspective concept in informatics', in *Computers and Democracy* (eds G. Bjerknes, P. Ehn and M. Kyng), Avebury, Aldershot.

Orlikowski, W. J. (1992) 'The duality of technology: rethinking the concept of technology in organizations', *Organization Science*, **3**, No. 3, 398–427.

Robey, D., and Markus, M. L. (1984) 'Rituals in information system design', *MIS Quarterly*, **8**, No. 1, 5–15.

Schäfer, G. (1988) (ed.) *Functional Analysis of Office Requirements: A Multiperspective Approach*, Wiley, Chichester.

Schneiderman, B., and Carroll, J. M. (1988) 'Ecological studies of professional programmers: guest editors' introduction', *Communications of the ACM*, **31**, No. 11, 1256–1258.

Wilson, B. (1984) *Systems: Concepts, Methodologies and Applications*, Wiley, Chichester.

Wilson, B. (1989) 'A systems methodology for information requirements analysis', in *Systems Development for Human Progress* (eds H. K. Klein and K. Kumar), North-Holland, Amsterdam.

Zuboff, S. (1988) *In the Age of the Smart Machine*, Basic Books, New York.

Chapter 10
IMPLEMENTATION

This chapter is concerned with the issue of implementation. The term implementation is used in different ways in the context of computer-based information systems. It is sometimes used to mean technical implementation, namely ensuring that system development is completed and that the system functions adequately in a technical sense. At other times, it is used to refer to human and social aspects of implementation, such as that the system is used frequently by organization members or that it is considered valuable to them in their personal work activities or co-ordination with others. The focus in this chapter will be on the second category, and the term organizational implementation will be used to summarize the human and social aspects of the implementation of IS in organizations.

The chapter is divided into four sections, and the first section reviews some *literature on implementation*. The second section compares and contrasts the findings on organizational implementation from the case studies in Part II, based around some selected *themes on IS implementation* arising from the earlier analyses. The third section then *synthesizes a perspective* on IS implementation drawing from the material in the previous sections. In the final section, this perspective is applied to a discussion of the *implementation practice*, based around the set of themes developed from the case material, and aimed to provide some issues for debate in any particular context.

RELEVANT LITERATURE ON IMPLEMENTATION

The purpose of this section is to describe and discuss some relevant literature on organizational implementation, and to relate ideas from this work to the earlier case studies where appropriate. The first subsection addresses some interesting work concerned with the relationship between policy and implementation, with a focus on ambiguity. The second subsection is centred on standard literature on the implementation of management science and information systems, taking a factor or process approach. The final subsection deals with some literature on IS implementation and organizational change.

Implementation and the Policy Process

The material in this subsection is largely derived from an article by Baier, March and Sætren (1988) dealing with the relationship between implementation and the policy process in large administrative organizations such as government bodies and commercial enterprises. The authors state that there are two common interpretations of implementation problems, namely bureaucratic incompetence in implementing policy and difficulties due to conflicts of interest. They consider that these interpretations are sensible, but emphasize the importance of a third interpretation, concerned with an appreciation of the ambiguity inherent in the policy-making process and its links to implementation problems.

Baier, March and Sætren argue that the details of a policy's execution can be less important to policy makers than its proclamation. They give an example of the United States Congress where the act of voting for legislation with appropriate symbolic meaning can be more important to legislators than its implementation. An interest in the support of constituents leads policy makers to be vigorous in enacting policies but lax in enforcing them. In order to secure agreement on policy, Baier, March and Sætren argue that policies are often oversold, the real level of support for the policy is exaggerated, and one common method for securing policy support is to deliberately increase the ambiguity of a proposed policy. The authors conclude that official policy as a consequence is likely to be vague, contradictory, or adopted without generally shared expectations about its meaning or implementation.

This theme of ambiguity inherent in official policies is an example of the more general phenomenon of ambiguity in all organizational activities. Martin and Meyerson (1988) identify three types of ambiguity: uncertainty, contradiction, and confusion. Uncertainty refers to a lack of predictability in, for example, the organization's technology or environment. Contradiction refers to cultural manifestations and interpretations that are capable of multiple meanings. Confusion is caused by ignorance or lack of information. Whilst these categories are rather indistinct and overlapping, all three types certainly influence the policy-making process and its results.

Baier, March and Sætren draw some interesting conclusions concerning likely responses to policy ambiguity. They argue that administrative agencies charged with the implementation of ambiguous policies may tend to adopt a posture of creative autonomy, involving the establishment of independent political constituencies, the treatment of policy as problematic, and the expectation that policy makers will be uncertain or in conflict about the expected consequences of a policy or its importance. Such agencies come to realize that they cannot escape criticism by arguing that they were following policy, but must establish an independent political basis for their actions. As the actions of administrative agencies become more flexible, it then becomes

212 INTERPRETING INFORMATION SYSTEMS IN ORGANIZATIONS

easier for policy makers to use policy ambiguity as a basis for forming coalitions. The authors conclude that it is not hard to see why we might thus observe organizations functioning with only a loose coupling between policies and actions, between plans and behaviour, and between policy makers and administrators.

Although the above literature did not address the implementation of computer-based information systems and its links to IS strategy or policy, we can view this as a special case, and use our earlier case studies to illustrate some of the ideas. In the Processing Company, the policy of installing a new MRP system had symbolic importance as a major effort towards improving organizational performance, which had been unsatisfactory for some time previously. However, the policy was ambiguous, at least in the sense that it was adopted without generally shared expectations about its meaning for new work activities and roles in the organization and how these were to be implemented. The response of the 'administrative agency' charged with implementation, which in this case was largely the IS project team, could certainly not be characterized as creative autonomy. For example, they were unable to establish any independent credibility with important stakeholder groups such as the sales order processing staff. The response of the IS project team to issues of organizational implementation was largely to ignore them.

Brown's broad IS policy at Sky Building Society, concerned with improved customer service via decentralized IS, can be viewed as sufficiently ambiguous to readily command general support. Brown was not, however, lax in the implementation of policy but pursued it with great vigour. One explanation for this vigour may be that, unlike politicians in the US Congress, Brown's personal performance would be measured by shareholders and potential future employers in terms reflecting implementation success, rather than in the symbolic attributes of general policies. The 'administrative agency' of the IS staff at Sky, with leadership provided by Brown, showed considerable creativity in responding to other stakeholder groups during the design and development phases of the new computer systems, and thus carried political credibility with these groups. In this case, the key player in the policy-making process was also directly involved in policy implementation, and ambiguity in general policy was not a hindrance to its creative implementation.

The Government Co-ordination Agency provides perhaps the most direct example of the earlier ideas. This correspondence may be due to its position as a government agency responsible to national-level politicians, which was one of the key areas used by Baier, March and Sætren to develop their analysis. The Polonian government's approach to policy fits well with the view of politicians concerned largely with symbolic affirmation of loyalty and support for the economic development of the disadvantaged, but much less concerned with the effective implementation of this policy via computer-based information systems. Official IS policy was invariably vague, and certainly adopted without generally shared expectations about its meaning for new work activities of agencies, and how these would be implemented. The administrative agency charged with implementation, the GCA, appeared to show no creative autonomy on the organizational aspects of policy implementation, for example by not establishing any independent credibility with the other central agencies. Instead, the GCA concentrated primarily on the technical aspects of the computerized systems. One can suggest that creative autonomy of government agencies is not a concept that was in tune with government thinking or cultural attitudes in Polonia at the time of the research.

Literature on MS/IS Implementation

A sizeable body of published work exists on implementation in the context of management science (MS) and operational research (see, for example, Ginzberg and Schultz 1987). This work is not always specifically concerned with computer-based IS, but there is invariably a strong overlap of interest. A major strand in this literature is the factor approach, which aims to identify a group of variables of relevance to implementation outcomes by sampling a series of successful and unsuccessful projects. Results from this approach include the importance of top management support and user involvement in implementing change. Walsham (1992) notes that these factors can be related to a broader view of the context and process of implementation. For example, top management support can be seen as a contextual condition, which is desirable in principle in terms of providing appropriate strategic vision and managerial authority. It is also relevant to a processual analysis to help bring about the process of cultural change with the right amount of political backing. However, the factors are merely elements which it may be helpful to include in a broader analysis, since an understanding of context and the management of process in any particular example, as demonstrated by our earlier case studies, goes far beyond such relatively simplistic concepts.

A more comprehensive list and classification of factors of relevance to IS implementation is given by Lyytinen and Hirschheim (1987) under the heading of 'reasons for IS failure'. These include technical features of the IS itself; features of the IS environment including individual, organizational, and environmental aspects; features of the systems development process such as the methods used or the amount of attention given to decision-making processes; and features of the systems development environment such as the organizational knowledge possessed by system developers or amounts of user education. This list of factors provides a useful classification of much of the IS implementation literature but, as noted by the authors themselves, interactions between the factors are crucial. In addition, the factors approach, whilst it takes some account of the human and social aspects of IS implementation, has a rather static feel to it, with no consideration of the dynamics of the process of organizational implementation.

An alternative approach to that of the identification of factors is to view implementation as a process, although much early work in this area was based on rather rigid models that see process as consisting of distinct, sequential stages. Srinivasan and Davis (1987) argue that this view is obsolete for contemporary computer-based IS, since the sequential handling of issues that is implicit in the process model literature does not adequately capture the complexity of the dynamics of change in such areas as user-developer interaction. They propose an alternative to the process model approach based on the centrality of users in the contemporary development of computerized systems. They characterize implementation as encompassing the vision of creating an environment in which a diverse array of users has convenient access to the development tools, training and support needed to carry out implementation tasks either on their own or through intermediaries. This view echoes earlier work on implementation with a user-centred focus (Lucas 1981). The case studies in Part II can be taken at one level to illustrate the importance of a user-centred focus, but such a focus provides a very limited view of the whole process of organizational implementation of computer-based IS, which involves complex interaction of stakeholder groups, and is a theme running all the way through strategy development, evaluation, and systems development.

IS Implementation and Organizational Change

The literature on organizational implementation of computer-based IS discussed in this subsection is directly concerned with the dynamics of organizational change. The work reviewed is broadly based on the political and cultural metaphors of organization, and includes both case descriptions of organizational change processes and more prescriptive material on practical methods of intervention for an IS implementer. Some of this literature was touched on briefly in Chapter 2, but a more detailed account is given here, and the focus is on organizational implementation.

An early article by Keen (1981) viewed information systems development and implementation as 'an intensely political' as well as technical process. Keen saw the organizational change associated with a computer-based IS as requiring a process of coalition building. He argued that this cannot be achieved by staff analysts, who are too easily caught in the middle with no formal powers, but requires information systems managers with authority and resources for negotiation. Keen suggested some tactical approaches to be adopted by such people to counter resistance from 'counterimplementers'. These tactics include ensuring that the implementer has a contract for change; seeking out resistance as a signal to be responded to; relying on face-to-face contact; becoming an insider and working hard to build personal credibility; and co-opting users early.

A similar political stance on implementation is taken by Markus and Pfeffer (1983) in the context of accounting and control systems. They argue that if the goal of the implementers is to minimize resistance and maximize system success, then the systems can be designed to be consonant with 'organizational power distributions and cultures'. If, however, the goal is to effect significant organizational change, the issues of resistance and organizational implementation need to be addressed explicitly. Under these circumstances, the authors argue that various political strategies and tactics are needed in order to achieve effective implementation. They note various political skills of value to implementers including facility with the use of political language, the ability to build coalitions with other interests, knowledge of the distribution of power, various personal characteristics, and the ability to argue one's position selectively using the information that is available.

The article by Markus and Pfeffer deals directly with the political aspects of organizational change, but an important subsidiary theme is concerned with the clash between cultures and the need for cultural change in order to address issues of organizational implementation. For example, the authors describe an attempt to implement a computerized information system in the cardiology division of a major teaching hospital. Their analysis showed that it was the symbolic aspects of the system which led to system failure. The system was designed in the spirit of statistical epidemiology, which was sharply at odds with the ethos of clinical care amongst its potential users. Markus and Pfeffer conclude from this case, and others, that unless design and implementation efforts address the structural features of organizations, involving power distributions and cultures, they will not be successful, even if they employ process strategies such as participative design. In other words, new social structures are needed to achieve high levels of implementation success on measures such as effectiveness in use or stakeholder satisfaction.

Some more recent work by Willcocks and Mark (1989) supports the hypothesis of the need for IS implementers to take cultural and political change seriously. The article describes approaches to the implementation of computer-based IS in the UK National Health Service, and criticizes aspects such as the lack of resources for information technology (IT) training. The authors suggest that such training should be aimed at producing a supportive culture for the introduction and operation of IT, and at helping users to develop the ability to use IT-based systems in their work. The article concludes that, if general management is to operate successfully and bring in IT to serve its purposes, it must establish political and cultural support for its objectives and their implementation, through identifying and responding to other group and individual objectives in the organization. This conclusion has a rather managerialist emphasis, since it implies that the purposes of general management are pre-eminent, which is only one view in the fiercely political climate of organizational change in the National Health Service.

A rather different area of implementation research is described by Land, Le Quesne and Wijegunaratne (1989), who investigated implementation in four different organizations of a new computer-aided software engineering tool, namely the Integrated Project Support Environment (IPSE), aimed at improving productivity and enhancing quality in software development processes. Although the results of the research are presented as a set of six 'factors' of importance to implementation success, which as commented earlier reflects a rather static approach to the implementation process, it is interesting to note that the factors identified are primarily related to cultural aspects of the organization. They include the motivation for installing an IPSE; the organizational commitment to it; organizational culture; management style; nature of the implementation process; and the organization's familiarity and experience with standard ways of working.

The final paper reviewed in this subsection describes a single case study of the introduction of an MRP system into a medium-sized manufacturing firm (Kling and Iacono 1984); elements of this Printco case were discussed earlier in Chapter 3. The emphasis of the article is on the political nature of implementation, and the authors note that political campaigns can continue throughout the life of a computer-based IS, including the period of post-implementation. Key actors built support for the MRP system by a variety of means including 'ideological training' on the merits of the system, and manipulating structural arrangements for allocating computing resources. In addition to building support for campaigns of action, 'opposition was quieted' by such means as the setting up of a legitimizing decision-making body, and later co-opting to this body an individual in charge of microcomputers, in order to gain control over the proliferation and development of microcomputing. Kling and Iacono conclude the paper by asking whether such 'politics of control' are always required to effectively implement large-scale computer-based IS, and whether 'ideologies' are essential to give meaning to an organizational strategy of computerization and to mobilize support.

Some of the ideas from the above literature can be illustrated by our earlier case studies. In the Processing Company, there was no serious attempt at coalition building with respect to the new MRP system, and political tactics such as becoming an insider with respect to critical stakeholder groups, and co-opting users early, did not happen. There was no clear ideology other than that of central control, and certainly no ideological training. Potential opposition was ignored rather than 'quieted', and only surfaced after the implementation failure of the sales order processing system.

Brown at Sky Building Society provides a good example of a skilled political tactician who followed many of the approaches suggested in the article by Keen, such as face-to-face contact and co-opting users early. At a more strategic level, Brown was involved in the development of ideology and in coalition building, and he used ideological training as a major tactical approach, with the branch staff for example. He consciously set about 'quieting opposition', using a variety of tactical means, including enhancing the status of the IS staff to 'sugar the pill' of reduced autonomy. Taylor at Sky was unable to successfully build coalitions and to quiet opposition in the time period following Brown's leadership, but Taylor was showing more interest in the politics of control by the end of this period.

There was no political 'fixer' or implementer at the Government Co-ordination Agency, and thus no serious effort seems to have been made to build coalitions at the level of the central agencies. There was a strong political ideology amongst the senior politicians based around the central control of development projects. However, the ideology on how IS was to be used to address this was very general in nature and contested by different parties, and there was no ideological training. Opposition to the new computerized systems was not quieted, and was able to express itself by non-use of the systems developed, rather than by open disagreement.

THEMES FROM THE CASE STUDIES

This section brings together material on organizational implementation arising directly from the case studies in Part II under the headings of content, social context, and social process. The discussion is organized around a set of themes derived from the case analyses; these themes are summarized in Table 10.1.

TABLE 10.1 Themes on IS implementation from the case studies

Content
• Implementation measures
• Learning
Social Context
• Leadership style
• Implementation responsibility
Social Process
• Linking theme
• Management of change

Content

Even if we restrict ourselves to the organizational aspects of implementation, the definition of 'successful' implementation remains problematic. Alternative *implementation measures* include the meeting of strategic objectives, a high level of system use, effectiveness in use in terms of supporting particular organizational activities or areas, and the expressed satisfaction of various stakeholder groups including system users. High achievement on all of these measures may not be feasible, and computer systems can normally be regarded as a relative success or failure in terms of organizational implementation, dependent on their performance on particular measures and the weight that is placed on those measures.

In the Processing Company, the sales order processing system performed badly across a wide range of implementation measures. The system was used after switch-over, but proved so ineffective in the support of work activities that chaos in order deliveries resulted and substantial business was lost. Stakeholder groups such as the sales order processing staff and the warehousemen were highly dissatisfied with the new system. The strategic objective of installing the first stage of an MRP system was achieved in the end, but at a very high organizational cost.

In contrast to the Processing Company, the computer-based IS developed at Sky under Brown can be considered to be successful across a range of implementation measures, including effectiveness in use, user satisfaction of groups such as the branch staff, and the meeting of the strategic objective of decentralized IS providing improved customer service. Indeed, the systems can be viewed as a cornerstone for the exceptional financial performance of Sky under Brown's leadership. Brown also achieved some key personal goals, as seen by a senior colleague, in terms of demonstrating a high level of capability enabling him to obtain a similar job in a larger organization. Success was achieved on most of the obvious implementation measures, but there were exceptions: for example, the systems staff assessed the computer systems badly in terms of the short-termism inherent in Brown's approach to systems development, and in terms of the high levels of work pressure they experienced during his time as leader.

With respect to the Government Co-ordination Agency in Polonia, the important implementation measure of effectiveness in use was largely not achieved by the Premis and Intis systems. The systems also scored poorly on assessment of satisfaction by stakeholder groups such as the other central agencies. It can be argued that the systems met important political stakeholder's strategic objectives of visible systems designed for central control purposes, reinforcing the norm of central control. However, in view of the ineffectiveness of the systems in use, closer central control of development projects was not actually achieved. One could not be certain how the Devplan system would perform on organizational implementation measures, but it seemed likely that value to the work activities of lower level staff would not be achieved unless there was a considerable change in approach.

No case study is ever one of implementation failure across all measures, since at the very least *learning* takes place which provides a changed social context for systems redesign and for the development of new systems. Several months after the disastrous switch-over at the Processing Company, the sales order processing system passed into routine use. In addition, senior management and the computer project team had started to take a more thoughtful stance on the role and impact of computerized systems. However, there were major direct costs of the initial implementation failure, and there was a serious delay in the technical implementation of the rest of the MRP system; discussions on how to proceed were still taking place two years later.

Learning could be considered to be built in for all stakeholder groups on a continuous basis in Brown's approach to the design and development of computer-based IS at Sky. With respect to other areas such as IS strategy, Brown was keen to learn himself; it is less obvious that this learning involved others, and this lack of involvement may partly account for the strategic vacuum after Brown's departure. The IS staff learnt about ad hoc systems development during Brown's leadership, which enabled them to exert vigorous pressure for more orthodox approaches after he left. Taylor can be considered to have learnt from the failure to implement an agreed way forward following his experiment in widespread participation. By the end of the research period, he had come to recognize the need for an action orientation, although it was uncertain exactly how this would translate into a changed implementation approach on his part.

In the Government Co-ordination Agency, the relative bleakness of the implementation picture can be brightened in a small way by the clear evidence of learning on the part of some of the IS staff in the GCA. They had realized that the systems which had been developed in relative isolation from users were not well regarded by these users and were not being utilized by them to any substantial extent. In consequence, they were starting to think somewhat differently with respect to the Devplan system; however, there was little evidence of a similar learning process on the part of senior politicians responsible for IS strategy.

Social Context

An important element of the social context for the whole IS implementation activity can be thought of as the *leadership style* normally provided by senior management or its equivalent. The senior management leadership in the Processing Company can be considered as relatively autocratic with respect to IS strategy, reliant on formal legitimation procedures with respect to IS evaluation, and basically uninvolved in design and development. Senior management were thus remote from other stakeholder groups during each of the major activities of the computerization project.

Brown's leadership style at Sky can be described as highly personal and autocratic with respect to IS strategy and evaluation, but participative and involved where design and development was concerned. In contrast, Taylor pursued a participative style with respect to strategy, although he was not deeply involved in the IS aspects of this. The Sky case study should not be taken to imply that Brown's leadership style is the 'right' way in a total sense. Some negative aspects of implementation such as short-termism and little encouragement for strategic learning of others have been noted above. In addition, Brown's style can be challenged from a radical standpoint, as discussed in the previous chapter, as to whether the computer systems developed were genuinely in the best interests of most of Sky's workforce. Nevertheless, Brown's hands-on leadership style during design and development ensured a depth of contact between senior management and other stakeholder groups in at least one major phase of the computerization process, enabling mutual learning between them to take place.

The leadership style provided by senior management in the Government Co-ordination Agency can be considered to be even more remote from lower level stakeholder groups than that in the Processing Company. The cultural context of Polonia was reflected in this top-down hierarchical approach to leadership, and such inbred social attitudes are slow to change in any society. One must question whether this style is compatible with the achievement of successful organizational implementation of computer-based IS, if we put emphasis on the support of changed work activities and social interaction between lower level stakeholder groups as an important implementation measure.

A related element to the social context provided by leadership style can be thought of as the *implementation responsibility* for computer-based IS. The term implementation is again being used in a non-technical sense here, and there is a danger in IS projects that this organizational responsibility is not perceived by any person or group to be their problem. This was largely the case in the Processing Company. The head of the project team was at least aware of the need for more user contact and training, but under the time and resource pressure exerted by senior management, he gave low weight in the end to any personal responsibility for organizational implementation.

The case of Sky Building Society under Brown is also relatively clear, although rather different to the Processing Company. Brown accepted full personal responsibility and provided the leadership for organizational implementation of the computerized systems, although he did not of course do all the detailed work himself. Taylor seems to have had a more ambivalent view, and at first appeared to tacitly assign implementation responsibility away from himself, even at the strategy stage. There was some evidence that this was changing by the end of the research period.

The Government Co-ordination Agency was similar to the Processing Company in that no one saw themselves as owning the responsibility for organizational implementation, except in such limited areas as data input for the Intis system. The location of the GCA in the Prime Minister's Department meant that it was very close to the centre of political power and could draw on facilities to ensure compliance on issues such as data supply. However, even if the IS staff in the GCA had felt that the broader aspects of organizational implementation were their responsibility, it would have been difficult for them to suggest a major change in the implementation approach, since it could have been perceived as political disloyalty.

Social Process

One way of thinking about the social process of organizational implementation is to see it as a *linking theme* which runs through all social aspects of computer-based IS, and in particular is interwoven with the key issues discussed in earlier chapters of IS strategy, evaluation, and design and development. If one takes this view, then the relative success or failure of the computer systems on the various implementation measures can be related to a synthesis of the organizational implementation elements of these three key processes.

In the Processing Company, senior management were relatively demotivated and lacked strategic and technical understanding of computer systems; organizational implementation was not considered as a major issue in deliberations on IS strategy. The evaluation process also ignored organizational implementation, emphasizing formal procedures and reinforcing the perspective of computerization as automation and control. Design and development was notable for its technical emphasis and lack of stakeholder group involvement. It is possible that a focal interest on organizational implementation in any of the main activities of strategy, evaluation, or design and development, may have been sufficient to ensure that the severe problems which occurred at switch-over were considerably reduced. However, it is not a coincidence that organizational implementation was largely ignored during all main stages, since the theme appears not to have been at the forefront of the minds of either senior management or the system developers.

Brown certainly had organizational implementation as a key theme throughout his action and intervention with respect to computer-based IS at Sky. He was directly involved in IS strategy, evaluation, and design and development, and succeeded in linking these together and orchestrating sufficient common purpose to enable new systems to be developed rapidly and effectively. Taylor also was keenly aware of organizational implementation issues with respect to computer systems. Indeed, the primary purpose of his participative approach can be seen to be his desire to arrive at shared views and approaches, and thus create the right prerequisites for implementation. This aspect of the case indicates that whilst the approach to organizational implementation through participation may be sound in principle, it is not sufficient in itself to generate consensus.

The absence of the organizational implementation theme in all phases of the Government Co-ordination Agency case study is similar in some ways to that in the Processing Company. However, in the GCA case, senior management were not demotivated, but their remoteness from stakeholder groups during discussions on IS strategy and evaluation can be seen to derive partly from cultural norms, and partly from their emphasis on political goals as the key driving force. The design and development activity emphasized technical implementation, since this was perceived by system developers as their main task, with the theme of organizational implementation not being regarded by them as their responsibility.

If organizational implementation is recognized as an important linking theme throughout all phases of computerization, and responsibility is accepted by an individual or group, the question then is how such an individual or group should approach the task of the *management of change*. In the Processing Company and Government Co-ordination Agency case studies, we have seen that neither of the conditions were satisfied regarding recognition of importance or acceptance of responsibility, and thus it is not possible to learn anything significant about the change management activity in these cases.

Brown's approach at Sky to the management of change in order to address organizational implementation issues can be seen as largely focused on the design and development activity, rather than any direct stakeholder group involvement in strategy or formal evaluation. The particular methods used by Brown during this phase were centred, in terms of cultural change, on the symbolic and learning aspects of participation and training, as discussed in the previous chapter. With respect to political change, Brown can be considered to have largely succeeded in deflecting political opposition from other interest groups, by a combination of methods involving enhancement of group status, symbolic commitment on his own part, and in some cases by suppressing opposing views, such as those of the systems developers on ad hoc systems. This latter suppression was feasible since Brown was able to exert a dominant position in power relations with all other groups in Sky, and this dominance was reproduced throughout the period of his leadership.

A SYNTHESIZED PERSPECTIVE ON IS IMPLEMENTATION

The purpose of this section is to synthesize a perspective on IS implementation drawing from the preceding material in the chapter. The first subsection presents a view of the nature of IS implementation, and the second subsection discusses the role of an IS implementer related to this view. Key features of this perspective are summarized in Table 10.2, and the ideas will be illustrated in more detail in the final section of the chapter.

The Nature of IS Implementation

The technical implementation of computer-based IS is clearly necessary, but is not sufficient to ensure organizational implementation with respect to such aspects as high levels of organizational use or positive perceptions by stakeholder groups. Organizational implementation involves a *process of social change* over the whole time extending from the system's initial conceptualization through to technical implementation and the post-implementation period. This change process can be facilitated and influenced by actions and activities aimed at producing *new social structures*, involving such elements as revised interpretative schemes on the nature and importance of work activities, or changed norms and values regarding the function and importance of the work of particular stakeholder groups to the organization.

Ambiguity in IS strategy or policy is inevitable, due to such factors as the need to ensure agreement amongst diverse parties, uncertainty in the organization's technology and environment, the multiple perspectives of different individuals and groups, and lack of information. Agencies charged with the implementation of strategy thus need to emphasize *creative autonomy*

TABLE 10.2 A synthesized perspective on IS implementation

The Nature of IS Implementation

- Organizational implementation of IS involves a process of social change, over the whole time from system conceptualization to post-implementation
- Implementation actions and activities aim to produce new social structures, involving such aspects as the nature and importance of new work activities
- Ambiguity in IS strategy is inevitable, and there is a need for creative autonomy on the part of implementation agencies
- Effective organizational implementation of large-scale IS may require coalition building, ideological training, and political tactics

The Role of an IS Implementer

- An IS implementer has a key role throughout all the interconnected activities of strategy formation, evaluation, and design and development
- An IS implementer needs personal skills and a knowledge of political tactics
- An IS implementer has a facilitator role in the process of cultural change
- The role of an IS implementer as moral agent emphasizes ethical choices concerning organizational change, and is not a role which can be avoided

in their roles and actions, involving a relatively loose coupling between policy and implementation actions, and the establishment of their own independent credibility with important stakeholder groups.

The effective organizational implementation of large-scale computer-based IS requires *coalition building* between stakeholder groups. Ideological training on the value of the systems to their work and the organization is one approach to the building of widespread support for IS action campaigns. The politics of control requires also the *quieting of opposition*, where political tactics are employed to ensure that opposition to organizational change associated with a particular information system is diverted or defused. Such activities necessarily reflect norms and values concerning the desirability of particular change processes.

The Role of an IS Implementer

An IS implementer, concerned with the organizational implementation process, has a *role throughout all the interconnected activities* involved in IS strategy formation, evaluation, and design and development. This does not necessarily imply that the same implementer needs to be involved directly in all these activities, but such an approach has merits in terms of co-ordination and continuity. In any case, there should be a significant focus on organizational implementation in all these activities, facilitated by people who see at least part of their task as being centrally concerned with IS implementation.

An IS implementer needs *political and personal skills*, and the ability to use appropriate *political tactics* in the organizational change process. Political and personal skills include the ability to argue one's position selectively using available information, and facility with language and person-to-person interaction. Political tactics include the deliberate seeking out of resistance as a signal requiring response, relying on face-to-face contact, and working to build credibility with stakeholder groups as a relative insider. An IS implementer is involved in cultural as well as political change, and can be regarded as a *facilitator in the enactment of new meanings* in the process of social action.

The roles of an IS implementer envisaged above imply active intervention by such an individual in the creation of new social structures, and this necessarily carries with it the role of *moral agent*, involved in ethical choices concerning desirable organizational change in connection with computerized systems. It could perhaps be thought that an acceptance of senior management pre-eminence in terms of organizational direction removes the need for the moral agent role on the part of the IS implementer. However, this acceptance represents an ethical choice and a particular moral position, even if this is not analysed as such by the IS implementer in a conscious way.

THE PRACTICE OF IS IMPLEMENTATION

The discussion which follows is oriented to the practice of an IS implementer who is concerned with the organizational implementation of computer-based IS. The approach taken derives from the perspective on the nature of IS implementation summarized in the previous section, and from the related view of the cultural, political and ethical roles of an IS implementer. The discussion below does not address technical implementation, although it is recognized that this is also vital to implementation success in the broadest sense. Indeed, an IS implementer concerned primarily with organizational issues also needs to have a thorough grasp of technical issues, not least in order to carry credibility with stakeholder groups, including the IS analysts themselves.

The material below is focused around the themes discussed in the second section of the chapter, derived from the three case studies in Part II. The discussion is divided into three broad task areas: considering implementation aims, understanding implementation context, and facilitating implementation process. Some issues for debate arising from the discussion are summarized in Tables 10.3 to 10.5.

Considering Implementation Aims

The definition of successful organizational implementation is problematic, and alternative *implementation measures* include the meeting of strategic objectives, high levels of system use, and the satisfaction of different stakeholder groups.

TABLE 10.3 Some issues for debate on considering implementation aims

Implementation Measures

- Recognition of ambiguity in strategic goals implies that one aim should be the creative implementation of strategy
- High levels of use are usually a desirable aim, but may be achieved at the expense of other short- and long-term implementation aims
- Stakeholder satisfaction is a sensible but limited implementation measure
- A key implementation aim should be the building of coalitions for change

Learning

- In all IS implementation, learning takes place, which provides a changed social context
- One aim is to capture what has been learnt as a basis for future change
- A related aim is to facilitate the development of a learning environment
- Resistance can be enacted by IS implementers as a threat to be overcome, or can be perceived as an opportunity for exploration and learning

With respect to the first of these, a recognition of the ambiguous nature of strategic goals implies that one aim should be the creative implementation of strategy, involving tailoring the broad strategic approach or vision for change to the details of the context, taking account for example of the complex and often tacit understanding of stakeholder groups concerning their work activities and organizational role. Some degree of implementation autonomy should thus be encouraged, rather than being perceived for example as disloyalty to those developing the broad strategy.

The implementation aim of high levels of system use is usually desirable in principle, but is inadequate as a measure viewed in isolation. High levels of use do not necessarily imply the effective use of systems in either economic or organizational efficiency terms. In addition, if high levels of use are achieved based only on short-term goals, this can create problems in the longer term. For example, the imposition of systems on unwilling stakeholder groups can create a climate of opposition for future initiatives. A further point to note is that systems with low levels of use may be very valuable if the use is of high importance; for example, in a safety system which is triggered only occasionally.

The measure of stakeholder satisfaction is again an implementation aim that appears desirable in principle, although it could be achieved by a 'no change' approach in some cases, which may not be in the best interest of any of the stakeholder groups in the organization. However, assuming that significant organizational change is involved, stakeholder satisfaction is a sensible target and, as noted previously, an early implementation aim should be the building of coalitions for change between stakeholder groups. This can be regarded as a prerequisite, although not a guarantee, of later stakeholder satisfaction with the implemented system.

A particular case study may be described as relatively successful or unsuccessful across various measures of organizational implementation discussed above, but in all cases some degree of *learning* takes place, which provides a changed context for later systems development. One deliberate implementation aim therefore should be to understand and capture where possible what has been learnt from any particular IS implementation, as a basis for future work. Such an attempt to describe and discuss previous experience will necessarily involve multiple interpretations and enactments, and no simple consensus view; nevertheless, the debate itself can form part of the process of building coalitions for future change.

A related but rather broader point concerning organizational learning is the desirability of facilitating the development of a learning environment or culture in connection with the implementation of computer-based IS. This implies that all participants in the implementation process, including IS implementers and the involved stakeholder groups, should be encouraged to see part of their role as self-learning and communication with others. For example, the resistance of a stakeholder group can be enacted by an IS implementer as a threat to be overcome, or alternatively can be perceived as an opportunity for exploration and learning on the part of both parties.

Understanding Implementation Context

An important element of the social context for any IS implementation activity can be thought of as the *leadership style* provided by IS implementers who may be senior management or members of the IS project team or both. It can be argued for a number of reasons that the approach to leadership on IS implementation should involve close contact with stakeholder groups. A first reason is that previous comments on policy ambiguity and the need for creative autonomy during the implementation process imply that implementers and stakeholder groups should interact closely to facilitate mutual learning. Secondly, the exercise of political skills and tactics by implementers can normally only take place during direct and close interaction. Finally, a cultural perspective on change sees an IS implementer as a facilitator in the enactment of new meanings, and this role cannot be carried out in a remote way.

Leadership style can vary considerably between different parts of the process of IS initiation and development. For example, a rather personal and autocratic style with respect to strategy is not incompatible with a highly participative style during system design and development. The discussion in the above paragraph would imply, however, that there needs to be substantial contact

TABLE 10.4 *Some issues for debate on understanding implementation context*

Leadership Style

- Need for close contact between IS implementers and stakeholder groups
- Such closeness facilitates mutual learning on strategy implementation, the exercise of political skills, and the enactment of new meanings
- Leadership style can vary between different parts of the IS process, but substantial contact is needed during at least one major phase
- A top-down hierarchical approach to leadership may create a context in which IS organizational implementation is particularly problematic

Implementation Responsibility

- Traditional roles of senior managers and systems analysts may lead to organizational implementation responsibility being unassigned
- Responsibility should be taken by a significant subgroup of IS analysts and at least one member of senior management
- Organizational implementation needs a high priority weighting, particularly when the IS project team is under time and resource pressure
- Senior management has a major role in providing adequate facilities for both technical and organizational implementation

between IS implementers and other stakeholder groups in at least one major phase of the computerization process. A top-down hierarchical approach to leadership during all phases, related for example to cultural attitudes in a particular society, may result in a context in which the organizational implementation of computer-based IS aimed to support lower level stakeholder groups is particularly problematic.

A related element in the social context of a computer-based information system can be thought of as the question of *implementation responsibility*. Traditional roles of senior managers and systems analysts, as strategists removed from detailed implementation and technical experts with little organizational knowledge respectively, lead to the danger in IS projects that responsibility for organizational implementation is not perceived by any person or group to be their problem. It is unrealistic to expect all members of an IS project team to have responsibility in this area, since for example knowledge and ability on organizational aspects of computer-based IS is likely to be thinly spread. However, a significant subgroup of the IS analysts should take responsibility for close interaction on organizational implementation issues with senior management, with stakeholder groups, and in a gatekeeper role to the rest of the IS project team. Similarly, at least one member of senior management should accept the responsibility for continuing in-depth contact with the other groups involved, including the IS project team.

Organizational implementation should thus be the responsibility of a combination of members of the IS project team and senior management, and it is important that the activities of this group be given a high priority weighting. Otherwise, there is an understandable tendency on the part of systems analysts to reduce their effort in this area when under time or resource pressure. This tendency arises from the higher visibility of technical activities such as code production when compared to the more nebulous organizational implementation aspects such as coalition building, combined with the natural preference of most systems analysts for technical issues related to their choice of this area of work. Senior management has an important role in this context in providing adequate support and facilities to ensure that neither technical nor organizational implementation is underprovided for in terms of resources at critical periods.

Facilitating Implementation Process

The process of organizational implementation can be viewed as a *linking theme* which runs through all social aspects of computer-based information systems, and in particular is interwoven with the key areas of IS strategy, evaluation, and design and development. It is possible that a focal interest on organizational implementation in any one of these areas would ensure an adequate consideration of relevant issues, but a more solid proposal is to argue for the

TABLE 10.5 Some issues for debate in facilitating implementation process

Linking Theme

- Organizational implementation can be viewed as a linking theme which runs through all social aspects of computer-based IS
- It should be a key element for consideration and debate in all phases of IS strategy, evaluation, and design and development
- An IS implementer should confront ethical issues of organizational change, even if they are only involved in design and development

- -

Management of Change

- The use of ideological training is one example of how to facilitate the creation of new social structures
- The political change process can be facilitated by the exercise of political skills and the use of political tactics
- Standards of morality should be a legitimate subject for debate in the context of the organizational implementation of computer-based IS

---

inclusion of the theme as a key element for consideration in all phases. An individual who is directly involved in all of the phases is well placed to play an integrative role with respect to organizational implementation, and can perhaps be thought of in some cases as a 'system champion', which has been argued in the IS literature (see, for example, Curley and Gremillion 1983) to be a factor in implementation success.

An IS implementer who is a member of the IS project team may not be consulted in earlier phases, and may only become involved during design and development. However, consideration of organizational implementation aspects during this phase may raise ethical issues concerning organizational change, for example in terms of possible impact on stakeholder groups. Traditional organizations may view these issues as having already been decided by senior management, and may consider that the IS implementer should see resistance from particular groups as something to be overcome. A broader view of IS implementers as moral agents would suggest that they should confront ethical issues directly, and be prepared to debate moral choices with all other stakeholder groups including senior management.

It has been argued that organizational implementation should be recognized as an important linking theme throughout all phases of computerization, and that responsibility should be accepted by a group of IS implementers; this leads to the question as to how the task of the *management of change* should be approached. The creation of new social structures can be facilitated by a variety of actions and activities, and the use of ideological training is one example. This involves the conscious effort to convince stakeholder groups of the merit of the computerized systems, and to use training both as a means of communicating that message and as a symbolic commitment to the message by all parties concerned, both trainers and trainees.

In addition to the cultural aspect of the management of change discussed above, the political change process can be facilitated by the exercise of political skills such as the ability to argue selectively and a general facility with language, and political tactics such as face-to-face contact and working to become an insider. It is worthwhile to mention the moral dimension again here. Political skills and tactics can be used for a variety of ends, and it is demotivating and degrading for an individual to use their political capacity to support and facilitate social processes which they consider to be aimed at goals with low standards of morality. It is not being argued here that such standards are easy to evaluate in practice or that they are always shared between different stakeholder groups. Instead, the argument is that such standards should be legitimate subjects for debate in organizations at all hierarchical levels, and in particular should be debated in the context of the organizational implementation of computer-based information systems.

REFERENCES

Baier, V. E., March, J. G., and Sætren, H. (1988) 'Implementation and ambiguity', in J. G. March, *Decisions and Organizations*, Basil Blackwell, Oxford.

Curley, K. F., and Gremillion, L. L. (1983) 'The role of the champion in DSS implementation', *Information and Management*, **6**, No. 4, 203–209.

Ginzberg, M. J., and Schultz, R. L. (1987) 'The practical side of implementation research', *Interfaces*, **17**, No. 3, 1–5.

Keen, P. G. W. (1981) 'Information systems and organizational change', *Communications of the ACM*, **24**, No. 1, 24–32.

Kling, R., and Iacono, S. (1984) 'The control of information systems developments after implementation', *Communications of the ACM*, **27**, No. 12, 1218–1226.

Land, F. F., Le Quesne, P. N., and Wijegunaratne, I. (1989) 'Effective systems: overcoming the obstacles', *Journal of Information Technology*, **4**, No. 2, 81–91.

Lucas, H. C. (1981) *Implementation: The Key to Successful Information Systems*, Columbia University Press, New York.

Lyytinen, K., and Hirschheim, R. (1987) 'Information systems failures: a survey and classification of the empirical literature', *Oxford Surveys in Information Technology*, **4**, 257–309.

Markus, M. L., and Pfeffer, J. (1983) 'Power and the design and implementation of accounting and control systems', *Accounting, Organizations and Society*, **8**, No. 2/3, 205–218.

Martin, J., and Meyerson, D. (1988) 'Organizational cultures and the denial, channeling and acknowledgement of ambiguity', in *Managing Ambiguity and Change* (eds L. R. Pondy, R. J. Boland, and H. Thomas), Wiley, Chichester.

Srinivasan, A., and Davis, J. G. (1987) 'A reassessment of implementation process models', *Interfaces*, **17**, No. 3, 64–71.

Walsham, G. (1992) 'Management science and organisational change: a framework for analysis', *Omega*, **20**, No. 1, 1–9.

Willcocks, L. P., and Mark, A. L. (1989) 'IT systems implementation: research findings from the public sector', *Journal of Information Technology*, **4**, No. 2, 92–103.

CONCLUSIONS

Chapter 11
THE FUTURE FOR INFORMATION SYSTEMS

The purpose of this chapter is to bring together some of the key themes in the book, and to draw some conclusions concerning the possible future with respect to computer-based information systems. The first section synthesizes a perspective on information systems in organizations derived from the analysis of the major issues in Part III. The second section then relates this organizational-level view to a broader picture of the social aspects of information systems in society at large. The final three sections draw implications from the whole book for future IS research, education, and practice.

A SYNTHESIZED PERSPECTIVE ON INFORMATION SYSTEMS IN ORGANIZATIONS

This section aims to bring together some key elements of the perspectives on information systems which were developed in detail in the four chapters of Part III. These chapters dealt with the major issues of strategy, evaluation, design and development, and implementation; although the issues were treated separately in this way, they are in fact inextricably interlinked. The social processes centred on each issue are overlapping, mutually informing, and stakeholder groups are normally involved in more than one of the processes. The rather artificial division of the issues for analytical purposes is dissolved in this section, which describes a perspective on the nature of IS in organizations and the role of the IS actor in the whole process of the initiation, development and use of computerized information systems.

The Nature of IS in Organizations

Computer-based information systems embody interpretative schemes in the sense that they provide ways of viewing the world and thus making sense of it. They also reflect norms and values concerning what are desirable states of the world or what can be achieved. Finally, they provide a facility that can be used in the control and co-ordination of material and human resources. These different aspects of a computer-based IS are interlinked. For example, the use of an information system as a co-ordination facility draws on its status as an interpretative scheme and the norms and values implicit in it; in so doing, social structures of meaning, power, and morality are reproduced or changed.

Stability in social structure arises from the routinized drawing on sets of established interpretative schemes, norms, and facilities. Change in social structure basically arises from the reflexive monitoring of knowledgeable human agents concerning such aspects as the unintended consequences of intentional conduct, the interaction between individuals with different views and perceptions, and the assessment of new material or non-material circumstances. New technology in general, and information technology in particular, offers fresh options and opportunities. A new computer-based information system may thus be associated with elements of changed social structures, but its use can also reproduce existing structures of meaning, power, and morality; or, in other words, computer-based IS are associated with a blend of social reproduction and change. The case material in Part II of the book gave detailed examples of the blending of continuity and change in social structures in connection with IS in three specific cases.

Important elements of change associated with IS include new forms of work activities, new roles and involvement with others, and thus new identities at work for individuals and their perception in the eyes of others. The reinforcement or change in social identities and social structures associated with a computer-based IS takes place through a process of continuous discourse and reflection on the part of the people involved. Strategy formation, evaluation, and design and development can all be conceptualized in this way as involving a social process of communication, learning, and negotiation both within and between individuals and stakeholder groups.

The social process centred on a particular IS issue is often mediated by formal procedures such as the use of strategy frameworks, evaluation methods, or design and development methodologies. An exercise using formal procedures may have overt or covert functions from the perspective of different stakeholders, and in some cases can be viewed as a ritual, expressing for example symbolic belief in management competence. However, in all cases, the social context of the use of a formal procedure includes the informal assessments of individuals and stakeholder groups, reflecting their own set of perceptions and rationalities. The outcome of a formal exercise does not therefore necessarily represent a shared interpretative scheme amongst the various stakeholders, and may not embody shared interests and values. A lack of shared interpretation or set of values with respect to a particular computer-based IS may create a major problem in terms of organizational implementation. A further point about formal methodologies is that those with a strong technical or economic focus may help to reproduce a narrow view of social process if used in isolation.

The organizational implementation of IS, with respect to such aspects as changed work activities and work roles and positive perceptions by stakeholder groups, results from a process of social change over the whole time extending at least from the system's initial conceptualization to its technical implementation, and indeed rather beyond those limits in terms of pre-conceptualization attitudes and relationships and post-implementation activities. The social processes centred on the issues of strategy, evaluation, and design and development, can be considered as constituent parts of the overall organizational implementation process. This process involves cultural and political debate and action, and ethical issues are implicit or explicit throughout all the discourse and activities of stakeholders in all phases. Individuals in an organization with assigned IS responsibilities are clearly of major significance, although not exclusively so, in the discourse and action associated with computer-based IS. We now turn specifically to a discussion of the roles of such individuals in the various social processes summarized above.

Roles of an IS Actor

The roles of an IS strategist, evaluator, analyst and implementer were discussed in Part III, and these are synthesized here into the roles of an IS actor who may be involved in any or all of the four processes discussed earlier. The synthesis is based on Habermas' concept of knowledge interests which was described briefly in Chapter 1 (Habermas 1972).

The first element of Habermas' categorization is the technical knowledge interest which, in the context of IS design and development for example, 'is concerned with purposive rational design of systems and technical functionality' (Ehn 1991). It has not been the aim of this book to focus on technical issues but, as stated previously, this should not be taken to imply a downgrading of the importance of such issues. It is essential that an IS actor in any capacity, and perhaps particularly the IS analyst, should have a good understanding of the technical aspects of computer-based IS. However, this role of an *IS actor as technical expert* should be regarded as a necessary but not sufficient part of the IS actor's skills and capacity, and we turn now to the two other knowledge interests which are central to the social roles of an IS actor.

The second knowledge interest according to Habermas is the practical, which is concerned with 'dialogues, participatory relations, and understanding' (Ehn 1991). This knowledge interest is reflected in the role of an *IS actor as an enactor of meaning*. The discussion in Chapter 7 viewed this role for the IS strategist being played through the discourse on IS strategy. The task of the strategist in this role is seen as contributing to 'organization making', the creation and maintenance of systems of shared meaning that facilitate organized action. The IS strategist is thus an agent of organizational stability and change through the medium of language. The choice of vocabulary implying particular enactments of the organization and its environment is a key element of the role of the strategist. The related role of an IS evaluator as an enactor of meaning takes place in a responsive evaluation design where the evaluator is seen as a facilitator of the evaluation discourse amongst stakeholder groups. The evaluator in this role can be seen as a collaborator, learner and teacher, and change agent.

The role of the IS analyst as management change agent is also related to the practical knowledge interest and the view of the IS actor as an enactor of meaning. The management change agent role is concerned with monitoring and facilitating the discourse between stakeholder groups on the design and development of the computer-based system. However, the role was seen earlier as implying the acceptance of the legitimacy of the authority of management to resolve conflict by the exercise of power where necessary. We will comment further on this below in connection with the third knowledge interest. One of the roles of an IS implementer was also seen as an enactor of new meanings, and it was noted that the role requires personal and political skills. This comment applies more generally to the IS actor when carrying out social activities centred on any of the major IS processes.

Habermas' third category is the emancipatory knowledge interest. This is the basis for critical theory, and is an interest in 'the process of critique as a means to reveal power relations embodied in our socio-cultural form of life as systemically distorted communication' (Ehn 1991). One can immediately see that an approach based on this view would challenge the role of an IS analyst as management change agent, with its acceptance of management's privileged position in the discourse on IS design and development. An alternative role is that of an *IS actor as a moral agent*, which was discussed in Chapter 9 for the IS analyst as involving, for example, the aligning of the analyst on the side of labour rather than management. A second approach for the IS analyst, still centred on moral values, does not align itself with any particular group in advance. It is addressed to the learning and emancipation of all parties to the discourse on design and development, and includes critical reflection in such areas as power and political action, social differentiation, and the bias and limitations of language use.

A similar role of moral agent was identified earlier for each of the areas of IS strategy, evaluation, and implementation. The IS strategist or evaluator is involved in the production and reproduction of normative values, and in the maintenance and change of power relations, even if they do not see themselves consciously in this light. The process of organizational change associated with a computer-based IS will contribute to the reinforcement or change of social structures. The role of the IS strategist or evaluator as moral agent implies a conscious and critical reflection on moral choices regarding such aspects as reinforcement or change in norms and power relations in connection with a computer-based system.

It may be possible for an IS strategist or evaluator to distance themselves from such aspects as the perceptions of stakeholder groups with less formal authority in the organization, and thus for them to be relatively unaware in a conscious sense of their role as moral agents. An IS implementer as envisaged earlier in Chapter 10 needs to actively intervene with stakeholder groups to facilitate the creation of new social structures, using such approaches as face-to-face contact and the building of personal credibility. It is thus difficult for the IS implementer to avoid the ethical choices concerning organizational change in connection with computerized systems, and the IS implementer is likely to be a conscious moral agent at least in some sense. The acceptance that management is always right in the case of disputes or different perceptions represents an ethical choice and a particular moral position, even if it is a rather uncritical one in Habermasian terms.

IS IN SOCIETY

The focal level of the book has been organizations, and the previous section provided a summary of some key elements of a perspective on information systems linked to this focus. This section aims to locate the organizational issues considered in the book in the broader social terrain of information systems within society at large. The section is divided into three subsections dealing with social issues in the computerization of society, a social choice model for information systems, and the theme of individual responsibility.

Social Issues in the Computerization of Society

The organizational aspects of computer-based IS discussed throughout the previous chapters are a subset of a broader set of social issues concerned with the computerization of society. A recent book edited by Dunlop and Kling (1991) provides a substantial contribution to this broader picture using a set of readings on a diversity of areas where there is controversy and scope for social choice concerning computing. The common focus of the readings is on exploring social and ethical issues, in a similar spirit to the philosophy of our book here, but the readings cover a wider range of issues. Dunlop and Kling (pp. 2–3) note a number of key areas for debate on the social aspects of computerized systems. These include links between such systems and worklife, class divisions in society, human safety, democratization, employment, education, gender biases, military security, health, and literacy. Other important areas not focused on by Dunlop and Kling include the role of computerized systems in the so-called developing countries (see, for example, Stover 1984, and Walsham, Symons and Waema 1988). It is not possible here to provide any substantial discussion of these issues, but they are listed to emphasize their breadth and importance. Two issues only are selected for brief illustration below, namely that of surveillance at work and that of the privacy of personal data. The first of these issues can be considered to be directly within the organizational focus of our book, whereas the second issue is in the broader societal arena.

Surveillance has been discussed at various points in the book, and provides an interesting example of a social issue of computerization involving controversy and the need for social choice. An article by Marx (1990) describes a fictitious organization which uses computer-based technology and systems to create an 'omniscient organization', and Marx then asks a number of 'experts' to comment on this vision. One expert, Moderow, notes that there is continuous monitoring and surveillance of virtually every movement of employees and that the vision removes the human element of management and evaluation. A second expert, Zuboff, comments that the omniscient organization has created transparency of human behaviour for the purposes of total control. The omniscient organization as envisaged by Marx could be dismissed as nothing more than a fiction, but Zuboff notes that elements of its organizational strategy have been practised for over 100 years in some real organizations. Developments in information technology have made the implementation of the omniscient organization more feasible in principle than it was at the time of the disturbing vision of Orwell (1949) on central surveillance.

Attewell (1991) discusses computer surveillance in the automated office, and provides a partial antidote to the view that new information technology will lead in practice to strict and pervasive personal surveillance. Attewell notes that it has not been a lack of technology that has prevented surveillance in the past, but there have been other reasons why work measurement has not been used more forcefully by managers to monitor employees. These reasons include concerns about office morale, a preference for group rather than individual measures, a trade-off between speed and quality, labour market explanations, organizational constraints on intervention and punishment, and the threat of sabotage. Attewell is not complacent about the possible dangers of a trend towards surveillance and speed-up in the workplace. However, his article supports a view that the levels of surveillance in a particular case are determined by the social choices made by managers and others, within a social context of considerable complexity which constrains and enables various choices.

The second computerization issue chosen to comment on here is that of the privacy of personal data on citizens. Such data include medical records, financial records, criminal records, and family data. A good example of a society where such data on citizens are widely available to central government is that of Singapore. For example, the majority of Singapore citizens live in housing provided through a particular government agency. The central database of this agency includes a wide range of data on individual citizens including their criminal record, if any. The priority allocated to an individual on the housing list takes account, in a negative sense, of any such record.

This example should not be taken to imply that such activity is necessarily undesirable. Part of the Singapore government's policy over many years has been aimed at reducing crime, and they have been very successful at achieving this. Government politicians would no doubt argue that reduced housing priority is one of the deterrents to criminal behaviour. However, there is little doubt that many people outside Singapore would not wish to see their own government adopt such an approach, and the broader issue of who should have access to what data on which citizens for what purposes is of major importance in any country.

A rather different context for social choice on the issue of personal data privacy is provided by the USA. Dunlop and Kling (1991, p. 411) note that proponents of unregulated computerization in this context have been wealthy, organized, and aligned with the anti-regulatory sentiments that have dominated US federal policies for 15 years. Dunlop and Kling argue that this wealthy elite have effectively blocked many attempts to preserve personal privacy through regulation. Thus, for very different reasons than in Singapore, the privacy of personal data in the USA is also not well protected, and remains a controversial and continuing issue for social choice. In this case, individuals and groups can impact computerization policy mainly by attempting to exert a counter-pressure on legislators to that provided by wealthy interest groups concerned with gaining relatively unlimited access to personal data.

A Social Choice Model for Information Systems

The discussion of two social issues related to computerization given above is illustrative of the importance and complexity of such issues in connection with computing. Each issue is different, and involves different individuals, groups, organizations, and sometimes the whole of society. Nevertheless, some broad conclusions can be drawn with respect to the social impact of computer-based information systems, and these conclusions will be discussed below, and then brought together as a social choice model for information systems summarized at the end of the subsection.

A first conclusion is that technological determinism, namely the view that technology determines social direction, is an inadequate model at any level. The individual, whether manager or citizen or employee, can exercise social choice. The way in which issues such as surveillance at the organizational-level, or the privacy of personal data at the societal level, are decided at any point in time involves a myriad of personal choices, and complex social interaction, which cannot be captured by a model with technology as the social driver.

Although individuals can choose amongst a range of possible actions, a second general conclusion is that the conditions or context within which they make a choice is not selected by them, except in the important sense that they enact this context in a personal way. Their perception of the context for action constrains and enables various personal choices. Giddens' structuration theory is one way of viewing this duality of individual choice as the agent of stability or change, but with social structures in human minds as a constraining and enabling social context. The fascinating if rather depressing analysis by Foucault (1979) of modern times, as having created 'disciplinary societies' in which individuals self-regulate their behaviour to conform to various materialistic norms which reproduce technologies of control by the powerful, places an emphasis on the constraining nature of the context of modern societies and their current enactments by human beings.

Kraemer (1991) addresses the issue of the role of computerization in processes of social choice and social change, drawing on a large programme of empirical work conducted in US local government agencies. He argues that, although information technology has long been viewed as capable of bringing about organizational change, it has not been shown to play this role in reality. Rather, information technology has tended to 'reinforce existing organizational arrangements and power distributions in organizations'. Kraemer considers that technology is not the driver of change and it is rarely even the catalyst; 'at most it is supportive of reform efforts decided on other grounds'. The view of technology not being the driver has been argued earlier, but the conclusion concerning the role of computer-based IS in reinforcing existing social structures is not generalizable. The social structures in the context of US local government agencies may have displayed a long-term history of stability, and their use of computer-based IS may have been generally supportive of these structures. Nevertheless, as our earlier case studies illustrated, computerized systems can be associated both with social stability and with social change, and the occurrence of one or other of these phenomena, or a combination of elements of both, is dependent on particular social choices and specific contexts.

This view of the diversity and specificity of the impact of computerized systems is supported by Kling (1991), who discusses the issue of the relationship between computerization and social transformations. He argues that, if we examine the evidence, then we have trouble in assembling a credible historical portrait of the links between computerization and the larger social order. Kling considers that the restructuring of social relations because of computerization has been much more important in some institutional areas than others, and he argues that it is a good point in time to ask what kinds of social transformation have or have not happened and why, and what social choices remain.

A summary of a social choice model for computer-based information systems derived from the discussion in this subsection is as follows. Technology does not determine social direction, but rather social stability and change arise from a myriad of personal choices. Individuals make such choices within perceived social contexts which constrain and enable various alternative actions. Computerized systems may be associated with the reinforcement of existing social structures, but may also be associated with significant social change. The focus of future attention should be on questions such as why transformations have or have not occurred in specific areas, what social choices there are now in these areas, and how we should approach the question of making ethical choices.

Individual Responsibility

The last question raised above is one of how to make ethical choices, and the discussion in this subsection shifts the focus to this individual level. A simple answer to the question is to say that people should assume personal responsibility for their actions, but there is more content to this assertion than might be assumed at first sight, and indeed it can be argued that personal responsibility is often avoided in many contemporary contexts. This viewpoint is eloquently argued by Weizenbaum (1991), who considers that we have moved on to an age of 'new conformism', which permits us to say anything that can be said in the functional language of instrumental reason. There are strong parallels here with Foucault's concept of the disciplinary society. Weizenbaum argues that the scientist and engineer, particularly, have responsibilities that transcend their immediate situation, and his description of individual responsibility is worth quoting at some length:

> At least, every individual must act as if the whole future of the world, of humanity itself, depends on him. Anything less is a shirking of responsibility and is itself a dehumanising force, for anything less encourages the individual to look upon himself as a mere actor in a drama written by anonymous agents, as less than a whole person, and that is the beginning of passivity and aimlessness . . . . It is a widely held but a grievously mistaken belief that civil courage finds exercise only in the context of world-shaking events. To the contrary, its most arduous exercise is often the small contexts in which the challenge is to overcome the fears induced by petty concerns over career, over our relationships to those who appear to have power over us, over whatever may disturb the tranquility of our mundane existence. (pp. 734 and 740)

Weizenbaum's description of individual responsibility provides rich background to our earlier view of the role of an IS actor as a moral agent in the specific context of computer-based information systems. Dunlop and Kling (1991, p. 657) argue that career-minded IS professionals find it difficult to make moral considerations paramount in the workplace. This is no doubt true, and applies to us all to some extent, but it is not an argument that it *should* be true for any of us to any extent. A common feature of many contemporary Western organizations is the sense that employees at all levels, but perhaps particularly managers and those in authority, are required to hang aspects of their humanity at the door as they enter their workplace, and only put them on again when leaving for home. Those who argue that the bringing of the full range of moral issues into the workplace would undermine the basis of successful enterprise are contemporary torch-bearers of those who argued in the past for the essential part played in business enterprise by child labour or slavery.

In case the above discussion could be taken as an argument for moral debate and action at the expense of economic efficiency, it is worth noting that there is no evidence that the two are mutually exclusive. Indeed, this author would argue that the evidence points the other way. A human being acting as a 'whole person' is likely to be more economically productive than one enfeebled by the adoption of an amoral role subservient to powerful interests. For example, in the context of computerization, Bullen and Bennett (1991) comment on the productivity of work groups and note that the most successful are not always the most computerized. Instead, they argue that success tends to occur where group members and their managers have worked hard to create environments that have clear elevating goals, and that support and reward commitment. The word elevating is critical to the key theme of this subsection, which is that human beings can only receive such elevation from activities which they perceive to be of positive moral purpose, and for which they accept full responsibility.

IMPLICATIONS FOR FUTURE IS RESEARCH

The purpose of this section is to generate and discuss some implications for future research on computer-based information systems, drawing from all the preceding material in the book. The section summarizes some of the approaches used in the work, relates these to elements of the literature where appropriate, draws some lessons from the research experience, and thus suggests some ideas, approaches, and issues of relevance to future work. The material is divided into three subsections addressing theory, methodology, and future research topics.

Theory

The broad theoretical approach used in the book has been to consider the social process of IS initiation, development, and use in an organization as being carried out by human actors in a knowledgeable and reflexive way within social contexts which are constituted by previous and present social actions. Garnsey (1992) describes such approaches as 'constitutive process' theories, which are concerned with the processes whereby social actors are engaged in producing and reproducing the social systems of which they form a part. Giddens' structurational analysis is one example of this type of theory, and has been used as an important underlying model in the theoretical analysis in this book. However, the empirical research that was carried out, and the resulting analysis in the book, drew from a wider range of sources. Theoretical ideas of considerable significance to the research were obtained from Morgan's work on organizational metaphors, Pettigrew's contextualism, and Habermas' work on critical theory. In the broad IS domain, valuable theoretical insight was provided by Kling's web models, Zuboff's work on the informating aspects of information technology, and Checkland's soft systems methodology. With respect to the specific IS issues focused on in Part III, a broad range of theory was drawn on which addressed these issues directly; reference can be made to the individual chapters for these sources.

It is worth mentioning at this point a brief aside on the relationship between theory and research. Although the above sources provided valuable theoretical background, the listing of sources does not capture anything of the processual, intermingled, and mutually informing nature of the relationship between theories and the research carried out. The actual research process did not match the linear presentation of the book whereby theory is described first, empirical research happens next, results are then analysed, and conclusions are drawn. Instead, the process involves such aspects as the use of theoretical insights at different stages, the modification of theory based on experience, the generation of intermediate results that lead to the reading of a different theoretical literature, and the continuing revision or new enactment of past research results. This book represents a particular point in this continuing process of attempting to understand the unknowable, namely the essence of human experience, using theoretical frameworks and ideas which at best only illuminate interesting elements of an infinitely variable and complex reality.

Returning now to an assessment of the theory used in the book, it is worthwhile to attempt to locate the work within particular IS research traditions, using classifications developed in the literature. Markus and Robey (1988) discuss the use of theory to address the relationship between information technology and organizational change. The research described in this book falls loosely within Markus and Robey's classification of an emergent perspective on causal agency, a process theory of logical structure, and a mixed level of analysis. An emergent perspective is described by Markus and Robey as one in which change is viewed as emerging from the complex interaction of people and events, rather than being driven solely by technology or by the intended results of coherent purposeful action. A process theory is said to be one in which the relationship between antecedents and outcomes involves a 'recipe of sufficient conditions occurring over time'. Whilst the research in this book is concerned with process, the above description does not capture the essence of 'constitutive process' theory as we have used it. This new theoretical category could usefully be added to Markus and Robey's classification of logical structure. Finally, the level of analysis in the book has been mixed in terms of individual, group, organizational, and societal levels of analysis, although the focal level has been organizational. However, the constitutive process approach does not fit neatly within Markus and Robey's classification of a mixed level of analysis, since an emphasis is placed, in structuration theory for example, on the way in which the various levels are inextricably interlinked and constituted by each other, whereas traditional mixed level analysis has tended to treat the levels rather more separately.

A second paper which attempts to classify IS research traditions is that by Orlikowski and Baroudi (1991), where they identify three broad research philosophies as positivist, interpretivist, and critical. The authors describe the interpretive philosophy of IS research as emphasizing the importance of subjective meanings, the need to understand social processes by 'getting inside' them, and the non-neutral stance of the researcher. They describe the critical philosophy of IS research as emphasizing the unfulfilled potentiality of people, the way that knowledge is grounded in social and historical processes, and the role of the researcher as being to bring to consciousness the restrictive conditions of the status quo in order to help eliminate the bases of alienation and domination. The research described in this book has elements of both the interpretive and critical traditions as described above, and does not fit in one of these two categories. Constitutive process theories, such as structuration theory, are indeed an attempt to dissolve the boundaries between such traditions, in emphasizing not only the importance of subjective meaning for the individual actor, but also the social structures which condition and enable such meanings and are constituted by them.

We have summarized the theoretical approach of the book and have related it above to two categorizations in the literature, but what can be concluded about theory for future IS research? The first main conclusion is that constitutive process theory, integrating interpretive and critical elements, provides a new approach to research on the social aspects of computer-based information systems, and that the theoretical approach can be used and further developed by other IS researchers. For example, Table 3.1 provides an outline analytical framework, based on the theory, which can be used to address issues of IS and organizational change in other contexts.

In addition to providing a broad theoretical approach for future work, new theory has been generated in more specific areas. The material developed in Part III includes theoretical descriptions of the nature of the social processes of IS strategy formation, evaluation, design and development, and implementation. These perspectives on the nature of the social processes surrounding specific IS issues were related to theory on the roles of an IS strategist, evaluator, analyst, and implementer. A synthesized view on the nature of IS in organizations and the roles of an IS actor was then provided earlier in this chapter. These theoretical outputs, described in detail in the book, can be used by others as a basis for future research on computer-based IS in general, and the specific IS issues in Part III in particular.

Methodology

The methodological approach adopted throughout the research described in the book has involved an exploration of the contexts of computer-based information systems, the processes of organizational stability and change associated with their introduction and use, and the linkages between context and process. The methodological vehicle has been the in-depth case study, where a combination of historical reconstruction and longitudinal analysis has been used to interpret events and actions over a period of a number of years. This style of empirical research is appropriate for the view of the nature of knowledge embedded in a broadly interpretive philosophy, which emphasizes the need for detailed understanding of human meanings in context. Indeed, if one adopts such a theoretical stance on the nature of knowledge, in-depth case studies are the only feasible method for empirical research.

Generalizability from small numbers of case studies relies on the plausibility and cogency of the inductive reasoning from them, rather than being based on statistical inference from a representative sample as is the case for many positivist research designs. The three case studies in the book produced interesting insights of general applicability to other situations, but nevertheless the criticism that three cases is a very small sample from the enormous diversity of the applications of computer-based IS has some validity. An attempt to compensate for this in the book has been made by drawing on other literature and case material, particularly when exploring the specific IS issues in Part III. A cumulative research approach is vital for the development of any field of academic work, and the theoretical outputs from Part III were developed from a combination of insights from the case material of the book and from previous empirical and theoretical work in the literature.

The approach to field research for the case studies carried out largely derives from the ethnographic research tradition in anthropology. Any IS researcher planning to carry out in-depth case studies in organizations would be well advised to read some of this literature as valuable background for their field work. It is beyond the scope of this book to try to describe this tradition in any detail, but one or two points may be of value here. Geertz (1973) describes the ethnographic approach as 'thick description', and gives a concise and illuminating view of the data collected by the approach:

What we call our data are really our own constructions of other people's constructions of what they and their compatriots are up to. (p. 9)

Van Maanen (1979), writing in the tradition of organizational ethnography, calls the interviewee's constructions first-order data and the constructions of the researcher as second-order concepts. He warns that assuming an ethnographic stance is by no means a guarantee that researchers will collect useful data no matter how long they stay in the field. He points out that researchers can be misled in a number of ways including deliberate deceit by the informant, and when the informants themselves are misled. In addition to these points, it should be noted that second-order concepts rely on good theory and insightful analysis, and the mere collection of in-depth case study data does not provide these concepts in itself.

Some conclusions can now be summarized on appropriate methodology and method for future IS research in the broadly interpretive tradition. Firstly, there is no choice but to adopt in-depth case studies for this type of work. Secondly, the cumulative approach is vital, and researchers should utilize previous work from the same tradition, and should try to contribute to a deeper understanding by building on it. Thirdly, theory has a major role to play here, since theory is a concise way of capturing insights from case study work, which can then be of value to future researchers. Finally, the adoption of an in-depth case study approach will not of itself guarantee interesting results. In addition to the need for good theory and the importance of building on the existing literature, IS researchers conducting research in the ethnographic tradition need good social skills to interact successfully with organization members and, last but not least, the ability to write up their results in a clear and convincing way. The last word in this subsection relates to this final point and is taken from a later article by Van Maanen (1989) on the importance of writing in the field of organizational studies:

> We try to persuade others that we know what we are talking about and they ought therefore to pay attention to what we are saying. We do this by means of text—the written word . . . what theory allows is for a coherent story to be told. But, I submit, it is the story which convinces, not the theory . . . the next generation of organizational researchers (should) be offered a writing course to help them build some sensitivity to matters of rhetorical force. (pp. 27, 30, 32)

Future Research Topics

The work described in this book has raised many issues which have not been resolved, and there are numerous IS research topics which could be further explored using a constitutive process approach to theory, and empirical work based on in-depth case study methods. The scope for further work is wide, but we will mention here only some topics which derive rather directly from the main themes explored in the book. A first general area for future research arises from the specific issues chapters in Part III, where theoretical perspectives were developed on the social processes of IS strategy formation, evaluation, design and development, and implementation. Each of these areas could be the subject of further research activity, designed to develop and enrich perspectives on these processes.

In addition to research aimed at improved theoretical insight, detailed research would be desirable with respect to the proposals for practice which were put forward in Part III. Proposals for the practice of IS strategy in Chapter 7 identified three areas of debate and action concerned with forming strategic content, understanding strategic context, and facilitating strategic change. From a research perspective, one can ask a whole series of questions concerning these activities. For example, is the proposed classification of areas for debate a useful one in describing events and processes in a particular case, how does the discourse on the areas and the issues within them take place, what other issues for debate and action should be included under the area headings, and how do participants to the discourse themselves view their actions in the areas? Similar research questions could be asked concerning the proposals for practice put forward with respect to the processes of evaluation, design and development, and implementation; or research could be carried out which attempted to investigate the linkage between these processes in a particular case.

The material in Part III also identified various roles for the IS strategist, evaluator, analyst, and implementer. Research questions here include whether these roles are a useful categorization for a particular context, whether there are other roles which could usefully be identified and analysed, how the various roles of the individual interact and overlap, and how the roles interrelate across the four issue areas. With respect to the role of an IS actor as a moral agent, such a role could be consciously adopted in an action research approach for example, and the researcher could then describe his or her experience of doing this, and any difficulties, dilemmas, or choices which they encountered, and how they resolved them.

Leading on from this last area of the IS actor as moral agent, it is worth noting that the choice of a research topic by a researcher or research team is itself part of a social process which is constrained and enabled by social structure. This is commented on by Cooper (1985) as follows:

> If research in information systems is to be socially useful and informing, then researchers in the subject will need to be more sensitive to the human and social context in which they work, including their own relationships to powerful interests in large corporations and the State ... Much research funding is dependent on the assessment by corporations or state agencies of the 'relevance' of the research ... Relevance is typically defined in managerialist terms ... What is needed is research that explores the social and human context and consequences of IS. What is unfortunate is that in many Western societies today such research is unlikely to be funded ... from governmental sources as from corporate sources. (pp. 93, 94, 97)

Cooper's views may be unduly gloomy about the funding for IS research with a non-managerialist agenda in the 1990s, although such views are echoed somewhat by Dunlop and Kling (1991, pp. 657–659) who comment on the extent of influence on research agendas by the military complex in the USA. They note that some fields of computer science, such as artificial intelligence and software engineering, get the lion's share of their funding directly from the military. An interesting area for future IS research would be to explore the social processes of research funding on computer-related topics from a critical perspective, although the researchers might have some difficulty in obtaining funding and access for their work.

IMPLICATIONS FOR FUTURE IS EDUCATION

Education with respect to computer-based information systems is a large and diverse topic area including such aspects as computer training in schools, mass education via such media as the television, on-the-job training, and formal higher education programmes. Rather than attempting to tackle all of these aspects, this section will concentrate on two important components, namely IS education in formal computer science and management courses. The purpose of the section is to discuss some implications for these areas, drawing from the philosophy and approach of the book.

IS Education in Computer Science Courses

It has been emphasized throughout the book that a good technical training is essential for computer scientists, and nothing which follows in any way detracts from this view. However, the argument is that the development of computer-based information systems in organizations requires more than technical expertise, and that the IS analyst, for example, has a role as an enactor of meaning and a moral agent in addition to that as a systems expert. The current education provided to most computer scientists in universities and other higher education institutions around the world does not fit them for these additional roles. Dunlop and Kling (1991) comment that:

> The dominant paradigms in academic computer science do not help technical
> professionals comprehend the social complexities of computerization, since they
> focus on computability rather than usability . . . Paradigms that focus on the
> nature of social interaction provide much better insights for designing computer
> systems in support of group work than does the computability paradigm. (p. 9)

There is an argument which says that computer scientists can learn about the human and social aspects of computer systems in organizations after they leave their university and enter the world of work. This is of course a legitimate argument, but there are at least four good reasons why such an approach may be problematic. Firstly, the productivity of such people in terms of implementable systems can be very low for a number of years until they gain an understanding of organizational functioning. Secondly, early education is highly formative and it can be much harder to introduce social ideas at a later stage if the individuals have not been exposed to such ideas as students. Thirdly, good on-the-job training on the social aspects of computer-based IS often does not occur in practice, due to factors such as lack of time and unavailability of appropriate trainers or mentors. Finally, training whilst working is typically atheoretical and with no critical dimension. It is ironic that our best trained computer scientists often receive no formal education on any aspect of social theory and are sometimes not even aware of its existence, despite the fact that their later jobs invariably rely just as heavily on social skills and knowledge as they do on the technical side.

With respect to possible curricula for computer scientists to expose them to the social aspects of computer systems, this is too large a topic to go into in detail here, but a few general guidelines can be offered. Firstly, some basic education on human organizations and their functioning is essential as a prerequisite to thinking about the purpose and impact of computer-based IS in organizations. With respect to the latter area specifically, in-depth case material such as that in Part II of this book can be valuable as a basis for learning. One does not necessarily need the full theoretical apparatus developed in Part I to gain some benefit from studying and discussing such cases. Finally, if time and resources permit, practical projects in real contexts, supervised by staff members with a good knowledge of human and social issues, are very worthwhile for student learning.

Dunlop and Kling (1991, p. 11) consider that computer science of the twenty-first century *will* be strong in areas that rest on the social foundations of computerization as well as in areas that rest on its mathematical and engineering foundations. Whilst agreeing with the sentiments that inspired the prediction, the statement is too deterministic for this author, whose own institution for example continues to teach a prestigious computer science programme with no vestige of non-technical interest. There is a need for a major change in attitude over the next few years if Dunlop and Kling's prediction is to come true by the start of the next century. A final observation is that computer scientists in formal education now will probably still be in the workforce in the 2030s. If early training is indeed highly formative, this lends an urgency to the need for a change to the provision of a broader social education for our young computer scientists.

IS Education in Management Courses

There is an enormous variety of management education and training provided in formal higher education institutions at the undergraduate, postgraduate and post-experience levels, together with in-house training schemes and other in-company programmes. There is no difficulty in any of these programmes, in contrast to those for computer scientists, in arguing for a good knowledge of the functioning of organizations, and for the importance of human and social issues in management. This could lead to the view that IS education in management courses will inevitably focus on social issues as a major theme, and nothing further need be said. Whilst there is some degree of truth in the first of these statements on social focus, the philosophy and approach in this book on such issues is rather different from what is typically taught in MBA programmes and the like, and we will now briefly explore these differences and possible reasons for them.

Much of the material which is taught in traditional IS courses that form part of a management programme concentrates on formal techniques and methods and is relatively lacking in any substantial theory on social aspects. Typical programmes include aspects such as competitive advantage frameworks for IS strategy, cost-benefit techniques for IS investment appraisal, and the use of structured design methodologies. Such approaches are not without value, but they largely ignore the subtleties of the human and social issues surrounding the initiation, development and use of computerized systems, or rely on relatively simple prescriptions such as participative design. There are of course exceptions to the generalization here, but it is fair to say that many management programmes do not incorporate any depth of analysis of human and social issues in connection with computer-based IS.

A second difference between the philosophy of this book and the typical orientation of management education programmes is the book's emphasis on moral issues in connection with computer-based information systems, and the discussion of critical approaches to analysis and understanding. The lack of emphasis on ethical issues in management programmes is not restricted to IS education, and is perhaps not surprising in the wider social context of our present-day societies. We often maintain the fiction that business and management activity can be conducted in some sense apart from the world of moral judgements, in a type of social vacuum driven by the engine of economic rationality. This can be thought of as serving the interests of the economically powerful, who can hide behind the smokescreen of economic determinism to justify the preservation or enhancement of existing inequalities.

In the specific context of computer-based information systems, management education programmes should permit the exploration and debate of the full range of ethical issues in connection with such systems. A number of these have been raised in the book, including issues of autonomy and control, surveillance, the enhancement and degradation of work, power relations between groups, and the possibilities for emancipatory discourse. There is every indication that management students are keen to be involved in studying and debating these ethical issues. It is hoped that such activities will contribute to the creation of a world of management in organizations in the future where successful enterprise and an explicit focus and debate on moral issues are not regarded as mutually exclusive.

IMPLICATIONS FOR FUTURE IS PRACTICE

The title of this final section could be a subtitle for the whole book, since the main rationale for writing the book was to attempt to influence IS practice. The previous two sections have generated some implications for future IS research and IS education, but these activities can themselves be largely justified on the basis of their eventual contribution to practice. The material in the book which was aimed most directly at practitioners was contained in the last sections of each of the chapters in Part III, and addressed the practice of IS strategy, evaluation, design and development, and implementation. It is hoped that this material will be of direct use to those concerned with such issues in organizations, whether they be IS managers, analysts, or other stakeholders.

The theories, ideas, models, issues for debate, and other constructs in the book were thus all, directly or indirectly, aimed to be of value to the practitioner. It is not the intention of this final section to repeat or substantially summarize this material here. Instead, the aim is to present a synthesized view of some broad implications for practice which derive from the philosophy and approach of the book. This brief finale is organized into three subsections dealing with human-centred practice; key themes of vision, learning, and autonomy; and some observations on individual action.

Human-centred Practice

It has been emphasized throughout the book that computer-based information systems are associated with organizational stability and change directly through the agency of human actors. Any approach to the development and use of such systems which concentrates solely on technical issues, or which treats human and social issues as of secondary importance, is likely to lead to failure in terms of most measures of organizational implementation. There is a need in the planning and development of computerized systems to build commitment to a common purpose or approach, and to take full account of stakeholder perceptions. These observations apply to all the IS issues discussed earlier in the book. A focus on human behaviour should not be limited, for example, to participation in the design and development process, but is also crucial during other processes such as IS strategy formation and evaluation.

The human behaviour focus discussed above is needed, but is not enough in itself to justify the term human-centred practice. This latter label implies that moral issues also are explicitly included in the discourse about computer-based information systems and their links with organizational change. It implies that people in organizations are treated as whole people, who do not want to divorce their work from their sense of ethical values, and who want to explicitly discuss such values in the context of the organizations for whom they work. The discourse and action of human-centred IS practice involves organization-making in its fullest sense, concerned with behaviourally feasible and ethically desirable organizational change in connection with computerized systems.

The above case for human-centred practice should not be taken to imply a simple idealism, based on the creation of situations of complete freedom of speech and action and equality between all parties. Such conditions cannot be achieved in practice, and asymmetries in power relations, linked to specific forms of language use and the ability to promote particular norms and values, are inevitable features of human life. The point of view which is being expressed here on the desirability of a human-centred approach to IS practice is that an explicit focus on moral themes, and their acceptance as legitimate subjects for debate by all stakeholders, would be an aid to emancipation of all parties to the discourse.

Vision, Learning and Autonomy

Many specific behavioural and ethical themes have been discussed in the book, but only three themes will be mentioned in this final section, illustrating the societal, organizational, and individual levels of analysis and their interlinking. The three chosen themes are societal vision, organizational learning, and personal autonomy. With respect to the first of these, the theme of vision was discussed earlier in the book in the context of organizational change, but we will broaden it out here to vision for a changed world.

The making of organizations is part of the making of human society, and we should ask what sort of world we wish to create in the future. Material prosperity as measured by increased per capita income is one goal which is held to be central in most contemporary societies; but other societal goals are important in addition to purely economic ones. With respect to the work which people carry out in organizations, and which occupies for most of us a large part of our lives, these goals should include the dignity of people's work; their sense of control over their work activities and scope for self-development; a degree of personal privacy in their work and non-work activities; and a sense that they are contributing through their work to something of positive benefit to society. Computer-based information systems are becoming increasingly central to these social goals and issues. We can design systems in ways which degrade or enhance work activities, which offer individuals more or less control over their work, which increase or reduce privacy, and which reproduce a narrow economic approach or see economic goals as merely one element of a desirable future. Computerized systems will thus be deeply implicated in the directions that we choose to move in, and in the nature of organizations, societies and the world which we thereby produce.

A key theme at the organizational-level is that of organizational learning in connection with computer-based IS. It was argued earlier in the book that organizations should attempt to create and support a climate in which learning flourishes, including in particular stimulating learning in the discourse and activities surrounding the issues of IS strategy formation, evaluation, design and development, and organizational implementation. Ways in which this can be achieved include the statement and the clear symbolic support for views such as that the questioning of goals and approaches is acceptable, that all assessments and issues are legitimate subjects for debate, and that everybody in the organization is a learner. A specific example is that resistance to a proposed new computer-based IS should not be enacted as something to be overcome, but rather as an opportunity for exploration and learning.

The final theme in this subsection is that of personal autonomy, which is linked directly to aspects of societal vision and organizational learning as discussed above. There is a need in all contexts to carefully balance an individual's need for autonomy of action in their work, and a sense of personal control, with the need for co-operation between people and groups in organizations, and thus the requirement for some group or organizational control. There are no simple prescriptions in this area as to how a middle way should be chosen between relatively unrestricted autonomy and high levels of control. However, it is clear that computerized systems will often be centrally involved in such questions in organizational life in the future. There is thus a need for explicit and continuing debate on issues such as task-related decentralization, ethical limits on surveillance, and approaches which enable group and organizational interaction, but at the same time help to stimulate creativity and a sense of self-worth in those using computerized systems.

Individual Action

Individuals are in some senses free to choose, but certainly not in conditions of their own choosing. The book has raised some themes, particularly those connected with moral issues, which an individual reader may feel cannot be tackled in their own context. A systems analyst could perhaps argue that they are employed to carry out technical systems development and that behavioural, and certainly ethical, issues are not their concern. A second example could be an IS manager who may feel that raising moral issues with senior management, such as ethical limits on surveillance, would not achieve anything worthwhile and may indeed threaten the manager's career prospects. These examples illustrate the view of the IS actor as a helpless agent in a drama for which the script has been written by others, and exemplify more generally the perceptions of employees of contemporary organizations who feel the need to cloak some aspects of their humanity whilst engaged in the world of work.

We are all influenced by our contexts to take actions which, with critical hindsight, we may feel were unduly affected by baser motives such as personal advancement, rather than taking a braver stance which could upset those in authority over us. This book is not saying that we can avoid such actions. Instead, it is suggested that, for the individual, small actions in local areas, rather than large gestures, may be the way forward. The raising of one new issue, such as user involvement by the systems analyst or empowerment by the IS manager, can be considered a step in the right direction. A second example of small positive change is for the individual IS actor to consciously reflect on his or her own actions. If a more self-critical attitude were adopted by considerable numbers of future IS actors, particularly in ethical domains, the cumulative effect would be a significant societal change.

It is hard for IS actors, or any human beings, to make a conscious and continuous effort to act in a better way. It is often easier to accept existing constraints as binding and existing attitudes as acceptable. However, a positive future role for computer-based information systems in organizations and human society requires that large numbers of individuals do not accept the existing status quo without question, but instead strive to achieve full personal responsibility for their actions. The way to move in this direction may be to tread across a series of small stepping-stones rather than to leap great distances, but the time to start is always now.

REFERENCES

Attewell, P. (1991) 'Big brother and the sweat shop: computer surveillance in the automated office', in *Computerization and Controversy* (eds C. Dunlop and R. Kling), Academic Press, Boston.

Bullen, C. V., and Bennett, J. L. (1991) 'Groupware in practice: an interpretation of work experience', in *Computerization and Controversy* (eds C. Dunlop and R. Kling), Academic Press, Boston.

Cooper, D. (1985) 'Comment by David Cooper', in *Research Methods in Information Systems* (eds E. Mumford, R. Hirschheim, G. Fitzgerald, and T. Wood-Harper), North-Holland, New York.

Dunlop, C., and Kling, R. (1991) (eds) *Computerization and Controversy*, Academic Press, Boston.

Ehn, P. (1991) 'The art and science of designing computer artifacts', in *Computerization and Controversy* (eds C. Dunlop and R. Kling), Academic Press, Boston.

THE FUTURE FOR INFORMATION SYSTEMS 257

Foucault, M. (1979) *Discipline and Punish*, Vintage Books, New York.
Garnsey, E. W. (1992) 'In defence of systems thinking: constitutive processes and dynamic social systems', unpublished paper, Management Studies Group, University of Cambridge.
Geertz, C. (1973) *The Interpretation of Cultures*, Basic Books, New York.
Habermas, J. (1972) *Knowledge and Human Interests*, Heinemann, London.
Kling, R. (1991) 'Computerization and social transformations', *Science, Technology, and Human Values*, **16**, No. 3, 342–367.
Kraemer, K. L. (1991) 'Strategic computing and administrative reform', in *Computerization and Controversy* (eds C. Dunlop and R. Kling), Academic Press, Boston.
Markus, M. L., and Robey, D. (1988) 'Information technology and organizational change: causal structure in theory and research', *Management Science*, **34**, No. 3, 583–598.
Marx, G. T. (1990) 'The case of the omniscient organization', *Harvard Business Review*, March–April, 12–30.
Orlikowski, W. J., and Baroudi, J. J. (1991) 'Studying information technology in organizations: research approaches and assumptions', *Information Systems Research*, **2**, No. 1, 1–28.
Orwell, G. (1949) *Nineteen Eighty-Four*, Harcourt-Brace, New York.
Stover, W. J. (1984) *Information Technology in the Third World*, Westview, Boulder.
Van Maanen, J. (1979) 'The fact of fiction in organizational ethnography', *Administrative Science Quarterly*, **24**, No. 4, 539–550.
Van Maanen, J. (1989) 'Some notes on the importance of writing in organization studies', in *The Information Systems Research Challenge: Volume 1* (eds J. I. Cash and P. R. Lawrence), Harvard Business School, Boston.
Walsham, G., Symons, V., and Waema, T. (1988) 'Information systems as social systems: implications for developing countries', *Information Technology for Development*, **3**, No. 3, 189–204.
Weizenbaum, J. (1991) 'Against the imperialism of instrumental reason', in *Computerization and Controversy* (eds C. Dunlop and R. Kling), Academic Press, Boston.

AUTHOR INDEX

SUBJECT INDEX

accounting, 20, 62–4
  systems, 42–3
action
  individual, 255–6
  rationality, 169, 170
  research, 17, 191
adhocracy, 144
ambiguity, 160
  in evaluation, 114
  in policy process, 211–13, 223, 227
analysis, mixed level, 245
anthropology, symbolic, 33
authority, in organizations, 19
automation, as technology strategy, 19, 152
autonomy
  and control, 44–6, 59–60, 85, 195, 252
  implementation, 226
  personal, 255
  see also creative autonomy
autonomy/control balance, 105, 130, 152–3, *160(tab.7.3)*, 161
autopoiesis, 32, 46

banks *see* financial services sector
breakdown, 8, 33
building societies, 97–8

case analysis
  context/process linkage, 86–91, *87(tab.4.3)*, 109–12, *110(tab.5.3)*, 132–6, *132(tab.6.3)*
  social context, 78–80, *79(tab.4.1)*, 100–1, 124–7, *125(tab.6.1)*
  social process, 81–6, *82(tab.4.2)*, 102–9, *102(tab.5.1)*, *106(tab.5.2)*, 127–31, *128(tab.6.2)*
case studies
  generalizability from, 14, 17, 19, 247
  insights from, 21
  value of 14–16
  see also longitudinal case study

coalition building, 214, 216–17, 224
cognition, 7–9
collective resource approach, 189
commitment
  and abstraction of work, 19
  and action rationality, 169
  and evaluation, 171, 177–8, 179
  and participation, 99
  as basis for language, 8
  of management, 81, 91, 104
  of users, 17
  shared, 95, 253
  symbolic, 103, 138, 163, 205
communication, 13, 61, 89
  learning, and negotiation process, 236
  of meaning, 19
computer science courses, 250–1
computer scientists, social knowledge, 251
Computer-Aided Software Engineering (CASE) tools, 66–7
computer-based technology, social impact, 3, 241
computer-supported co-operative work (CSCW), 192–3
computerization of society, social issues, 239–41
computing in organizations, effects of, 31
computing skills, 81
conflict, 11, 12, 85
  in development process, 191
  in systems development, 202
  perspective, on organizations, 189
  see also stakeholder, conflict
consciousness raising, 38
constitutive process theory, 244, 245, 246
consultants
  lack of experience, 127
  role of, 83, 206–7
  technical focus, 139

and IS failure, 215
and management, 38, 62, 84, 103,
    205
and policy, 211, 212
in IS development, 35
of concern, 139
see also information use, symbolic
systems design
    as ritual, 35, 191
    case study of, 16–17
    participative approach, 30, 188, 189,
        190, 201
systems development, ad hoc, 103, 105
systems expert, role of, 202–3

technological determinism, 241
theory, 244–7
    relationship with research, 245
    value of 6–7, 70–1
Third World, 118
see also developing countries
training, 94, 103–4, 139, 200–1,
    207(tab.9.5), 208
    ideological, 216–17
triangulation, 18

understanding, 9
unintended consequences, 61, 89, 133,
    185
users
    attitude of computing team, 82
    interacting with, 17
    see also participation, user

vision
    for a changed world, 254–5
    for change, 113, 150–2, 160–1,
        160(tab.7.3), 196, 204
vocabulary
    for learning, 19
    in evaluation, 182
    of strategic discourse, 158, 161,
        237–8

web models, 55, 57, 67–8, 78, 245
work
    activities, 236
    nature and purpose of, 155–6, 192,
        253, 254–5
    new forms of identity, 202, 236
writing, importance of, 248